THE DOMINION

OF THE DEAD

THE DOMINION
OF THE DEAD

ROBERT POGUE HARRISON

THE UNIVERSITY OF CHICAGO PRESS
CHICAGO AND LONDON

The University of Chicago Press, Chicago 60637
The University of Chicago Press, Ltd., London
© 2003 by The University of Chicago
All rights reserved. Published 2003.
Printed in the United States of America

20 19 18 17 16 15 14 13 12 11   3 4 5 6 7

ISBN-13: 978-0-226-31791-5 (cloth)
ISBN-13: 978-0-226-31793-9 (paper)
ISBN-10: 0-226-31791-9 (cloth)
ISBN-10: 0-226-31793-5 (paper)

Library of Congress Cataloging-in-Publication Data

Harrison, Robert Pogue.
    The dominion of the dead / Robert Pogue Harrison.
        p. cm.
    Includes bibliographical references and index.
    ISBN 0-226-31791-9 (hardcover : alk. paper)
    1. Death—Psychological aspects.   2. Death—Social aspects.
I. Title.
BF789.D4 H375 2003
306.9—dc21

                                                          2003002158

To a feast of friends and the giant family

CONTENTS

Whatever the rift that separates their regimes, nature and culture have at least this much in common: both compel the living to serve the interests of the unborn. Yet they differ in their strategies in one decisive respect: culture perpetuates itself through the power of the dead, while nature, as far as we know, makes no use of this resource except in a strictly organic sense. In the human realm the dead and the unborn are native allies, so much so that from their posthumous abode—wherever it be—the former hound the living with guilt, dread, and a sense of responsibility, obliging us, by whatever means necessary, to take the unborn into our care and to keep the story going, even if we never quite figure out what the story is about, what our part in it is, the end toward which it's progressing, or the moral it contains. One day the science of genetics may decode the secrets of this custodianship, but meanwhile we may rest assured that there exists an allegiance between the dead and the unborn of which we the living are merely the ligature.

Our basic human institutions—religion, matrimony, and burial, if one goes along with Giambattista Vico, but also law, language, literature, and whatever else relies on the transmission of legacy—are authored, always and from the very start, by those who came before. The awareness of death that defines human nature is inseparable from—indeed, it arises from—our awareness that we are not self-authored, that we follow in the footsteps of the dead. Everywhere one looks across the spectrum of human cultures one finds the foundational authority of the predecessor. Nonhuman species obey only the law of vitality, but humanity in its distinctive features is through and through necrocratic. Whether we are conscious of it or not we do the will of the ancestors: our commandments come to us from their realm; their precedents are our law; we submit to their dictates, even when we rebel against them. Our diligence, hardihood, rectitude, and heroism, but also our folly, spite, rancor, and pathologies, are so many signatures of the dead on the contracts that seal our identities. We inherit their obsessions; assume their burdens; carry on their causes; promote their mentalities, ideologies, and very often their superstitions; and often we die trying to vindicate their humiliations. Why this servitude? We have no choice. Only the dead can grant us legitimacy. Left to ourselves we are all bastards. In exchange for legitimacy, which humans need and crave more than anything else, we surrender ourselves to their dominion. We may, in our modern modes, ignore or reject their ancient authority; yet if we are to gain a margin of real freedom—if we are to become "absolutely modern," as Rimbaud put it—we must begin by first acknowledging the traditional claims that such authority has on us.

This book offers some broad perspectives on only *some* of the manifold relations the living maintain with the giant family of the dead in Western culture, both in past and present times. In themselves these relations are so vast, profound, and numerous that no book could hope to deal with their topics except fractionally and selectively. I use the word *topics* advisedly here, for in the following pages I seek out places or topoi in our midst where the dead exert their power, press their demands, grant or deny their blessing, become loquacious, and in general cohabit our worlds. Such places where the dead carry on a secular afterlife (I have little to say about any other, nonsecular afterlife they may or may not enjoy) include graves, homes, laws, words, images, dreams, rituals, monuments, and the archives of literature, whose voices always have a posthumous character of sorts. Like human dwelling, the afterlife needs places to take place *in*. If humans dwell, the dead, as it were, indwell—and very often in the same space. I am interested here above all in the nature and modes of this indwelling of the dead in the worlds of the living.

My main objective in investigating these places is not to pursue an anthropology, even less a psychology, but to uncover what I call the humic foundations of our life worlds. A humic foundation is one whose contents have been buried so that they may be reclaimed by the future. The humic holds in its conserving element the unfinished story of what has come to pass. If it is true that we move forward into the future only by retrieving the past, it is because, through burial, we consign the future of our legacies to this humic element, with its vast, diversely populated underworlds. Thus burial does not mean only the laying of bodies to rest in the ground (although religion and matrimony are more likely to disappear among humans than burial customs are). In a broader sense it means to store, preserve, and put the past on hold. Dead etymons, latent meanings, and lateral connotations lie buried in the roots and phonemes of our living words, where they carry on an active afterlife. Our psyches are the graveyards of impressions, traumas, desires, and archetypes that confound the law of obsolescence. Vico, who devoted his career to "unearthing" it, believed that all the poetic wisdom of the ancients lies buried in the Homeric epics. In some instances the buried is indeed consigned to oblivion; in others it is in fact given up to repetition and reinheritance.

If I were to try to phrase the principal thesis of this study—a hazardous proposition, to be sure, since a number of diverse theses come together here—I would say that humans bury not simply to achieve closure and effect a separation from the dead but also and above all to humanize the ground on which they build their worlds and found their histories. And since I will be referring to the human rather often in these pages, let me put forward a premise here to the effect that humanity is not a species (*Homo sapiens* is a species); it is a way of being mortal and relating to the dead. To be human means above all to bury. Vico suggests as much when he reminds us that "*humanitas* in Latin comes first and properly from *humando*, burying" (*New Science* §12). By *properly* he means essentially and irreducibly. And if I have mentioned Vico more than once already it is because his *New Science* (1744) is the major inspiration for this study. Certainly it was Vico who first helped me understand how the human is bound up with the humus and why burial figures as the generative institution of human nature, taking the word *nature* in its full etymological sense (from *nasci*, "to be born"). As *Homo sapiens* we are born of our biological parents. As human beings we are born of the dead—of the regional ground they occupy, of the languages they inhabited, of the worlds they brought into being, of the many institutional, legal, cultural, and psychological legacies that, through us, connect them to the unborn. Vico's thinking on the nature of this dominion is full of unrealized potential for self-knowledge in its broad historical scope. If my book does not take the form of a conventional commentary on his work, it is because sometimes the best way to

retrieve a legacy is by freeing it from its original framework and rein-
scribing it in new ones. Today Vico needs heirs more than commentators.

Before turning this book over to its audience I would like to state
that it is above all a reader's book. Some books are writers' books, in
that their authors undertake the largest share of the labor, do most of
the thinking, circumscribe (as much possible) the horizon of reference, and draw the final conclusions. *The Dominion of the Dead* is different. It is more like a net than a cloth. Its articulation is full of empty
spaces for the reader to enter and wander about in. It calls on its interlocutor not only to think along with the author but to establish independent connections, leap over abysses, pursue his or her own paths of
inquiry, bring to bear adventitious considerations, and, through the
tracings offered here, discover the topic for him- or herself. Given its intrinsic limitations (of which I am all too aware), I have tried to turn my
approach into one that opens rather than closes the horizon of speculation. The result is a book that only the reader can finish writing.

NOTE ON REFERENCES

The following book does not contain numbered footnotes or endnotes. Notes and references have been placed in separate sections, "Notes" and "Works Cited," at the back of the volume.

CHAPTER 1

THE EARTH AND ITS DEAD

One of the blessings of our planet, along with life itself, is that it allows for the disposal of its dead. The characters in a Jules Verne story realize to what extent they, like us, take that circumstance for granted after they eject a dead dog from their space capsule, only to find that the dog (named Satellite) faithfully follows them on their journey toward the moon—a veritable satellite holding close to the rocket as it travels through empty space. The dead like to stay close to the living, to be sure, yet not in this nondisposable fashion. To realize their fate and become truly dead they must first be made to disappear. It is only because their bodies have a place to go that their souls or images or words may attain an afterlife of sorts among the living. We should be infinitely grateful, therefore, for the hiding and receiving power of this terracqueous globe, which Michel Serres, reflecting on the image of Jules Verne's dog, rightly calls "a tabernacle, a receptacle for all decompositions" (*Statues*, p. 39).

Nietzsche once declared: "Let us beware of saying that death is opposed to life. The living is merely a type of what is dead, and a very rare type" (*Gay Science* [§109], p. 168). Certainly to the degree that its heavy elements were formed by the death of stars—the so-called supernovae—our planet as a whole, like all solid bodies in the universe, is a species of what is dead. Yet its biosphere—host to such an abundance of life—is necrogenic in an even more pertinent sense. Through the action of fire the corpse gives itself up to air; through inhumation or simple putrefaction it returns its composite substance to the earth; through the force of gravity it sinks into the sea's underworlds. Whatever biomass it receives after the extinction of life becomes part of the planet's receiving matter—matter from which life, its imponderable origins, in turn emerges. Because the earth has reabsorbed the dead into its elements for so many millions upon millions of years, who can any longer tell the difference between receptacle and contents? Take away the millennial residues that consecrate them, human or otherwise, and our waters, forests, deserts, mountains, and clouds would lose the spirit that moves in and across their visible natures.

Human bodies, when they perish, share in this organic afterlife of the dead. They are "rolled round in earth's diurnal course, / with rocks, and stones, and trees," to speak with Wordsworth. The human returns to the humus, to be sure, yet the fact that Wordsworth wrote those verses at all or that we revisit their utterance over a century and half later shows that human culture, unlike nature, institutes a living memory, and not just a mineral retention, of the dead. Culture is the condensed residue of such perpetuation, unless we prefer to think of it as the nonorganic residue-forming process itself.

We know by now that in the great span of geological time, human history figures as no more than the briefest, evanescent instant; yet it is in that self-sedimenting instant that we nevertheless dwell insofar as we are human. If to be human means to translate our mortality into history, as I believe it does, then one could say that the ethos or dwelling place of humanity remains mortal time, which we transmute into historical durations that are themselves radically finite. We are through and through temporal, that is, finite, in our mode of being. Even our perception of space is thoroughly temporal in character. Immanuel Kant claimed as much when he threw up a barrier between the noumenal realm of nature, unknowable in itself, and the world as it appears to us phenomenally, through the so-called pure intuitions of space and time. I invoke Kant here because, according him, while all our sense data is spatialized and temporalized by these two a priori forms, there is an important difference between them. In addition to determining our perception of the external world, time also determines the immediately experienced flow of our inner lives: "Time is nothing but the form of inner sense, i.e., of the intuiting we do of ourselves and of our inner state. . . . Time is the formal a priori condition of all appearances generally. Space is the pure form of all outer appearances; as such it is limited, as an a priori condition, to just outer appearances intuitions" (Kant, *Critique of Pure Reason*, p. 88). In short, our access to the world passes through the temporal flow of human consciousness. This explains why even our perception of space is temporal and, I would add, mortal in nature.

Unlike music and poetry, whose rhythms participate in, arise out of, or echo the flow itself, most visual artworks cannot directly represent the temporal flow of our inner lives, precisely because they are committed to the spatialization of form and the formalization of space. As for architecture, it belongs to a category of its own. Insofar as it builds the worlds we dwell in, architecture actually *creates* the places where human time, in its historical and existential modes, takes place. Such places—be they homes, buildings, cities, or landscapes—are recesses of mortal time in which we go about inhabiting the earth historically rather than merely naturally. One could say that, in its world-forming capacity, architecture transforms geological time into human time, which is another way of saying it turns matter into meaning. That is why the sight of ruins is such a reflexive and in some cases unsettling experience. Ruins in an advanced state of ruination represent, or better they literally embody, the dissolution of meaning into matter. By revealing what human building ultimately is up against—natural or geological time—ruins have a way of recalling us to the very ground of our human worlds, namely the earth, whose foundations are so solid and so reliable that they presumably will outlast any edifices that we build on them.

Precisely because it is the faculty that schematizes our intuition of time, the human imagination is also able to conceive images of the end of time. Or perhaps we are so governed by its law and so haunted by its implications that we can't help but project our finitude onto the cosmos in apocalyptic visions of ultimate cessation. Take one of oldest English poems to have come down to us, entitled "The Wanderer," which contains an extended meditation on Roman ruins in the early medieval English landscape. Evoking the implacable, destructive forces of nature, especially of the sea, whose "storms break on the stone hillside," wearing down the earth's solid mass, the poem concludes with a hyperbolic projection of the past's ruination into an ultimate, ultratemporal future: "In earth's realm all is crossed; Weird's will changeth the world. Wealth is lent us, friends are lent us, man is lent, kin is lent; *all this earth's frame shall stand empty*" (Alexander, *Earliest English Poems*, p. 51). Here a landscape of retrospection sponsors a transhuman or even inhuman vision of the eschaton, understood not only as the end of history but as the surcease of the earth itself—that same earth where history's ruins leave behind their trace. A truly extreme or self-consuming vision of annihilation takes the form of the earth's demise, for the forces of destruction, when pushed to their cosmic extreme in the human imagination, not only destroy all that human labor builds in time, they also destroy the supporting element of time, namely the land on which we erect our worlds.

In the eschatological imagination where such visions are born, earth and sea belong to different, even opposing orders. In its solidity and stability the earth is inscribable, we can build upon its ground, while the sea offers no such foothold for human worldhood. No doubt that is why the sea, in its hostility to architecturally or textually imprinted memory, often figures as the imaginary agent of ultimate obliteration. When John describes the eschaton at the end of the Book of Revelation he evokes the architectural marvel of the new Jerusalem and, in an exalted rhetoric, speaks of a "new earth" and "new heaven." He then declares, almost as an aside: "And the sea was no more" (21:1). The demise of the sea here signifies the final victory of providential history over its antagonistic element. For Revelation does not project the absolute ruin of human history, as "The Wanderer" poem does; on the contrary, it foresees the fulfillment of history and final perfection of time. In the plenitude of time—given the anthropotheistic tradition to which this vision belongs—the sea is bound to disappear.

In other types of eschatological visions, where it is the earth as such that succumbs to ruin, it is the sea that emerges as the victor. Consider a poem by Swinburne, entitled "A Forsaken Garden," which shows the extent to which the human imagination is able to strain against the bounds of its own conditions of possibility. The first of its ten stanzas sets the scene for the poetic meditation that follows:

> In a coign of the cliff between lowland and highland,
> At the sea-down's edge between windward and lee,
> Walled round with rocks as an inland island,
> The ghost of a garden fronts the sea.
> A girdle of brushwood and thorn encloses
> The steep square slope of the blossomless bed

Where the weeds that grew green from the graves of its roses
  Now lie dead.

In such heavy anapests the anonymous third-person speaker goes on to describe the garden's desolation, its paths overgrown with weeds, its dilapidated structures, its bygone roses reduced to thorns. The ruined landscape lies exposed now to the remorseless abrasion of wind, storm, and sun. The speaker goes on to imagine two lovers wandering among the once blossoming garden paths a hundred years earlier, only to conclude that "love deep as the sea as a rose must wither." The poem ends as follows:

All are at one now, roses and lovers,
  Not known of the cliffs and the fields and the sea.
Not a breath of the time that has been hovers
  In the air now soft with a summer to be.
Not a breath shall there sweeten the seasons hereafter
  Of the flowers or the lovers that laugh now or weep,
When as they that are free now of weeping and laughter
      We shall sleep.

Here death may not deal again for ever;
  Here change may come not till all change end.
From the graves they have made they shall rise up never,
  Who have left nought living to ravage and rend.
Earth, stones, and thorns of the wild ground growing,
  While the sun and the rain live, these shall be;
Till a last wind's breath upon all these blowing
      Roll the sea.

Till the slow sea rise and the sheer cliff crumble,
  Till the terrace and meadow the deep gulfs drink,
Till the strength of the waves of the high tides humble
  The fields that lessen, the rocks that shrink,
Here now in his triumph where all things falter,
  Stretched out on the spoils that his own hand spread,
As a god self-slain on his own strange altar,
      Death lies dead.

                    (Swinburne, pp. 210–13)

The anapests here produce an almost intolerable, pounding effect on the inner ear, evoking the harsh rhythm of the sea as it wears down the earth with its surf and storms, until rhythm itself succumbs to ruination in the remorseless paradox of the concluding half-verse: "Death lies dead." What is imagined here is something other than the triumph of geological time over human time. It is the sea's noumenal core reabsorbing the entire geophenomenal realm into its anachronic element. In its extreme projection of the fate of past ruins, the poem effectively deschematizes the forms of human intuition, with the result that the generative and degenerative law of death that informs mortal time is overturned or cancelled out in and by the sea.

The forsaken garden is merely the preludic image of this ultimate ruination of form. For what are ruins if not the partial, still incomplete dissolution of the solidity of form? If we usually view ruins retrospectively, as metonyms of what they once were in their integrity, in Swinburne's vision they turn into prospective metaphors of an incomplete liquefaction. For all their suggestive or mimetic magic, visual artworks can't represent ruins from this impossible, transhuman perspective. The domestication of terror in the picturesque is all the more palpable in those sketches and paintings, so popular during the nineteenth century, that include the presence of human beings in their so-called perspective views of ruins. The tiny human figures amid towering ruins of bygone eras give a sense of scale and diminishment, to be sure, yet they offer the consolation, if not the security, of perspective. Not so with Swinburne's poem, where the sea overwhelms perspective and devours the framework of scale as a whole.

Consider another poem that plunges into the sea, and, in so doing, stages the shipwreck of single-point perspective. "A Grave," by Marianne Moore, begins:

> Man looking into the sea,
> taking the view from those who have as much right to it as
>   you have to it yourself,
> it is human nature to stand in the middle of a thing,
> but you cannot stand in the middle of this;
> the sea has nothing to give but a well excavated grave.

We should give full weight to the words "it is human nature to stand in the middle of a thing," which affirm that human beings need an earthly

foundation for their perspectives, just as they need an earthly foundation for their buildings. The inhuman nature of the sea—of the *this* in
the middle of which you cannot stand yet from within which the poem
situates its speech act, precisely in the act of saying *this*—is revealed as
the poem sinks beneath the water's phenomenal surface in the final
verses:

> men lower their nets, unconscious of the fact that they are
> > desecrating a grave,
> and row quickly away—the blades of the oars
> moving together like the feet of water spiders as if there were
> > no such thing as death.
> The wrinkles progress among themselves in a phalanx—
> > beautiful under
> > networks of foam,
> and fade breathlessly while the sea rustles in and out of the
> > seaweed;
> the birds swim through the air at top speed, emitting catcalls
> > as heretofore—
> the tortoise shell scourges about the feet of the cliff, in motion
> > beneath them;
> and the ocean, under the pulsation of lighthouses and noise of
> > bell buoys,
> advances as usual, looking as if it were not that ocean in which
> > dropped things are
> > bound to sink—
> in which if they turn and twist, it is neither with volition nor
> > consciousness.
>
> > (Moore, *Complete Poems*, pp. 49–50)

The light and descriptive texture of these verses makes the abyss
whose surface they float upon all the more sinister in its nihilism.
Moore's poem is in many ways more perturbing than Swinburne's in
that it involves no hyperbolic temporal projections. The "neither-nor"
of its conclusion—"neither with volition nor consciousness"—uncovers the end time in the everyday presence of the sea, whose brilliant surface veils an underworld of extinction in which no spirits carry on an
afterlife. The poem perturbs in another way as well, for if the sea's sub-

surface element marks the limit of volition and consciousness, what are we to make of the men who are *unconscious of the fact that they are desecrating a grave* when they lower their nets? Confined to their superficial perspective, caught up in their daily activities "as if there were no such thing as death," are they not in some sense dead to the mortality that defines their condition? Is it only by looking deliberately into the abyss of what we stand in the middle of that we come alive to the world? And is that what poetry is in Moore's concept of its vocation—a transphenomenal way of looking that sees an inhuman darkness beneath the phenomena themselves?

I would invoke here another remarkable poem, authored by the contemporary poet Eleanor Wilner. Like several other poems in her collection *Reversing the Spell* (1998), this one, entitled "Reading the Bible Backwards," envisions the reversal or undoing of the Creation story told in Genesis. What it describes is a redemption, not of history but of nature, a redemption that takes the form of a universal flood that would "reverse the spell" of human history's disasters and tragedies by submerging history's elemental correlative altogether. After describing in extraordinary visual imagery the sea's slow and deliberate inundation of the earth, the poem concludes as follows:

> Now nothing but the wind
> moves in the rain-pocked face
> of the swollen waters, though far below
> where the giant squid lie hidden in shy tangles,
> the whales, heavy-bodied as angels,
> their fins like vestiges of wings,
> sing some mighty epic of their own—
>
> a great day when ships would all withdraw
> the harpoons fail of their aim, the land
> dissolve into the waters, and they would swim
> among the peaks of the mountains, like
> eagles of the deep, while far below them, the old
> nightmares of earth would settle
> into silt among the broken cities, the empty
> basket of the child would float

abandoned in the seaweed until the work of water
unraveled it in filaments of straw,
till even that straw rotted
in the planetary thaw the whales prayed for,
sending their jets of water skyward
in the clear conviction they'd spill back
to ocean with their will accomplished
in the miracle of the rain: *And the earth
was without form and void, and darkness
was upon the face of the deep. And
the Spirit moved upon the face of the waters.*

(pp. 156–57)

It is a prehuman and prehistorical Spirit that answers the prayers of the whales here. An earth without form after the end of the world is humanly inconceivable, since we are creatures of form and perspective; yet this is as close as we will get to an image of its pre- or postformal facticity—even if, or perhaps even because, the image traffics in multiple perspectives and contains a number of anthropomorphisms. Epics, prayers, convictions, accomplished wills are all attributed to the liberated whales, whose ecstatic deliverance from human oppression we share in here only through the poem's humanization.

Wilner's image of restored formlessness reveals, meanwhile, that the form the earth takes under the dominion of humans brings only death and enslavement to its other creatures, and mostly misery to the offenders. For Wilner the sins of the seed of Adam are sins against nature, not God, hence the guilt of history is neither punishable nor atonable. It is only oblivionable through the miracle of the rain. If history is at bottom a natural disaster, the general extinction of human volition and consciousness in a sea that preexisted the anthropogenic nightmare is the accomplishment of an elemental, planetary will. Wilner's sympathy with—and personification of—such a will is of course deeply human in its impulse insofar as it turns against the impulse of history. Such a turn is itself historical in nature, even and especially when it projects a diluvian, humanly depopulated universe that is at once beyond, below, and above history as we know it. And who knows whether the end of time, if and when it were ever to come about, would in fact be the accomplishment of a *human,* not natural, will? I mean the death drive that lurks at the heart of history itself.

Let us query one more text about the sea, this one in prose, authored by someone who actually earned his living on it for several years before going on to become a writer. Joseph Conrad's book *The Mirror of the Sea* describes a very different kind of ruin from the sort I have discussed so far. This work of nonfiction, composed in 1904–6, a decade or so after he retired from his seafaring career with the British merchant marine, contains a loosely interwoven series of reflections on seamanship. Conrad, we recall, never set eyes on the sea while growing up in Poland, yet as a young boy he was seized by an irrepressible desire to become a seaman. It was a wildly romantic fantasy that he had occasion to realize when, at age 17, he left for France and enlisted in the French merchant marine. Chapter 36 of *The Mirror of the Sea* recounts what Conrad called his "initiation," an incident early in his career that caused him to lose his youthful illusions about the sea. On a calm and luminous morning in the mid-Atlantic, "when the might of the sea indeed appears lovable," the crew aboard the ship on which he was serving as junior officer spotted the ruins of a brig on the horizon—a fragment of a ship, smashed up and completely dismasted. When they discovered through the binoculars that there were men aboard it waving rags at them, a silent yet frantic "race against time" got under way as the ship's two rowboats set out toward the wreck across a languorous and becalmed sea. It was a race on both sides of the placid divide, for while the men in the rescue boats pulled at their oars with superhuman efforts, their brothers on the Danish brig were working at the pumps, "bowing from the waist to each other in their back-breaking labour." They won the race, but only barely.

The survivors had been adrift for weeks, working the pumps day and night after their ship had sprung a leak and broken apart in a hurricane. Their travails had reduced them to an almost inhuman condition. As the rowboats made their way back to the mother ship with their human booty, the rescued captain of the brig suddenly "stood up with a low exclamation." Conrad:

> He was steadying himself on my shoulder with a strong grip, while
> his other arm, flung up rigidly, pointed a denunciatory finger at

the immense tranquility of the ocean. After his first exclamation, which stopped the swing of our oars, he made no sound, but his whole attitude seemed to cry out an indignant "Behold!" . . . I could not imagine what vision of evil had come upon him. I was startled, and the amazing energy of his immobilized gesture made my heart beat faster with the anticipation of something monstrous and unsuspected. The stillness around us became crushing.

Let's freeze the Danish captain in his demonstrative gesture for a moment and remark that he is pointing to the *this* in the middle of which one cannot stand. The account continues:

Something startling, mysterious, hastily confused was taking place. I watched it with incredulous and fascinated awe, as one watches the confused, swift movements of some deed of violence done in the dark. As if at a given signal, the run of the smooth undulations seemed checked suddenly around the brig. By a strange optical delusion the whole sea appeared to rise upon her in one overwhelming heave of its silky surface where in one spot a smother of foam broke out ferociously. And then the effort subsided. It was all over, and the smooth swell ran on as before from the horizon in uninterrupted cadence of motion, passing under us with a slight friendly toss of the boat. Far away, where the brig had been, an angry white stain undulating on the surface of steely-gray waters, shot with gleams of green, diminished swiftly without a hiss, like a patch of pure snow melting in the sun. And the great stillness after this initiation into the sea's implacable hate seemed full of dread thoughts and shadows of disaster. (*The Mirror of the Sea*, pp. 257–58)

This was Conrad's initiation into the sea's irresponsibility, its refusal or inability to respond to human appeal. On that day he realized that "the sea has no generosity. No display of manly qualities—courage, hardihood, endurance, faithfulness—has ever been known to touch its irresponsible consciousness of power" (p. 251). In short, he realized that the sea is unearthly. Whereas the earth sympathizes with human virtue, in the sense that it rewards backbreaking labor with generous harvests, or gives us the ground on which to build our destinies, commemorate our achievements, and honor our dead, the sea is dumb to human petition. It defies any and all humanization. "The amazing wonder of the deep," writes Conrad, "is its unfathomable cruelty" (p. 259).

The insight into this cruelty comes at the climactic moment when the sea swallows and covers up all traces of the floating ruin. The shocking or "monstrous" aspect of this spectacle consists in the sheer punctuality of the brig's demise as it disappears "swiftly without a hiss," leaving only a "smother of foam" at the spot where it sank. The eschatological erasure that Swinburne's and Wilner's poems envision over the course of geological time here takes place locally and in an instant. We are thankful to the sea that, unlike empty space, it receives, hides, and reabsorbs the dead. It is its passion for erasure that makes it inhuman. Erasure does not mean disappearance only; it means that the site of disappearance remains unmarkable. There are no gravestones on the sea. History and memory ground themselves on inscription, but this element is uninscribable. It closes over rather than keeps the place of its dead, while its unbounded grave remains humanly unmarked.

As for the loved ones of those who sink into its unfathomable grave, they suffer a special form of anguish. Before embarking on the *Pequod,* Ishmael visits the Whaleman's Chapel in Nantucket and reflects on the numerous marble tablets inscribed in commemoration of so many whalers who never made it home. The chapel is full of women who "wear the countenance if not the trappings of some unceasing grief" (Melville, *Moby Dick,* p. 130). Their grief is unceasing in that it lies at an enormous, untraversable remove from their husbands' remains, almost as if the intimacy of human time at the heart of natural time depended on keeping one's dead close by, within an earthly realm of presence. Ishmael exclaims: "Oh! ye whose dead lie buried beneath the green grass; who standing among flowers can say—here, *here* lies my beloved, ye know not the desolation that broods in hearts like these" (ibid.). Even as they commemorate those who perished at sea—"This marble is placed here by their surviving shipmates," "This tablet is erected to his memory by his widow," and so on—the inscriptions only aggravate the cause of so much anguish, confirming and, as it were, sealing the unearthly exile of the seamen in question. Hence Ishmael's reaction: "What bitter blanks in those black-bordered marbles which cover no ashes. What despair in those immovable inscriptions! What deadly voids and unbidden infidelities in the lines that seem to gnaw upon all Faith, and refuse resurrection to the beings who have placelessly perished without a grave" (ibid.). The very hypothesis of resurrection depends on an earth that receives and holds the place of our mortal remains. It is almost as if these frigid testaments were written in water, for it is the vast and inhuman sea that wells up in the empty space between the words and lines chiseled into the memorial stones, whose placement in the chapel has no effective bearing on their adventitious horizon of reference. Ishmael: "As well might those tablets stand in the cave of Elephanta as here" (p. 52).

But let us return to the Danish captain who stood up in the rescue boat and pointed to the spot where his ruined ship was sinking beneath the surface of a calm yet treacherous sea. If it is human nature to stand in the middle of a thing, it is human nature also to mark the passage from life to death in some way—to give meaning to the matter of it, as it were—even when, as in this case, it is a ship, and not its mates, that dies. It was left to the captain to answer the ship's passing with passing words:

> The captain of the brig lowered his rigid arm slowly, and looked at our faces in a solemnly conscious silence, which called on us to share in his simple-minded, marvelling awe. All at once he sat down by my side, and leaned forward earnestly at my boat's crew, who, swinging together in a long, easy stroke, kept their eyes fixed upon him faithfully.
>
> "No ship could have done so well," he addressed them firmly, after a moment of strained silence, during which he seemed with trembling lips to seek for words fit to bear such high testimony. "She was small, but she was good. I had no anxiety. She was strong. Last voyage I had my wife and two children in her. No other ship could have stood so long the weather she had to live through for days and days before we got dismasted a fortnight ago. She was fairly worn out, and that's all. You may believe me. She lasted under us for days and days, but she could not last for ever. It was long enough. I am glad it is over. No better ship was left to sink at sea on such a day as this." (Conrad, *The Mirror of the Sea*, p. 258)

Conrad remarks that there was "nothing wanting" in the captain's improvised "funeral oration"—"neither piety nor faith, nor the tribute of praise due to the worthy dead"—and that "by the merits of his sea-wise forefathers and by the artlessness of his heart, he was made fit to deliver this excellent discourse" (ibid.). Brought forth by the captain's human breath, that discourse would have dissipated in the air and been forgotten long ago by now had Conrad not written down its intent for us. Indeed, *The Mirror of the Sea* as a whole could be read as an expansive dilation of the captain's "excellent discourse," given the book's stated intention to honor the dead—be they seamen of the past or the worthy ships in which they had served. In his author's note of 1919, Conrad declares that "this book . . . is the best tribute my piety can offer to the ultimate shapers of my character, convictions, and, in a sense, destiny—to the imperishable sea, to the ships that are no more, and to the simple men who have had their day" (p. 135).

That is why I believe that the other equally inexplicable and improbable drive that defined Conrad's life—I mean his drive to become a writer—had its genesis in the initiation incident described in chapter 36. The sea is indeed imperishable, but "the act of blackening pages," as he called it, was Conrad's act of piety toward the perishable—his response to the sea's irresponsibility, its hostility to memory, its impatience with ruins, and its passion for erasure. In the final analysis Conrad's career as a writer represents his allegiance to the earth, not the sea, for the earth is our ultimate stone, tablet, or inscribable page. The words on Keats's grave in the Protestant cemetery of Rome—"here lies one whose name was writ in water"—were not written in water but on a headstone that continues to hold the place of its reference. Just as we build on the earth, so too we write in its element, regardless of the medium.

With the exception of Eleanor Wilner, all of the authors whose testaments I have visited here are dead. This is evidence enough that the act of blackening the page constitutes a gift of the dead to the future. Even if the "bleak tablets" in the Whaleman's Chapel "sympathetically cause the old wounds to bleed afresh" (Melville, *Moby Dick*, p. 51) in the widows who obsessively return to their inscriptions, *Moby Dick*, as a gift of literature, recalls the irreducibly human character of those wounds. In giving voice to the wound of mortality itself, literature houses or gives a home to even the most desolate kinds of grief. It gives us *back* that which we keep on losing, namely a cognizance or recognizance of our passionate and mortal natures. Hence the intrinsically posthumous character of the literary voice, which I insist on time and again throughout these pages. Works of literature, then, are more than enduring tablets where an author's words survive his or her demise. They are the gifts of human worlds, cosmic in nature, that hold their place in time so that the living and the unborn may inhabit them at will, make themselves at home in their articulate humanity—all thanks to the ultimate gift of the earth, which renders their testaments possible.

If the intuition of time is in fact schematized by the imagination, as Kant believed, then one could say that these various visions of ruin and annihilation I have reviewed—be they imaginary or real—throw the imagination back upon its source in human finitude. Ruins are in that regard apocalyptic, or revelatory. As images of posteriority they reveal the primordiality of the temporal law that holds sway over their obsolescence. Certainly in some of the visions I have discussed, ruins and the sea have at least this much in common: just as ruins have outlasted the worlds to which they once belonged, the sea will outlast the earth on which they stand. Yet I believe this is an anticorrelation, in the way the Antichrist is a false or deceptive semblance of Christ. The spectacle of ruins reveals the fact of destruction, yet at the same time it also reveals the fact of survival—the survival not so much of the ruins themselves as of the earth on which they stand or fall. I have insisted from the start that this is the true correlation: time and earth. While human worlds in their built character succumb to the law of finitude, the earth where they lay their foundations, and where the law finds itself at home, persists. It persists not merely as the material substrate of human dwelling but as the elemental correlative of the coffer from which human beings retrieve their legacies from out of their futures. History is made of and written into this conservative element that outlasts its bygone worlds even as it allows for the opening of crypts and folds of human time in the midst of nature's transcendence.

If the issue is the persistence *of* time and not persistence *in* time, and if time has an earthly correlate, then one could say that the sight of ruins in a landscape offers images of the postdiluvian covenant between God and humankind. When Abraham Lincoln ends his famous address at Gettysburg with the words "shall not perish from the earth," he declares his faith in the founding idea of the American republic, yet at the same time he confesses a much more basic faith in the providential ground of history, namely the earth, which is the basis for the durability of any nation whatsoever. This address, which I reflect on more fully in the next chapter, makes sense only on the basis of his trust in the covenant. Yet in truth there is nothing in this covenant that stipulates the eternity of the earth; on the contrary, the covenant holds, says Genesis, "as long as the earth endures." In its full articulation: "As long as the earth endures, seedtime and harvest, cold and heat, summer and winter, day and night, shall not cease" (8:22). Who knows anymore how long the earth will endure or what the covenant demands of us?

If we understand the covenant not so much as a contract between God and man as between man and earth—for it is the latter contract, I believe, that lies at the basis of the former—then we can speak of something like humankind's obligations toward the earth, as well as its failures to meet those obligations. I speak here not so much of the planet in its material determination as of the humic earth, which will endure as the elemental correlative of human history only as long as history itself endures. When history turns against its own memorializing and self-conserving drive, when it is perceived to have become a force of erasure rather than of inscription, of assault on the earth rather than humanization of the earth, then images of an apocalyptic sea inevitably surge up in the human imagination. Such images remind us that history exists in a covenant that has a history of its own, and a finite one at that; and remind us furthermore that only an ever-vigilant awareness of the covenant's finitude assures its perpetuity.

CHAPTER 2

HIC JACET

In an interview with the German magazine *Der Spiegel* in 1966, Martin Heidegger declared that "only a god can save us" (Sheehan, *Heidegger*, p. 57), but I live in a part of the country where new houses and buildings are cropping up everywhere—expensive ones at that—and hardly a day goes by that I don't think to myself, "only an architect can save us." As a layperson I get the impression that a discrete catastrophe is taking place in America these days: the loss of the basic art of building. It seems that we can no longer design a simple, inoffensive home that does not somehow show false. Nor can we erect a public edifice in which "truth of feature is related to truth of being," as Frank Lloyd Wright once expressed his wish for American architecture (Wright, *American Architecture*, p. 256).

The fracture between the truth of feature and truth of being seems to be growing ever wider, for reasons that we can speculate about endlessly and probably not very fruitfully. Manfredo Tafuri believed that any substantial reforms in architecture would have to wait until after the existing social and economic structures of society have been overturned. Heidegger believed that only a new epochal revelation of the sacred could alter the way we dwell, hence the way we build. Must we change our way of existing before we can change our way of building? Or would changing the way we build change the way we exist? Frankly it's undecidable. Yet if human being is a "being in the world," as Heidegger maintained, then nothing is more essentially related to our being than our building practices, given that the world into which we are thrown is always a *built* world. We take our measure of being from what surrounds us; and what surrounds us is always, to some extent, of our own making. Building, which starts from the ground up, is where the fundamental ontology of our mundane lives both begins and ends.

This chapter engages one of the basic questions around which such an ontology inevitably revolves, that of place. What is a place? How is it established? On what foundations? How does building define or articulate its wherewithal? In what exactly does placehood consist? Much has been written about place of late, by philosophers and historians of architecture alike; and while much of the literature is extremely good, some of it suffers from a lack of what Vico called "philological certainty" when it comes to identifying the ground on which places have traditionally been founded. I intend the term *ground* both literally and nonliterally. Indeed, it is because places come into being through acts of human grounding that the term possesses its literal and nonliteral senses. We know by now that the wherewithal of place does not preexist the act of building but is created by humanity's mark—its edified sign or signature—on the landscape. It is the substance of such marking that interests me here, for it is impossible to understand the nature of place without taking into account the origin and founding power of that marking.

Let me begin with an unproblematic proposition: a place is defined by its boundaries, its intrinsic limits, its distinctly local "here" that remains fixed in space even as it perdures in time. I follow with a slightly more controversial claim: places are located in nature, yet they always have human foundations. They do not occur naturally but are created by human beings through some mark or sign of human presence. A wilderness in itself is placeless, for it has no human center or point of convergence around which nature can gather and become bounded. Wallace Stevens's poem "Anecdote of the Jar" describes the minimal conditions of this sort of place making:

I placed a jar in Tennessee,
And round it was, upon a hill.
It made the slovenly wilderness
Surround that hill.

The wilderness rose up to it,
And sprawled around, no longer wild.
The jar was round upon the ground
And tall and of a port in air.

It took dominion everywhere.
The jar was gray and bare.

It did not give of bird or bush,
Like nothing else in Tennessee.

(*The Collected Poems*, p. 76)

I would draw attention first of all to the way in which "a hill" in the second verse becomes "that hill" in the fourth, suggesting that the placement of the jar has established a horizon of reference for the demonstrative pronoun's deictic gesture. The jar is not a piece of architecture, properly speaking, yet it brings about the domestication of space that we associate with architecture's place-creating functions. Tamed by the object's presence, the "slovenly wilderness" now "rises up to" and "surrounds" this center of orientation. The jar provides the surrounding nature with a measure of containment—of *human* containment, I would insist, by virtue of the fact that the object is man-made and has been placed there by a human being. It lies there as a kind of urn in the midst of the wilderness. The entire transfiguration of the scene of nature—its topical convergence in one place—is due to the introduction of this sign of human worldhood.

I argued in the preceding chapter that human worldhood is defined above all by time and that even our perception as well as inclusion in space is temporal in character. In *The Ethical Function of Architecture* Karsten Harries sympathizes with this claim when he writes that "[a]ny view that understands architecture as the art of establishing place by the construction of boundaries in space is inevitably one-sided. While dwelling requires the establishment of place, place must also be understood temporally" (p. 223). I would go even further and say that a place is where time, in its human modes, takes place. A place cannot come into being without human time's intervention in nature's eternally self-renewing cycles—the cycles of "bird and bush," as it were. What intervenes in natural time is human finitude, which is unlike other finite things in that death claims our awareness before it claims our lives. We dwell in space, to be sure, but we dwell first and foremost within the limits of our mortality. Those limits are not merely restrictive but are in fact *generative* of the boundaries—spatial and otherwise—of the worlds where history, in its temporal unfolding, takes place. When we build something in nature, be it a dwelling, a monument, or even a fire, we create the rudiments of a world and thereby give a sign of our mortal sojourn on the earth.

The most aboriginal sign of this history-making mortality, of which Stevens's jar is a kind of everyday correlate, is the grave marker. Adolf Loos once remarked: "If we find a mound in the forest, six feet long and three feet wide, heaped up with a spade in the shape of a pyramid, then we become solemn and something tells us: somebody lies buried here.—This is architecture!" ("Architektur," p. 318). You know, in other words, that a mortal, world-forming creature created it. A grave marks the mortality of its creators even more distinctly than it marks the resting place of the dead. It is not for nothing that the Greek word for "sign," *sema*, is also the word for "grave." For the Greeks the grave marker was not just one sign among others. It was a sign that signified the source of signification itself, since it "stood for" what it "stood in"— the ground of burial as such. In its pointing to itself, or to its own mark in the ground, the *sema* effectively opens up the place of the "here," giving it that human foundation without which there would be no places in nature. For the *sema* points to something present only in and through its sign. Prior to gaining an outward reference, its "here" refers to the place of a disappearance. It is that disappearance—death as such—that opens the horizon of reference in the first place. The grave marker's reference is first and foremost a self-reference. A. R. Ammons puts it best in his poem "Tombstones":

what does it matter if
a stone falls or slides and
misidentifies a mound:
the stone's outward
reference given up it
calls to itself
(*Sumerian Vistas*, p. 50)

Once the stone is uprooted and the outward reference of its "here" gets lost, the stone now refers solely to its own power of reference, which persists. More precisely, the stone now reveals that its power of reference resides in its power to mark the fact of passing. It is through the institution of such power, I submit, that places come into being.

In his book *Statues*, Michel Serres reminds us that the archaic statue originated as a kind of anthropomorphic stele, a lapidary representative of the person who lied buried at the site of its erection (p. 281). Indeed, in its earliest instantiations there was no such "representation" to talk of, since the first statue, according to Serres, was the mummified corpse itself. If, as Serres writes, "the cadaver and the mummy lie where their statue is raised" (ibid.), and if the latter bodies forth the figure of the former, then the statue is indeed a *sema* in the full multivalent Greek sense. Earlier I suggested that Stevens's jar lies in the Tennessee land-scape like a kind of urn, to which I would now add that it stands there like a kind of primitive statue, not because it "represents" a deceased person or marks a grave in any explicit sense, but because in its creat-edness and deliberate placement on the hill it "embodies" the mortality of whoever forged it, placed it there, or recognizes it as the object it is, either in itself or in the poem that names it. One could say that the sub-ject in the poem is not simply the placer of the jar, since all that takes place as a result of that emplacement takes place in and for the pres-ence of this same human "I," who is at once speaker, placer, poet, and reader. To be human means to be the surrounding center of such world-forming intentionality.

I agree with Harries, David Kolb, Edward Casey, and others who have meditated in depth on this topic and concluded that no one has thought more radically and originally about the nature of place than Heidegger. However, as I will insist time and again throughout this book, I believe that Heidegger's ontology is in need of some Vichian certainty, call it some genetic anthropology. This is especially the case when it comes to his thinking about the conditions under which places come into being. Heidegger speaks abstractly about the disclosure of the world in and through the *Da* of *Dasein,* but surely the *Da* is first opened, and subsequently kept open, by what Vico called the institu-tional order, about which Heidegger has next to nothing to say. And surely Vico was right to consider burial of the dead one of the three "universal institutions" of humanity, along with religion and matri-mony.

What does burial have to do with *Dasein*'s place—with *Dasein* as the *discloser* of place? In what way does the enclosure of the tomb open the *Da* of *Dasein*'s world? Serres remarks that the term *être-là* could be said to transcribe in another idiom the phrase *ci-gît,* or "here lies," which one finds in the epitaphs of old French tombstones (*Statues,* p. 63). The Italian for "here lies"—*qui giace*—is even closer to the Latin matrix of this tombstone deictic: *hic jacet*. If one wanted to speak Heideggerese, one could say that the *hic* of *hic jacet* is the aboriginal *Da* that grounds *Dasein*'s situatedness and historicizes its being in the world, especially since *jacet* alludes to the finite temporality that *Dasein* makes its own in its so-called being-toward-death. Certainly the *hic* of *hic jacet* is no ordinary locative adverb. Like the ancient *sema*, it is an indicator that appropriates the ground of indication, drawing a boundary of belonging around it. It is a shifter that refuses to shift. In its pointing always to the same place, it points to that persistent finitude that underlies the placehood of place and pervades the *Da* of *Dasein*. No human words need be inscribed on the tombstone. A crude gravepost is sufficient to indicate this mortal *hic*, or "here." Yet it *must* be indicated, one way or another.

In his 1939 essay on the meaning of *physis* in Aristotle's *Physics* Heidegger talks about the deeper commonality that underlies the difference between the two terms by which the Greeks thought about and named the "beingness of being": *hypokeimenon* and *hypostasis*. The former means literally "that which lies under." Its Latin equivalent is *subjectum*, literally "that which is thrown under." The latter term— *hypostasis*—means "that which stands under." Its Latin equivalent is *substantia*. Heidegger claims that while "to lie" and "to stand" are quite opposite, "only what stands can fall and thus lie; and only what lies can be put upright and thus stand" (McNeill, *Pathmarks*, p. 200). And I would claim in turn that there is at least one case in which this dialectic fails, namely in the case of the dead. The dead cannot "be put upright and thus stand," except vicariously, as when their statues, for example, are erected on the ground under which they lie.

Be that as it may, if Heidegger can get away with saying that "both [*hypokeimenon* and *hypostasis*] have equal weight, for in both cases the Greeks have one and the same thing in view: being-present of and by itself, presencing" (ibid.), then perhaps I can get away with saying that this "equal weight" derives from the "subjective" commonality that links the living to the dead in the modes of memory, genealogy, tradition, and history. It is as if we the living can stand (culturally, institutionally, economically, in other words humanly) only because the dead underlie the ground on which we build our homes, worlds, and commonwealths. To speak once again in Heideggerese, *Dasein* can inhabit its *Da* only because the *Da* is preinhabited by the predecessor. The essence of human "subjectivity" may well consist in such preinhabitation. In chapter 5 I will show how human "understanding," in its analytic and synthetic modes, derives from the same underlying source.

The preceding has, it is hoped, made us appreciate the extent to which we cannot understand the early institution of places on the earth independently of the institution of burial. For what is a place if not its memory of itself—a site or locale where time turns back upon itself? The grave marks a site in the landscape where time cannot merely pass through, or pass over. Time must now gather around the *sema* and mortalize itself. It is precisely this mortalization of time that gives place its articulated boundaries, distinguishing it from the infinity of homogeneous space. As the primordial sign of human mortality, the grave domesticates the inhuman transcendence of space and marks human time off from the timelessness of the gods and the eternal returns of nature. That is why gods are not the original founders of place—mortals are. An immortal god may bless a place that has already been founded, but such a god cannot introduce the mark of finite time necessary to ground it. Let us reflect on what the historian Walter Burkert has to say about the difference between the cult of heroes and the cult of gods in ancient Greece:

> An important difference between the hero cult and the cult of the gods is that a hero is always confined to a specific locality: he acts in the vicinity of his grave for his family, group or city. The bond with a hero is dissolved by distance. . . . In the newly established colonial cities, the founder generally becomes the *Hero Ktises* who is often buried in the market place. In this way the new land is immediately given a centre which, even if not from a greater past, nevertheless symbolizes the good fortune and obligations that flow from the new beginning. (*Greek Religion*, pp. 206–7)

The hero's burial here performs the function of Stevens's jar in that it provides the newly inhabited land with a center, makes of it a proper place. A god cannot do this, cannot as it were emplace human finitude. We know that Athens had in Athena its protective goddess, but even Athens needed the presence of Oedipus's grave in its vicinity to assure its founding and good fortune into the future. For all the enigmas and mytho-historical opacities surrounding the story of Oedipus's burial, we may perceive in its myth a poetic character of the founding power of the hero's grave. If it is true that the cult of heroes to which Burkert alludes in this passage is more ancient in origin among the Greeks and Romans than the cult of the gods, and that it goes back to the very earliest worship of their Indo-European ancestors, at a time when people venerated their own forebears and when the only gods who existed were domestic, mortal gods, then we can understand why, even after the advent of immortal gods, the hero's grave retained its ancient founding power in the classical world.

Let me put forward another proposition here, to the effect that places are not only founded but also appropriated by burial of the dead. The Sicilian baron in one of Pirandello's stories is no doubt a savvy realist when he remarks to his daughter that the reason he stubbornly refuses to allow his peasants to bury their dead on his land is because they would promptly come to believe that the land belonged to them by natural right. The surest way to take possession of a place and secure it as one's own is to bury one's dead in it. Consider in this regard the controversy that erupted in Israel a few years ago between religious leaders and Jewish archaeologists who were disinterring ancient Hebrew graves. Jewish religious law holds the profanation of graves a sacrilege, hence the rabbis were demanding an end to the excavations. The archaeologists, in turn, argued that the more evidence they could uncover confirming that Jews had been buried there in ancient times, the more it would legitimate Israel's claim to its territories. The rabbis responded with a devastating logic: by attempting to legitimate the claim, the diggers were violating its basis.

Not all cultures mark the graves of their ancestors, to be sure, or assert proprietary rights over the land through burial of their dead. In some nomadic Bedouin societies, for instance, the dead are buried in the desert with anonymous and temporary markers that the desert effaces over time. Such consignments do not entail possession and leave the desert unmarked by specific, bounded places in the sense I have discussed so far. Yet while the desert remains unpossessed as such, it remains nonetheless the Bedouins' native place of belonging, thanks in part to their ancestors' discrete and diffuse presence there. Something analogous applies to the native Americans, with their strong sense of an ancestral presence in the landscapes that have received the bones of their dead. There is a difference, then, between proprietary claims and the claims of belonging, this despite the fact that in Western culture these two claims have a way of blending into each other.

In the West the establishment of belonging through burial has origins dating to the very beginning of the Neolithic way of life. In his *New Science*, which, among other things, offers a genetic psychology of early Neolithic consciousness, Vico argues that the remote ancestors of what would later become the patrician families of Europe originally laid claim to their lands by pointing to the wooden graveposts of their own forefathers. Through that gesture they would legitimate their ownership of the land: "Thus by the graves of their buried dead the giants showed dominion over their lands, and Roman law called for burial of the dead in a proper place to make it religious. With truth they could pronounce these heroic phrases: we are sons of this earth, we are born from these oaks" (§531). He goes on to state that "the most noble houses of Europe and almost all its reigning families takes their names from the lands over which they rule" (ibid.). In this passage Vico is probing specifically the earliest origins of the ancient house, which was not merely a place of residence but an institution that linked the living to the dead, the dead to the unborn, and the family to its native ground. And since I have mentioned Vico let me invoke another author who is dear to me and who was himself influenced by Vico—Numa Denis Fustel de Coulanges, the nineteenth-century French author of *The Ancient City*. The crux of this masterpiece of classical philology is the claim (abundantly substantiated) that the ancient city was built on the foundations of the ancient house, and that the ancient house was built in turn upon the ancestor's grave. Fustel de Coulanges, who boasted of having read every word in Greek and Latin that had come down to his age from antiquity, claimed that every Greek and Roman house featured an altar on which burned a sacred fire, which was to remain perpetually lit and which the occupants identified with their domestic gods, that is, their buried forebears. There is even evidence, of the order of textual traces, suggesting that the dead were sometimes placed *inside* these altars, hence that the house was literally and figuratively erected upon their tombs, forming a sort of mausoleum around them. We will never know to what extent Fustel de Coulanges's specific claims are historically exact, yet there is little doubt that the ancient house, and in its turn the ancient city, were founded upon such sepulchers.

Unless we understand the binding terms of this genealogical contract between the living and the dead we will never understand the burden of Aeneas, leader of the Trojan refugees and mythical founder of Rome. After the destruction of Troy, Aeneas was entrusted with the responsibility of transporting the House of Troy from one land to another, so as to save the house itself. More exactly, he was charged with carrying the ancestral gods of his family to a new home. In a dramatic passage of *The Aeneid* the ghost of the dead Hector appears to Aeneas in a vision to give him instruction:

> "Ah, goddess-born, take flight [cries Hector] and snatch
> yourself out of these flames. The enemy
> has gained the walls; Troy falls from her high peak.
> Our home, our Priam—these have had their due:
> could Pergamus be saved by any prowess,
> then my hand would have served. But Troy entrusts
> her holy things and household gods to you;
> take them away as comrades of your fortunes,
> seek out for them the great walls that at last,
> once you have crossed the sea, you will establish."
> So Hector speaks; then from the inner altars
> he carries out the garlands and great Vesta
> and, in his hands, the fire that never dies.
>
> (Virgil, *The Aeneid*, 2.285–95)

The household gods, or *penates,* live on in that fire that never dies, except once a year, when it is ceremoniously extinguished and rekindled. To save the House of Troy and preserve its continuity in time, Aeneas must not only relocate the *penates* to a new land, he must also domesticate the *terra nova* by interring his people there. *The Aeneid* is punctuated by such ritual burials. Aeneas buries his father Anchises in Sicily; Palinurus he buries at the bottom of the mainland; Misenus he buries near Cumae; his nursemaid Gaeta he buries at Gaeta (naming the place after her), a hundred miles south of the future imperial city. Each one of those sites becomes in its turn a place in Rome's future history. In this retrospective epic of Rome's founding—all the more revealing insofar as its mythic burials *are* retrospective—Virgil makes of Aeneas a tamer of the Italian peninsula, a hero who founds places in its wilderness by giving them the names of those whom he buries there. It is as if, by planting his dead at various sites as he makes his way up the coast, he lays the ground for Rome's future political claims on those territories.

It is not only places, then, but also nations and empires, which repose on such human—call them humic—foundations. And lest we think that this claim relies on ancient myth and outdated French philology, we have only to look at the founding of a modern, "enlightened" nation like the United States of America. The American republic, we're told, is founded upon its Constitution. But how does or how must the Constitution ground itself upon that continent where its otherwise abstract, universalizing laws are supposed to apply? For it is one thing to frame a Constitution. It is quite another to give it a grounding that will secure the place of its authority. At a critical moment in American history, when the nation was divided over the issue of slavery, Abraham Lincoln realized that the Constitution needed to be rescued by those who, in coming to the rescue, would decide the fate of its authority. He realized, in other words, that the nation's founding scripture was in need of a refounding that the scripture itself could not provide:

> Four score and seven years ago our fathers brought forth on this continent, a new nation, conceived in Liberty and dedicated to the proposition that all men are created equal.
>
> Now we are engaged in a great civil war, testing whether that nation, or any nation so conceived and so dedicated, can long endure. We are met on a great battle-field of that war. We have come to dedicate a portion of that field, as a final resting place for those who here gave their lives that that nation might live. It is altogether fitting and proper that we should do this.
>
> But, in a larger sense, we can not dedicate—we cannot consecrate—we can not hallow—this ground. The brave men, living and dead, who struggled here have consecrated it, far above our poor power to add or detract. The world will little note, nor long remember what we say here, but it can never forget what they did here. It is for us the living, rather, to be dedicated here to the unfinished work which they who fought here have thus far nobly ad-

vanced. It is rather for us to be here dedicated to the great task remaining before us—that from these honored dead we take increased devotion to that cause for which they gave their last full measure of devotion—that we here highly resolve that these dead shall not have died in vain—that this nation, under God, shall have a new birth of freedom—and that government of the people, by the people, for the people, shall not perish from the earth.

Ralph Waldo Emerson's essay "Experience" opens with a question to his countrymen: "Where do we find ourselves?" (*Essays*, p. 45) To this haunting, deeply American query, Lincoln at the Gettysburg cemetery replies: *hic*. The word *here* occurs a full eight times in his brief address. In each case it points to the ground—"this ground"—to which the martyrs and victims of the nation's contradiction, its civil war, have been consigned. A discrete grammatical breakthrough—from "that nation" at the beginning of the address to "this nation" at the end—indicates that the securement of the nation's *hic* has taken place, precisely through the sepulchering act of the address itself.

The Latin word *sepulcrum* comes from *sepelire*, which means "to bury" but which has an Indo-European root that means "to render honor." The historical irony of Lincoln's speech is that, had it not been for its honoring gesture, the world would not much have noted what happened at Gettysburg. In other words it does not suffice to place the dead in the ground; as I stressed earlier, it is also necessary to mark that burial. In this case Lincoln's address is the *sema*, or grave marker. Its speech act makes of that ground a place or *the* place where the nation finds itself, on which it must found, or refound, its republic. Not only in their sacrificial deaths, but above all in their ritual sepulture, the remembered dead enable the nation to make its own the continent on which it first came forth. The "here" in Lincoln's speech is where nation and continent come together on that plot of "earth" from which "government of the people, by the people, for the people, shall not perish." Henceforth the continent becomes a veritable place—a place where the idea of America can take root geographically.

Yet the most important place secured in Lincoln's address is perhaps that of the nation's time. Its *hic* does not only mark a geographical "here" but also a historical "now": "Four score and seven years ago. . . ."

Now we are engaged in a great civil war." The speech locates the nation's place in time, in an ongoing, critical history, at a moment of decision about whether such a nation can temporally perdure. America, in short, needs a place to take place historically. That place is not only upon the earth of "this continent," but also in the hearts of those who would assure, through their rededication to the cause for which the dead here have died, that the idea of America shall endure—that this *hic* shall henceforth be the place where history, geography, and the Constitution intersect.

It was Lincoln's destiny to rescue the new nation's "new birth of freedom" by securing for it the sacrificial basis of the most ancient nations: the blood of the brother. In his martyrdom he embodied or stood for all the victims of a civil war waged on behalf of, and against, the union. That martyrdom brought together dispersed and diverse wounds into a unified history and geography of grief. Walt Whitman, in a series of unforgettable images, evokes the sacrificial binding power of the dead president in his poem "When Lilacs Last in the Dooryard Bloom'd":

Coffin that passes through lanes and streets,
Through day and night with the great cloud darkening the land,
With the pomp of the inloop'd flags with the cities draped in
    black,
With the show of the States themselves as of crape-veil'd women
    standing,
With processions long and winding and the flambeaus of the
    night,
With the countless torches lit, with the silent sea of faces and the
    unbared heads,
With the waiting depot, the arriving coffin, and the sombre
    faces,
With dirges through the night, with the thousand voices rising
    strong and solemn,
With all the mournful voices of the dirges pour'd around the
    coffin,
The dim-lit churches and the shuddering organs—where amid
    these you journey,
With the tolling bells' perpetual clang,

Here, coffin that slowly passes,
I give you my sprig of lilac.

(Whitman, in *American Poetry*, p. 897)

Whitman addresses the dead Lincoln as a living "you," for the corpse is still very much alive. Not only is it making an actual journey, it is also an animate force acting upon and drawing together the new nation, reborn now of the tolling bells and shadowy light. Once could say that the temporal passage of Lincoln's body across the spatial expanse of the nation effectively brings an end to, or better, "buries," the Civil War— "buries" in the sense of becoming the enduring foundation of a nation "so conceived and so dedicated." In the magnitude of its tragedy, his death became, and to this day remains, a source of unity in the Union, a unity that the Constitution, for all its enlightened provisions, could not provide.

To these reflections I would add the following reminder: foundational acts are never completely primordial. Latium was anything but an inhuman wilderness when Aeneas arrived there. The second half of *The Aeneid* recounts the wars the Trojans waged against the indigenous inhabitants of the new land. Likewise with the American continent. Stevens's poem about the jar may seem like an allegory of place-founding in the midst of a wilderness—I even read it as such—but there was already a place there in which to place the jar. The place-name itself—Tennessee—speaks of this indigenous prehabitation. As Thoreau wanders through the so-called wilds of New England, he finds arrowheads everywhere in the soil. We are all latecomers. To be human means to come after those who came before. Just as we are always preceded by our forebears, so too the ground in which we lay them to rest has always already received the bones of others—"others" in the most radical sense of the term, including that of other species, many of whom have died on our behalf.

• • •

So far my claims about the foundation of place have drawn mostly on the archives of our cultural past. I will now briefly turn my attention to the present and then, by way of conclusion, comment on how all this might relate to the concerns and vocation of architecture.

If cultural memory has a future, which at present seems doubtful, the twentieth century will one day be remembered as the fitful and prolonged continuation of a process that began in earnest a century earlier: the end of the Neolithic era. Throughout this era, which got under way with the domestication of animals and discovery of agriculture, the great majority of human beings lived and toiled on the land where their ancestors were interred, where they and their children and their children's children would also be interred. This is no longer the case in Western societies. For the first time in millennia, most of us don't know where we will be buried, assuming we will be buried at all. The likelihood that it will be alongside any of our progenitors becomes increasingly remote. From a historical or sociological point of view this is astounding. Uncertainty as to one's posthumous abode would have been unthinkable to the vast majority of people a few generations ago. Nothing speaks quite so eloquently of the loss of place in the post-Neolithic era as this indeterminacy.

It goes hand in hand with another indeterminacy that until recently would have been equally unthinkable for the majority. Most of us have no idea where the food we eat comes from. We are oblivious of the fields that yielded our grain, the gardens our vegetables sprouted in, the orchards where our fruits are gathered. We are not familiar with the individual animals we eat: we don't tend to them, we don't watch them grow, we don't know what flock they came from or on which pastures they grazed, and above all we have no hand in their sacrifice. The daily holocausts that supply the world markets' demands for meat, fish, and poultry take place in another world than the one most of us inhabit. And yet we live off such holocausts, inevitably.

The fact that so many of today's children have never seen a cow is not necessarily a problem for the cows, but some of us would say it's a problem nonetheless. Milk remains more or less the same substance whether we know where it comes from or not; but when a staggering proportion of first-world children respond to the question "Where does milk come from?" with answers to the effect that "it comes from the carton," or, in the case of meat, "it comes from the supermarket," there is reason to believe that more is at stake here than urban distantiation from the conditions of food production. Origins are in some ultimate sense unknowable, yet there is a difference between not knowing where life in its original impulse comes from and not knowing where milk comes from. When the "from" of the things we consume becomes not only remote but essentially unreal, the world we live in draws a veil over the earth we live on—a veil that obscures not only the source of our foodstuffs but also the source of our relation to the earth, namely our death. For the earth is both our *unde,* or "from," as well as our *quo,* or "whereto."

Uncertainty about the provenance of one's food and the destination of one's corpse relate to each other not accidentally but essentially. Both stem from a single-minded effort undertaken by the West in the last few centuries to emancipate ourselves, by whatever means necessary, from our millennial bondage to the land and our servitude to the dead. Who can blame us for striving for this emancipation? The sweat and tears of untold generations—an ocean of them—have gone into our labors. We have worked the earth to death and borne the curse of our earthbound race in every way imaginable. We have suffered endless hardships and indignities in the name of our obligations to the dead and the land. Haven't we paid our dues several times over? Don't we have the right to settle, once and for all, our debts with the dead, with the earth, even with God, if it comes to that?

This remains to be seen. A genuine modernity or post-Neolithic freedom would consist in a genuine settlement of this sort, but we are not genuinely modern, and for the most part we have presumed to settle our debts merely by ignoring them. Certainly no amount of emancipation, be it through mechanized food production, technological innovation, or genetic engineering, can absolve us from the humus that makes up the "substance" of humanity, regardless of whether biomedical science will eventually find ways to prolong human life indefinitely. Endless prolongation of life does not amount to absolution. Mortality is absolved only by dying. The destruction of place that is occurring almost everywhere at present, and that has been occurring for some time now, is linked in part to an anxious and even frenzied flight from death. We are running away from ourselves, not so much in the sense that we are abandoning our traditional homelands but in the sense that we are forsaking or destroying the places where our dying can make itself at home.

In his interview with *Der Spiegel,* where he asserted that "only a god can save us" from the nihilism that is uprooting us from the earth, Heidegger declared: "We do not need atomic bombs at all [to uproot us], the uprooting of man is already here. All our relationships have become merely technical ones. It is no longer upon an earth that man lives today" (Sheehan, *Heidegger,* p. 56). These are the kind of solemn pronouncements that render Heidegger so irksome to many people. Certainly he managed to irk his urbanite interviewers over the course of their long interview. Well prepared and in no way intimidated by the philosopher's lofty stature, they responded to Heidegger's lament with the following challenge:

> *Spiegel:* Well, we have to say that indeed we prefer to be here [on the earth], and in our age we surely will not have to leave for elsewhere. But who knows if man is determined to be upon this earth? It is thinkable that man has absolutely no determination at all. After all, one might see it to be one of man's possibilities that he reach out from this earth toward other planets. We have by no means come that far, of course—but where is it written that he has his place here? (p. 57)

This is the most crucial "philosophical" question posed by the interviewers during the entire interview, for it goes to the heart of Heidegger's faith in the irreducible ontological relationality between "man" and the earth, indeed, his faith that Being, in the final analysis, is nothing other than this relationality. Heidegger answered awkwardly enough: "As far as my own orientation goes, in any case, I know that, according to our human experience and history, everything essential and of great magnitude has arisen only out of the fact that man had a home and was rooted in a tradition" (ibid.). There is something feeble about the response, not only because the talk of "home" and "tradition" smacks of Swabian provincialism, but also because Heidegger, who had nothing but contempt for all forms of empiricism throughout his career, invokes his personal "orientation" and appeals uncharacteristically to the authority of "experience and history." If Heidegger cannot justify the faith that underlies his philosophy on philosophical grounds, then the statement that effectively culminates the interview—"only a god can save us"—appears, if not inevitable, then at least coherent. Such a god would presumably save our connection to the earth and thus save "man" from the homelessness, or indetermination of nature, posited by the interviewers' question.

I would have answered the interviewers somewhat differently, in any case more anthropologically. To begin with, I would have pointed out that it is in the earth itself that it is "written" that we have our "place here." Dig up its fossils, unearth its graves, excavate its cities, and read the scripts for yourselves. They all say: *hic jacet.* To this I would have added that it may well be the case that "man," in his species being, is not determined to be upon the earth, but that the same cannot be said for humanity. Humanity is not a species; it is a connection with the humus. The Neanderthals belonged to a different species than we, yet the fact that they buried their dead is evidence enough that their mode of being was human. If one day we colonize other worlds, then we might be able to say, empirically and definitively, that "man" was not "determined" to be upon this earth after all. But such a "man," when and if he comes to exist, will no longer be human, at least not in the sense in which Vico talked of *homo humandi,* or in which his giants pointed to "this earth" and "these oaks" as their place of belonging.

Of course it is not necessary to colonize other worlds in order for the species to become unearthly or to dehumanize its nature. It may well be that what we are witnessing today is the end not only of the Neolithic era but of the human epoch as such—the end, that is, of a mode of being on the earth that rests on humic foundations. One must ask here whether an intrinsic, millenarian drive in us is responsible for this uprooting, or whether the posthuman era, about which so much ink is spilt today, is in fact the "slovenly" result simply of an all too human failure to meet the challenges of modernity. If the former is the case, that is, if the end of the Neolithic era means the final demise and dissolution of our domesticity and the beginning of a new phase in our species being, then this book is no more than a retrospective probing of the obsolete ground of an obsolete human nature. If the latter is the case, then we are faced with the task of reclaiming the claims that the earth and our dead make on that nature—no easy task, given that we hardly know what a genuinely modern response to those claims would consist in. Meanwhile we find ourselves in a situation where each of us must choose an allegiance—either to the posthuman, the virtual and the synthetic, or to the earth, the real and the dead in their humic densities.

Architects too face the same kind of choice. If Heidegger is right that "[p]hilosophy will be unable to effect any immediate change in the current state of the world" or offset in any way the "world movement that is bringing about an absolutely technical state" (Sheehan, *Heidegger*, p. 57)—a state divorced but not detached from the earth—the same need not be said for architecture, which determines the configuration of our life worlds. When I declared at the outset that only an architect can save us, I was being only half-facetious, for architecture has it within its power to house our mortality, and, in so doing, to re-place the jar in our slovenly post-Neolithic habitat. I would hope that we need not wait for a global revolution or the advent of a god before we can re-humanize the basis of our building practices. I would like to believe that our constitutive finitude is accessible to us at any moment, and that we can build or rebuild upon that foundation here and now. For as long as we think of our houses, cities, and nations as merely places to live, and not as places to die, those houses, cities, and nations can never become homes or take their stand within the limits of containment from which all shelter and placehood ultimately derive.

I see no reason why architecture, for all its past delinquencies, could not lead the way to a fully modern redemption of our debt to the earth, hence to a new economy of habitation, by taking its measure from the *sema* of our mortality rather than from the empty expanse of a false transcendence—false in the sense in which earlier I spoke of our false modernity. We do not need an architecture of the milk carton that poses as the origin of its contents but an architecture of the cow, as it were, which brings to bear in its lineaments and materials the *unde* and the *quo* of human dwelling on the earth. Its buildings must not only rise from but also redescend into the ground of their edification. They must not only stand there but also lie there. In short, an architecture not so much of the humanistic (in the grand modernist sense) as of the humic.

I would expect a humic architecture of this sort to be vertical in the downward and not only upward sense, and its rising to be more of an emerging than a soaring. I would expect it to be mortal and matrical, haunted in its visible aspects by the earth in which the existential and historical past ultimately come to rest. By that I do not mean that it would be funereal, commemorative, or self-consciously pious toward the has-been, but that its buildings would sink into and emerge out of the recesses of mortal time, or out of the subterranean abodes of the dead, in whom the "spirit" of place ultimately resides. If a house, a building, or a city is not palpably haunted in its architectural features— if the earth's historicity and containment of the dead do not pervade its articulated forms and constitutive matter—then that house, building, or city is dead to the world. Dead to the world means cut off from the earth and closed off from its underworlds. For that is one of the ironies of our life worlds: they receive their animation from the ones that underlie them.

CHAPTER 3

WHAT IS A HOUSE?

According to an ancient strain in Western philosophy, a knowledge of essences figures as the precondition for making; thus the house builder must know what a house is before going about the business of building one. Such knowledge is both theoretical and practical, yet it is not necessarily reflective, at least not in the way philosophy presumes to be reflective. The question in my chapter title is intended reflectively. It does not sound like one, yet it may well be *the* philosophical question of our time—a time when traditional philosophy, or so we are told, has come to an end, leaving us confused about who or where we are, insofar as we are human. Heidegger believed that the confusion stems from modern homelessness; indeed, that modernity and homelessness are at some level necessary correlates. Even if that is true *(dato non concesso),* is the correlation itself amenable to domestication? Is something like the housing of modern homelessness conceivable? What would such housing look like? On what foundations would it rest? What would it shelter? These are questions that we cannot begin to answer until we first clarify, in a reflective way, the essence of a house.

To which philosophers can we turn for help? To Heidegger himself? Certainly he did not make things any easier on his commentators when, in his "Letter on Humanism," after enigmatically declaring that "language is the house of Being," he went on to caution that his dictum should not be taken metaphorically: "The talk about the house of Being is no transfer of the image 'house' to Being. But one day we will, by thinking the essence of Being in a way appropriate to its matter, more readily be able to think what 'house' and 'to dwell' are" (*Basic Writings*, pp. 236–37). This is an astonishing piece of reasoning, even for Heidegger, who frequently reasons backwards. It is not by thinking the essence of being more appropriately that we will come to know what a house is; if anything, it is by thinking the essence of a house that we will come to know what being is.

Let us begin with an anthropological fact that, when we reflect on it, unsettles our everyday conception of the house as natural shelter or dwelling place: human beings housed their dead before they housed themselves. Lewis Mumford puts it well in the opening pages of *The City in History:* "Mid the uneasy wanderings of paleolithic man, the dead were the first to have a permanent dwelling: a cavern, a mound marked by a cairn, a collective barrow. These were landmarks to which the living probably returned at intervals, to commune with or placate the ancestral spirits" (p. 7). Mumford's summary statement, to the effect that "the city of the dead antedates the city of the living . . . is the forerunner, almost the core, of every living city" (ibid.), is reminiscent of Fustel de Coulanges's argument that the ancient house (on whose foundations rested the ancient city) had its origins in ancestor worship. The Greek and Roman house typically featured an altar on which burned the sacred fire of the so-called *lares.* The *lares* were ancestral spirits associated with the hearth, just as the *manes* were spirits linked to the ancestral graves.

And then there were the *penates,* household gods closely related the *lares.* The word *penate* is etymologically akin to *penitus,* meaning "inwardly, in the innermost part, deep inside." More directly it is connected to the word *penus*—the cellar or cupboard inside of which perishable provisions and victuals were stored and preserved. The origins of this association of the *penates* with the storage place for victuals are obscure, yet the *penates,* or gods of the pantry, may well have been the source of provisions in the *penus,* since the dead inhabited the soil from which came the harvests. Be that as it may, for Fustel de Coulanges the ancient house was first and foremost an institution by which, or *in* which, the dead were lodged and preserved in their being. To be at home meant to reside within the blessing sphere of the sacred fire, in and through which the dead maintained a presence among the living. The latter thought of the hearth not as a fireplace but as the glowing coals on their altars; they thought of the house's shelter not so much as a defense against the elements but as the ancestor's awesome power to protect the family against misfortune and calamity. A house, in sum, was a place where two realms—one under and the other on the earth—interpenetrated each other.

We no longer think of the house in the ancient way; yet even if we find it difficult to phrase exactly how we *do* think of it, we nevertheless know, more or less, what we want or expect or need from our houses. I cannot imagine, for example, that an architect would design a house without windows. Can we even imagine a house without windows? Yes, but we would say of it that it is more like a tomb than a house. It is appropriate for the dead to inhabit such coffined spaces in which they are protected from the bluster of the world (and the world from them), but we the living make other demands on our homes. In the same way that we expect a coffin to be as hermetically sealed as possible, we expect a house to open onto its surroundings. We require or desire that it contain within its space the presence of what is external to its walls. Thanks to its windows, yet thanks also to its enclosure, a house differentiates the inside from the outside space in such a way that, in and through such differentiation, it creates a relation between interior and exterior whose dynamic field of interpenetration the dwellers inhabit. How now? Is a house something that combines the closure of the tomb and the openness of nature? Is it, even for us, essentially a halfway house, a site of intersection between these two realms?

Nature has shelters, recesses, caves, and burrows, yet it has no houses in which the being (and not only the vestiges) of the bygone is preserved. A fox in its den finds itself in nature, yet we in our houses find ourselves both inside and outside of nature. A mouse that makes its home inside a house is *in* the house in some literal sense, but it does not inhabit the house in the human or humic mode. To inhabit the world humanly one must be a creature of legacy. That explains why the living housed the dead before they housed themselves. They placed them in graves, coffins, urns—in any case they placed them *in* something that we call their resting place so that their legacies could be retrieved and their afterlives perpetuated.

The retrieval and perpetuation by which humankind creates a memory and opens its future take place primarily within the human house. The "in" that the dead abide in—whether it be in the earth, in our memory, in our institutions, in our genes, in our words, in our books, in our dreams, in our hearts, in our prayers, or in our thoughts—this "in" of the dead's indwelling defines the human interiority which our houses build walls around and render inhabitable. The domestic interior is thus in some fundamental sense mortuary, inhabited not only by the dead but also by the unborn in their projective potentiality. It is because we are the ligature between the dead and the unborn—and not because we are vulnerable to the elements and predators—that we humans require housing. All of which corroborates the following proposition: A house is a place of insideness in the openness of nature where the dead, through the care of the living, perpetuate their afterlives and promote the interests of the unborn.

In the history of Western philosophy there is only one thinker whose vocation *as a philosopher* took the form of building a house—not the "house of Being," but a house to live in: Henry David Thoreau. In 1845 Thoreau went into the Walden woods to discover what exactly a house is through the act of making one, as if to declare allegiance to the Vichian principle that we can only know what we ourselves have made *(verum et factum convertuntur)*. When it comes to our question, then, Thoreau enjoys the special authority of someone who not only built a house from the ground up but who also built a philosophy on that act of edification. Thoreau's answer is at once trivial and astonishing. In *Walden* he speaks of food, clothing, and housing in terms of their literal function in the economy of survival: to nourish and preserve the body's "vital heat." That much seems trivial. What is astonishing is that the primordial house of man is his shirt: "I believe that all races at some seasons wear something equivalent to the shirt. . . . Our shirts are our liber or true bark, which cannot be removed without girding and so destroying the man" (p. 16). Thoreau invariably speaks literally, but he never speaks only literally, which is why we could take his remark to mean that a man lives *inside* something which is not his body but which is as connatural to the body as the bark is to the tree, hence that human beings are not naked, merely instinctive creatures, but creatures who inhabit recesses of time in which the past is carried forward into the future. For it is unlikely that Thoreau uses the word *liber* redundantly, to mean "bark," without evoking the word's other meaning of "book," thereby suggesting that our shirts, and by extension our houses, are linked to our possession of language and memory in their futural projections (a "liber" is a record book).

We live inside our shirts because our vital heat is more than a natural heat. It is an inward human heat akin to—perhaps even the source of—the sacred fire that burned on the altars of the ancient house. Both perpetuating and perpetuated, it shelters and requires shelter in turn. Hence Thoreau's disquieting remark: "How can a man be a philosopher and not maintain his vital heat by better methods than other men?" (p. 10) *Walden* is, among other things, a "discourse on method" about how to nourish that vital heat. The allusion to Descartes is not casual, for Thoreau's vital heat is strangely akin to the mystical heat that emanated from the stove in the small room in Germany where, during the religious wars, René Descartes experienced his visionary insight into the method for pursuing truth. It was in the full grace of such a heat that Descartes composed his *Meditations,* seated near a fireplace, doubting the sensations that came to him from without, but certain of the thinking self that thought the fire within. Just as Thoreau's vital heat is the descendant of Descartes's great fire of the First Meditation, so too the latter—whether it burned inside or outside the sanctuary of the thinking self—is the modern descendant of the fire by which Heraclitus warmed himself in his humble kitchen, much to the astonishment of a group of curious visitors, the likes of which would drop by Thoreau's cabin at Walden from time to time. "Here too the gods are present," Heraclitus is reported to have declared on that occasion, alluding no doubt to the *lares.* Those gods take up residence in a place (be it the soul, mind, self, memory, or logos) that philosophy, through its various methods, seeks to know in its ultimate foundations. It is astonishing how few philosophers in the long history of Western metaphysics—including Heidegger—came even close to suspecting what the archives of cultural memory tell us unambiguously: that the dead underlie those foundations.

Thoreau declares, "I am not aware that any man has built on the spot which I occupy. Deliver me from a city built on the site of a more ancient city, whose materials are ruins, whose gardens cemeteries. The soil is blanched and accursed there, and before that becomes necessary the earth itself will be destroyed" (*Walden,* p. 175). The statement defines, in the mode of revulsion, the ancient houses and cities built on the bones of the dead, or on the ruins of former, fallen cities. Under every Old World metropolis lies an older necropolis. Under Thoreau's self-built American house, by contrast, there were no bones—at least not that he was aware of. Nevertheless, no one will deny that it was crammed with ghosts: the ghosts of his Puritan ancestors, for example, whose gesture of departure across the Atlantic Thoreau repeated in his departure from Concord to the shores of Walden Pond. There were also several ghosts from classical and heroic literature that made a home there—the home-seeking Odysseus, for instance, or the refugee Aeneas looking to refound the House of Troy in a *terra nova* (in Thoreau's case, the house was American culture as such, and the *terra nova* was the American continent in its unrealized promise). There were the ghosts of romanticism as well, who had claimed Thoreau's imagination early on and who followed him into the woods. At Walden he encountered other less intimate ghosts—those of vanished "former inhabitants" who left behind them in the surrounding landscape subtle vestiges of their broken, unredeemed lives. And then there were the more aboriginal ghosts of the region—those of the Indians—whose spirit was inseparable from the land and waters of Walden, and whose bones probably haunted the subsoil of his house without his being explicitly aware of it. All these spiritual predecessors and presences— some internal, some external to the author's selfhood—were invited into the Walden cabin and into Thoreau's authorship. His house is where they congregated. His book is where they live on.

To the question "What is a house?" *Walden* gives only one frank and programmatic answer: "The house is still but a sort of porch at the entrance of a burrow" (p. 30). By *burrow* Thoreau means literally the cellar dug into the earth for the purpose of storing and conserving perishable provisions and victuals. Later in the book, precisely in the chapter that resurrects the ghosts of Walden's former inhabitants, he speaks of such burrows as the grave markers of the vanished houses that once populated the surrounding woods: "Now only a dent in the earth marks the site of these dwellings" (p. 174). These burrows are not quite pantries or kitchen cupboards, yet they serve the same purpose as the ancient *penus:* preservation. Was Thoreau aware of the connection to the *penates,* or gods of the pantry, when he defined the house in terms of its cellar? All we know for sure is that he emphasizes the word *still* in his definition: the house is *still* but a sort of porch at the entrance of a burrow.

A visitor to Thoreau's cabin at Walden would have found it distinctly unencumbered by those sundry passed-on objects, mementos, and portraits in and through which a household's ghosts typically make their presence felt in the traditional domestic space, yet he or she would have noticed at least this much: a table with a few books on it, Greek and Roman classics no less, in their original (dead) languages. If nothing else, a house is a place to keep books in. Books require storage places because they themselves store time. They are places where the past comes to meet us from out of the future, provided we learn the art of reading—no easy task if we follow Thoreau's prescriptions. Certainly reading was Thoreau's primary act of edification at Walden. He read not antiquarianly but as part of his effort to invent a "father tongue" for his new nation. It was this effort that turned him toward the literatures of antiquity as the only source for such a pedagogy: "That age will be rich indeed when those relics which we call Classics, and the still older and more than classic but even less known Scriptures of the nations, shall have still further accumulated . . . and all the centuries to come shall have successively deposited their trophies in the forum of the world. By such a pile we may hope to scale heaven at last" (p. 70). Of the ancient scriptures of nations Thoreau declares that they "are the only oracles which are not decayed, and there are such answers to the most modern inquiry in them as Delphi and Dodona never gave" (p. 68).

One of the lessons learned at Walden, and transcribed in *Walden,* is that the new must repose on, or literally *renew,* the foundations of the old. Unprecedented in its genre and idiom, Thoreau's book is comprehensible only on the basis of the traditions it transfigures in its retrievals. Thoreau conceives of the promise of American freedom not as liberation from legacy but as the freedom to become heirs to the "noblest recorded thoughts of man," which reach us from the depths of history. A house, or a nation, is where such inheritance takes place, which is why Thoreau's friend Emerson spoke about the "domestication of culture" as America's greatest challenge.

The burrow at the entrance of which Thoreau would have us build our houses as well as our nations is a cellar that leads into, and arises out of, the underworld of the dead. It is no doubt *in* us as much as it is in the earth. To say that this burrow is *in* us means that it is the source of the unfolding interiorities the vital heat of which our shirts, houses, books, and words maintain through more or less efficient methods. Those interiorities allow us to hold our place in time and to give time its human as opposed to merely natural character. If human beings are "sojourners on the earth," as Thoreau declared, it is because we domesticate our transience in historical, institutional, and linguistic modes that turn that transience in upon itself and make of it a force of conservation, a cellar or *penus*. In our houses time, in its stored or tumulous character, makes itself historical. We don't house ourselves because we speak, nor do we speak because we house ourselves; we house ourselves for the same reason that we speak—because we are a fold, a crypt, a wrinkle of insideness in the fabric of nature's externality. This insideness exudes a vital heat which our houses, when they house us humanly, preserve.

• • •

When it comes to probing the modern fate of this burrow of interiority, no one is more relentless or compelling than Rainer Maria Rilke, the so-called poet of human inwardness. In one way or another his entire corpus speaks to the question of home and homelessness in the modern era. Thus he too, along with Thoreau, enjoys a special authority regarding our query. Now if we put to Rilke the question "What is a house?" we hardly know where to start, since his poetry expands the notion of a house so greatly as to include not only historical but also cosmic forces. As good a place as any to start is with *The Notebooks of Malte Laurids Brigge*, a prose work, autobiographical in nature, published in 1910, one of the most pivotal years in European modernism. Malte, the book's protagonist, is a foreigner in Paris. He is lodged in a shoddy room, but he is in every other respect homeless, which is why the beggars, prostitutes, and street vagabonds seem to recognize him as one of their own—an outcast. Malte has a refuge from the street life of the city, however. It is the public library, whose glass door he opens "as if I were at home," and whose books offer him a place to dwell in—offer him a hospitality that stands in contrast with the nihilism of the hospital, which throws its analogical shadow over the city of Paris from the opening sentences on: "So, then people do come here in order to live; I would have sooner thought one died here. I have been out. I saw: hospitals" (p. 13). The library for Malte is an asylum from the hospital.

Today he is reading a poet who has "a quiet home in the mountains" and whose mahogany desk—or so Malte imagines—contains "faded letters and the loosened leaves of the diaries, recording birthdays, summer parties, birthdays." (p. 44). Imagining that house in his mind, Malte exclaims to himself: "Oh, what a happy fate, to sit in the quiet room of an ancestral house, among many calm, sedentary things. . . . And to think that I too would have become such a poet, had I been allowed to live somewhere, anywhere in the world, in one of those many closed-up country houses about which no one troubles. . . . There I would have lived with my old things, the family portraits, the books" (p. 44). But Malte is fated to become another kind of poet than the one he is reading—a homeless poet in a city which has undergone an uprooting and outcasting similar to his own. The estrangement that binds the poet's interiority to the city through which he wanders finds a powerful objective correlative in a wall that Malte comes across shortly after he leaves the library that day. The extended passage reads as follows:

Will anyone believe that there are such houses? . . . To be precise, they were houses that were no longer there. Houses that had been pulled down from top to bottom. What was there was the other houses, those that had stood alongside of them, tall neighboring houses. Apparently these were in danger of falling down, since everything alongside had been taken away; for a whole scaffolding of long, tarred timbers had been rammed slantwise between the rubbish-strewn ground and the bared wall. . . . [I]t was, so to speak, not the first wall of the existing houses (as one would have supposed), but the last of those that had been there. One saw its inner side. One saw at the different stories the walls of rooms to which the paper still clung, and here and there the join of floor or ceiling. Beside these room-walls there still remained, along the whole length of the wall, a dirty-white area, and through this crept in unspeakably disgusting motions, worm-soft and as if digesting, the open, rust-spotted channel of the water-closet pipe. Grey, dusty traces of the paths the lighting-gas had taken remained at the ceiling edges, and here and there, quite unexpectedly, they bent sharp around and came running into the colored wall and into a hole that had been torn out black and ruthless. But most unforgettable of all were the walls themselves. The stubborn life of these rooms had not yet let itself be trampled out. It was still there; it clung to the nails that had been left, it stood on the remaining handsbreadth of flooring, it crouched under the corner joints where there was still a bit of interior. One could see that it was in the paint, which, year by year, it had slowly altered: blue into mouldy green, green into grey, and yellow into an old, stale rotting white. But it was also in the spots that had kept fresher, behind mirrors, pictures, and wardrobes; for it had drawn and redrawn their contours, and had been with spiders and dust even in these hidden places that now lay bared. It was in every flayed strip, it was in the damp blisters at the lower edges of the wallpapers; it wavered in the torn-off shreds, and sweated out of the foul patches that had come into being long ago. And from these walls once blue and green and yellow, which were framed by the fracture-tracks of the demolished partitions, the breath of these lives stood out—the clammy, sluggish, musty breath, which no wind had yet scattered. There stood the middays and the sicknesses and the exhaled breath and the smoke of years, and the sweat that breaks out under armpits and makes clothes heavy, and the stale breath of mouths, and the fusel odor of sweltering feet. There stood the tang of urine and the burn of soot and the grey reek of potatoes, and the heavy, smooth stench of ageing grease. The sweet-lingering smell of neglected infants was there, and the fear-smell of children who go to school, and the sultriness out of the beds of nubile youths. To these was added much that had come from below, from the abyss of the street, which reeked, and more that had oozed down from above with the rain, which over cities is not clean. And much the feeble, tamed domestic winds, that always stay in the same streets, had brought along; and much more was there, the source of which one did not know. I said, did I not, that all the walls had been demolished except the last?—It is of this wall I have been speaking all along. One would think I had stood a long time before it; but I'm willing to swear that I began to run as soon as I had recognized that wall. For that is the terrible

thing, that I did recognize it. I recognize everything here, and that
is why it goes right into me: it is at home in me. (pp. 46–48)

The descriptive virtuosity of this passage, unmatched in all of modern literature, offers a concrete instance of language acting as the "house of Being," even if in this case the house under description has been demolished. It is a house that did not know the secret of endurance, which is why it now seems so dead in its afterlife, despite all the tenacity with which what Malte calls "life" sticks to its vestigial wall. That tenacity is described meticulously, insistently, expansively, until the dilapidated "being" of the wall, in all its stubborn thingness, clings to the poet's page like the life that refuses to abandon this remnant of a house that once was. As a result of the demolition process the wall's interior has been exposed to the exterior. Such exposure is precisely what the writing accomplishes: the description lays bare the brutal domestic essence of the wall much the way the demolition has. Hence the distinctly "modern" character of this writing, in style and narrative declension as well as its representative participation in the historical processes that have destroyed the foundations of the old world and thereby left the human spirit homeless, or so Rilke believed, both inside and outside of our houses. In Rilke's vision of history, the walls of our domestic containment have been torn down, leaving the "vital heat" of the human spirit exposed. Such exposure defines the spiritual fate of modernity as such. Under such conditions, the spirit is in need mostly of hospitals.

What does it mean for a wall that no longer houses anything to be at home in a poet who is essentially homeless? For let's not forget that Malte is not like the poet who resides in an ancestral house; he is a poet whose inner life, just like the wall, lies open to the abrasive bluster of a world in full disaggregation (the Great War would erupt four years after *Malte Laurids Brigge* was published). Yet it is precisely through this shelterlessness, or new historical estrangement, that the work of rehousing the being of the old world must occur. Our homelessness must now transfigure our mode of inhabiting the earth in such a way as to allow a superannuated earth to inhabit us in turn. I am alluding here to Rilke's cryptic doctrine, articulated in the *Duino Elegies*, to the effect that our cultural vocation in modern times must be that of gathering up our ob-

solete domestic relations with the earth into the exposed inwardness of
the human soul. It is not only the poet's task, but also the task of culture
as a whole, to offer the earth and its perishing human past a saving sanctuary. The only way to pull off such a rescue is by turning the hosted
into the host, or the housed into the house. The following verses from
the *Duino Elegies,* published in 1922, some twelve years after *Malte Laurids Brigge,* allude to this work of conversion:

> The wanderer does not bring a handful of earth,
> the unutterable, from the mountain slope to the valley,
> but a pure word he has learned, the blue
> and yellow gentian. Are we *here* perhaps just to say:
> house, bridge, well, gate, jug, fruit tree, window—
> at most column, tower . . . but to *say,* understand this, to say it
> as the Things themselves never fervently thought to be
>
> . . . .
>
> Here is the time for the *utterable, here,* its home.
> Speak and acknowledge it. More than ever
> the things that we can live by are falling away,
> supplanted by an action without symbol.
> An action beneath crusts that easily crack, as soon as
> the inner working outgrows and otherwise limits itself
>
> . . . .
>
> Praise the world to the angel, not the unutterable world
>
> . . . .
>
> Tell him about the Things
>
> . . . .
>
>   And these things that live,
> slipping away, understand that you praise them;
> transitory themselves, they trust us for [their] rescue,
> us, the most transient of all. They wish us to transmute them
> in our invisible heart—oh, infinitely into us.
>   Whoever we are.
>
> Earth, isn't this what you want: *invisibly*
> to arise in us? Is it not your dream

to be some day invisible? Earth! Invisible!
What, if not transformation, is your insistent commission?

(*Duino Elegies*, pp. 69–71)

Rilke was neither a historian nor a sociologist but a poet in whom homelessness became a collective historical condition and a personal poetic vocation. He believed that he belonged to an age when the "visible earth" was falling away, slipping into oblivion, giving way to a new order of "virtual" reality, an age when an entire mode of being that rested on humic foundations was being uprooted by forces that swept away the old in order to usher in a paltry newness based on "action[s] without symbol[s]," replacing the old things with things we can no longer "live by" precisely because their connection with the earth has been severed. House, bridge, well, gate, jug, fruit tree, window: these words now evoke the superceded domesticity of a culture that Rilke associates with the earthly-utterable, as opposed to the unearthly-unutterable. What is the nature of this correlation between the earth and the utterable? How does the post-Neolithic exposure of the modern age conspire with or promote the unutterable?

The unutterable lies beyond us. It may be signified, imagined, and even aspired to but not mortally resided in or lived by. Mortals partake of a different destiny than the angels, whose transcendence, if we get too near it, annihilates us. The human finds its place *here*, in the "time of the utterable," which is the time of transience as such. The historical unfolding of what passes away comes to rest in the earth, its humus. The utterable gives the "lived things" of our human worlds a domestic interior in which to make themselves at home. "Here is the time for the *utterable, here*, its home." This *here* stands at the entrance of a burrow.

If Aeneas's commission was to rescue the House of Troy by moving his household gods to a new land, our commission—our "insistent commission," as Rilke puts it—is to rescue the earth by becoming the agents of its conversion. By the earth Rilke means both more and less than this planetary body orbiting the sun; he means the soil in which all that has come to pass, in its historical modes of being, was rooted and now lies buried. Merely preserving a memory of what vanishes falls short of the task of conversion; so too does environmental and cultural conservation. In addition to those undertakings, conversion calls for a retrieval of the earth's "human" and "laral" value. In a letter to his Polish publisher, dated November 13, 1925, in which he attempts to explain the deeper import of the *Duino Elegies,* Rilke uses these terms interchangeably:

> [F]or our grandparents a "house," a "well," a familiar tower, their very clothes, their coat, were infinitely more intimate; almost everything a vessel in which they found the human and added to the store of the human. Now from America, empty indifferent things are pouring across, sham things, *dummy life.* . . . Live things, things lived and conscient of us, are running out and can no longer be replaced. *We are perhaps the last to have known such things.* On us rests the responsibility not only of preserving *their* memory (that would be little and unreliable), but their human and laral value ("laral" in the sense of the household gods). The earth has no way out other than to become invisible: *in* us who with a part of our natures partake of the invisible, have (at least) stock in it, and can increase our holdings in the invisible during our sojourn here,—*in* us alone can be consummated this intimate and lasting conversion of the visible [earth] into an invisible [earth] no longer dependent upon being visible and tangible, as our own destiny continually *grows at the same time* MORE PRESENT AND INVISIBLE in us. The elegies set up this norm of existence, they celebrate this consciousness. (*Letters of Rainer Maria Rilke,* p. 375; emphasis in the original)

While the conversion of the earth may sound like an extravagant and quasi-mystical undertaking, human beings are no strangers to the conversion process itself. It is what takes place in mourning. Just as burial lays the dead to rest in the earth, mourning lays them to rest *in us.* The analogy between these two parallel rites of internment rests on an intimate and age-old kinship between the earth and human inwardness— a kinship that makes the earth the caretaker of cultural memory and cultural memory the caretaker of the earth. There is so much of us in the earth, and so much of it in us, that the groundwork for its conversion has already been laid. Just as through burial and mourning we turn the deceased's material absence in the visible world into a "laral" presence in the invisible world, so too we have the capacity in us to "transmute [the things] in our invisible heart—oh, infinitely into us. Whoever we are." It is because we are by nature veterans of mourning— veterans of the "elegy," as it were—that we have it within our power to do for the earth what we have traditionally done for our dead, that is, to transmute its mode of being *in us*. In the broadest sense, a house for Rilke is where such a conversion takes place.

• • •

Before examining in the next chapter the mechanisms of conversion that take place in the mourning process, we might ask the following question: why are we putting our question—what is a house?—to poets and thinkers rather than to house builders, house dwellers, or house designers? The answer should be clear by now. If nothing else the discussion so far has revealed that to house does not necessarily mean to enclose within walls. It means to open the place of an afterlife. A living space may have walls that keep out the cold but not maintain our vital heat; it may be residential but not laral; it may have a basement for storage but no burrow where time in its stored character is preserved for future retrieval—for retrieval from out of the future. It is because we are probing the depths of this burrow that we turn principally to poets, who from time immemorial have been the ones who have most often sought out its recesses, descended into its underworld, communed with its ghosts, and made themselves at home among its shadows. Hence it is from them that we have the most to learn.

When we speak of the house as the place of an afterlife it need not be the afterlife of the dead per se but also of a simple sound, note, or voice. The burrow in question can also be the chamber where such a sound, note, or voice echoes. Let us listen to such an echo in a poem by a contemporary poet, the Italian Valerio Magrelli. Composed in 1992, it is titled "They're Talking":

But why always behind my wall?
Always there, the voices, whenever
night falls they start
talking, yelping, even thinking
it's better to whisper. (All the while

the cold wind of their words
chills and binds me,
torments me in my sleep).
At the edge of the Arctic circle
A couple cried in its room
Beyond a transparent wall, crying, the wall
A luminous, tender, tympanic membrane.
(And I would vibrate all the while, a soundbox
for their story.) Until at my house
they redid the roof, the pipes,
the façade, everything, pounding
everywhere, upstairs, downstairs, always pounding
chattering between themselves only when I slept
only because I was asleep,
only because I was the soundbox
of their stories.

(*The Contagion of Matter,* p. 43)

Whether the talking couple is real or imaginary, dead or alive, we can't say. That they live at the edge of the Arctic Circle, that they yelp as well as talk, that the wall of their room is a "luminous, tender, tympanic membrane," that they seem to be redoing the poet's house, talking only when he sleeps—all this indicates that they are no ordinary neighbors and that, even though they talk *behind* his wall, they in fact inhabit a more intimate recess of the poet's house. Indeed, the poet becomes the "soundbox" for the couple's stories, which echo in and through the house the way the notes of a stringed instrument resound in its hollow cavity. Whoever the two may be who haunt the poet with their voices during sleep, the fact that their existence comes to us through the poem's sound box is evidence enough that their voices belong to the afterlife. What is a house? To the various answers that have accrued over the course of this chapter, we may add this one as well: a house is a sound box.

In Italian the term used by Magrelli is *cassa armonica,* which almost certainly puns on the Italian word for "house," *casa. Cassa* means "chest, safe, coffer, chamber." It is also the word for "coffin"—*cassa di morto.* These linguistic connections are not casual, for they bring together within a single word (as only poems can do) the house, the dead, and the poet's medium of expression. The *cassa armonica* is the sound box of the Orphic lyre, for it is not only *with* his lyre that Orpheus descends into Hades, it is *in* its resonance chamber that the descent takes place. The poet's voice is itself a *cassa;* it does to words what the sound box does to notes: it restores their power to house. Magrelli confirms as much in a prose piece published in 2001, in which he remarks, regarding this poem, that "the house becomes a musical instrument, or better, the lining of the voice" ("Il ventunesimo compleano," p. 127). In the same article he declares that it was only after he came upon a passage from *Moby Dick* that he understood to what extent his *cassa armonica* shares an affinity with the coffin, in its containment of the dead. The passage occurs in chapter 127 and features an exchange between Ahab and the ship carpenter, who is turning a coffin into a life buoy to save a sailor adrift on the sea:

> "Hark ye, dost thou never sing working about a coffin? The Titans, they say, hummed snatches when chipping out the craters for volcanoes; and the grave-digger in the play sings, spade in hand. Dost thou never?"
>
> "Sing, sir? Do I sing? Oh, I'm indifferent enough, sir, for that; but the reason why the grave-digger made music must have been that there was none in his spade, sir. But the caulking mallet is full of it. Hark to it."
>
> "Aye, and that's because the lid there's a sounding board; and what in all things makes the sounding-board is this—there's naught beneath. And yet a coffin with a body in it rings pretty much the same, Carpenter." (Melville, *Moby Dick*, p. 755)

In Cesare Pavese's famous Italian rendition of *Moby Dick*, "sounding board" is translated as *cassa armonica*, and the phrase "there's naught beneath" as "il niente che c'e' sotto." [Gia', ed è perchè il coperchio fa da cassa armonica; e ciò che sempre fa da cassa armonica è questo, il niente che c'è sotto.] Taking up the Melville trope in Pavese's translation, Magrelli speaks of poetry as "il niente che suona," the nothing that sounds—making of the house a house of echoes (*Il ventunesimo*, p. 128). But what exactly does it mean for the nothing to sound? What is this "naught" from which words derive their sounding power? In what sense is the burrow similar to a coffin, a resonance chamber, or a musical sound box? These are questions that take us into the matter of the next chapter. For if poetry has the power to make the naught resound, if it has the power to house, bury, and commune with the dead, it is because its rhythms, accents, and elegiac tones have their elemental source in human grief. If the transmutation of the earth into invisibility is at bottom a poetic task, and if we have the ability to undertake such a task, it is because human beings are veterans of mourning.

CHAPTER 4

THE VOICE OF GRIEF

Benedetto Croce put it well when he declared that "in its first stages grief is a kind of madness: one is prey to impulses which, if they lasted, would lead to actions like those of the crazed Giovanna." (The allusion is to Ferdinand and Isabelle's daughter, who succumbed to psychotic behavior and suicide after her husband's death.) In its insane desire to be reunited with the deceased, grief puts the griever at odds with reality and turns him or her into its helpless antagonist: "One wants to revoke the irrevocable, call out to one who can't answer, feel the touch of a hand that has gone cold forever, see the flash in eyes that will no longer smile at us and that death has covered with a veil of sadness." To this psychology of self-immolation Croce adds that, in the wake of a loved one's death, "we feel guilty for living, it seems that we are stealing something that doesn't belong to us, we would like to die with our dead" (*Frammenti di etica*, pp. 22–24). This desire—"to die with our dead"—runs as deep in human nature as both love and the death drive, whose impulses it commingles and combines, making grief one of the most dangerous and potentially self-destructive psychic crises.

What Croce described in the present tense is all the more true of antiquity. We who have been civilized, modernized, and above all Christianized—we who today are allowed to mourn publicly for a day or two and left to grieve interminably in private—can hardly fathom the paroxysms of despair that the death of a protector or loss of a loved one provoked among the ancients, to say nothing of our remote prehistoric ancestors, whose "wild and savage natures," as Vico reminds us, "we cannot at all imagine and can comprehend only with great difficulty" (*New Science*, §338). Who among us can fathom the depths of primitive grief? In Attic tragedy we hear only echoes of the barbarous howls and shrieks of primal lamentation. In the Homeric epics we see powerful afterimages—but afterimages nonetheless—of the deranged behavior of prehistoric mourners. Achilles gives us such an afterimage when, upon learning of the death of Patroklos, he rolls in the dust, tears out his hair, and scratches his face (*Iliad* 18.22–27), or when, once his friend's body is presented to him, he falls upon it wildly and locks himself in a stubborn embrace. We know from the laws of Solon and other records that even in the archaic period legislators in Greece were trying to curb the terrible outbursts and self-violent behavior at funerals (Griffin, *Homer on Life and Death*, p. 142). To say nothing of the wives, virgins, servants, warriors, and jesters whom public grief sent into the underworld to attend the hero-kings in death. These traces in the archives of cultural memory point both to the power of ancient grief as well as to the predominantly public and gestural nature of its displays.

In the passage quoted above, Croce goes on to remark that "by expressing grief, in the various forms of celebration or cult of the dead, one overcomes heartbreak, rendering it objective" (*Frammenti*, p. 24). This work of objectification is what mourning rituals, with their traditional iterative gestures, are all about. It would be a naïve modern projection on our part to assume that wailing, hair-pulling, cheek-scratching, and breast-beating represent an inability or failure to subject the impulses of grief to proper control. Far from representing spontaneous outbursts of sorrow, the extravagant antics of the bereaved attested to throughout the ancient world were for the most part highly scripted and choreographed affairs that mimicked the gestures of spontaneity in order to distantiate and thereby master the emotions involved. What we find in Homer and throughout the ancient Euro-Mediterranean world is an elaborate ritualization and formalization of mourning behaviors. If violent grief threatens the bereaved with conniption, catalepsy, or psychic dissolution, then ritualized mourning, in its ancient protocols, performed what Croce calls the work of objectification.

The Italian philosophical anthropologist Ernesto De Martino— himself a Crocean of sorts—has given us one of the most probing books to date on ancient forms of ritualized objectification. In *Morte e pianto rituale* (1958) he undertakes a comprehensive analysis of traditional Euro-Mediterranean mourning practices, bringing to bear on his research cultural anthropology, philology, psychology, literary criticism, and speculative philosophy, in the best Vichian tradition. He and a team of collaborators spent six years observing and collecting data on lamentation rituals in the interior of Basilicata, in southern Italy, where mourning practices had remained largely unchanged over the centuries. The results of that fieldwork were added to other documentary and literary sources to produce a vast archive of "philological certainty" for his underlying claim that ritual lament consists in rehearsed and highly formal gestures of externalization whose purpose is first and foremost to *depersonalize* the condition of grief by submitting it to a set of public, traditionally transmitted codes. By dictating the rules for "how one mourns," ritual lament helps assure that the psychic crisis engendered by loss, especially in its initial stages, will not plunge the mourner into sheer delirium or catalepsy—or into what De Martino calls "irrelative" manifestations of grief. Ritualization thus serves to contain the crisis of grief in the very act of objectifying its content through scripted gestures and precise codes of enactment.

Morte e pianto rituale gives any number of examples of ritualized performance, some coming from directly observed ceremonies, others from ethnographic records, and still others from literary sources. A single example will suffice for our purposes. It is reported by the nineteenth-century ethnographer Bresciani in his study of Sardinian customs, and commented on by De Martino. Here is how Bresciani describes a mourning ritual observed firsthand in a village in the interior of Sardegna:

At first, when entering the resting place of the deceased, they [the women] keep their heads bowed, their hands composed and their faces restrained. They proceed in silence, almost together, as if they hadn't happened to notice that a coffin and a corpse were there. Afterwards, lifting their eyes as if by chance and seeing the deceased lying there, they give a sudden cry, clap their hands together and let out strange, distressing plaints. Raising a painful lamentation, some tear out their hair. They rend with their teeth the white handkerchiefs each has in her hands, they scratch and disfigure their cheeks, they let out screams, groans and plaintive, suffocating sobs. Others abandon themselves on the coffin, others throw themselves on their knees, others fling themselves to the ground, roll on the floor, covering themselves with dust. Others, in the desperate extremes of grief, close their fists, their eyes bulging, teeth chattering, and they seem to threaten the sky itself with their uplifted, savage faces. After such inordinate displays, the suffering women—beaten, livid and disheveled, seated here and there on the ground or on their heels around the room—fall suddenly into a profound silence. Taciturn, sighing, wrapped in coats gathered around them, with hands joined and fingers intertwined, they lower their faces and contemplate the bier with fixed eyes. At that moment, one of them, as if touched and lit by some sudden powerful spirit, jumps to her feet, shakes herself, becomes animated, reawakens, her face becomes flushed, her eyes sparkle and, turning towards the deceased, she breaks into a song. (p. 109)

Ceremonies of this sort, with minor local variations, occur throughout the southern regions studied by De Martino, some of their elements being perfectly consistent even with Homer's descriptions of grief-stricken behavior. A strict set of norms passed down through generations, with determinate time frames for each gesture, governs the entire proceeding, such that even the pathological behavior of shrieks, self-mutilation, and embrace of the dead—indeed, these pathological manifestations above all—are brought under the governance of a rule-bound performance. Far from being a spontaneous or cathartic expression of grief, the ceremony enacts at the symbolic as well as psychic level the movement from "irrelative" grief (i.e., chaotic or unreappropriated emotivity) to an objective or socially shared language of lament. It is through that shared, objective language of grief that the work of separation begins to take place. It is essential that this work fulfill its purpose, for if and when it fails, instead of the dead dying in me, I die with the dead—either through excessive identification with the corpse (Achilles locked in his embrace of Patroklos's body) or through an inability to articulate my grief, which leads to any number of discrete, yet no less dangerous, pathologies. The Sardinian mourning ceremony exemplifies how the threat of psychic disaster is both confronted and overcome through a series of the normative gestures and mimetic enactments. The song with which the ceremony comes to a close mournfully acknowledges the divide that separates the dead from the living, yet for all its rueful tones it signifies a final mastering of the self-destructive impulses that precede its resolution.

We should not be astonished, De Martino remarks, by the obvious theatricality of these kinds of mourning ceremonies; nor by the fact that paid professional lamenters (usually women) would frequently preside over the proceedings; nor by the reiteration, in village after village, of the same basic models of lamentation, with their scripted gestures, stock phrases, and literary stereotypes. Ritualization "submits the *planctus* to the rule of rhythmic gestures that are conventionally fixed" (*Morte e pianto rituale*, p. 80), precisely in order to depersonalize grief and provide a formal articulation of its accents. Why is this important? It is important because "if one were to face the actuality of the situation nakedly, in its strictly personal reality [of loss], one would be exposed to catastrophe" (p. 95). Thus on the one hand objectification prevents sorrow from degenerating into a "dehumanized, merely mechanical discharge of psychic energy" (p. 80); on the other, it opens the possibility of communal sharing by casting it into generic or "universal" modules. As De Martino points out, "it is precisely the impersonal character of the stereotypes that makes possible an interpersonal participation in the lament, with multiple successive recitals, planned exchanges, substitutions and collaborations, [a participation] which would be wholly inconceivable under a strictly personal regime of mourning" (p. 125). We could rephrase this by saying that, as ritual lament submits the emotive spontaneity of grief to impersonal forms of externalization, it *creates a chorus* or community of voices sharing in the lament of the bereaved.

Such a chorus of voices—the very possibility of it—comes into being primarily through the lamentation chant, which both sings and speaks the condition of grief. De Martino devotes a good portion of his book to identifying the prototypes that dominate lamentation chants in Basilicata—few yet presumably ancient in their historical or transgenerational reach. Here too the formal elements abound—recurrent emotive refrains, traditional melodies, stock verbal phrases, and controlled rhythmic motion of the body accompanying the recitals—all of which serve the same purpose of objective distantiation and emotive denotation (p. 80). *Morte e pianto rituale* analyzes the rhythmic and tonal structure of a great many chants, the transcriptions of which are ac-

companied by musical scores. The following lament of a sister for her
dead brother was recorded by De Martino in the village of Ferrandina,
in the area of Lucania, and illustrates what he calls the "organic nexus
between melodic and verbal modules":

1. O Ciccille mie, o belle
2. O frate, o frate
3. O Ciccille mie, o frate, o frate
4. Come vogghie fá, o belle
5. O frate me, o frate mie
6. 'O vogghie bé
7. O frate, o frate, o frate, o frate
8. Come 'o vuogghie bé, o frate, o frate
9. Mo te n'aie scí, o frate
10. Come agghia fa, o frate
11. O frate mie, frate mie
12. O Ciccille mie, o frate, o frate
13. Come vuogghie fa senza di te, o frate
14. Je me n'agghia scí, o frate
15. Agghia murí pur' ie, o frate
16. O frate mie, o frate mie
17. O come vogghie fa, o frate mie
18. Vogghie murí pur' ie, o frate mie
19. O frate mie, o frate mie
20. O frate mie belle belle, or frate mie
21. O frate mie, o frate mie
22. Frate mí!

(pp. 90–91)

[1. O my Francesco, o fair
2. O brother, o brother
3. O my Francesco, o brother, o brother
4. How will I cope, o fair
5. O my brother, o my brother
6. How I love him!
7. O brother, o brother, o brother, o brother
8. How I love him, o brother, o brother

9. Now you must go, o brother
10. What must I do, o brother
11. O brother, o brother
12. O my Francesco, o brother, o brother
13. How will I survive without you, o brother
14. I must go, o brother
15. I must die too, o brother
16. O brother, o brother
17. O how will I cope, o my brother
18. I want to die too, o my brother
19. O brother, o brother
20. O my brother fair fair, o my brother
21. O my brother, o my brother
22. My brother!]

The lament's verbal and musical characteristics are analyzed by De Martino as follows:

> The verbal text of this lamentation consists of short verses each of which iterates the same emotive refrain (my brother, brother) and relies entirely upon conventional phrases that "one utters" in laments. Each verse is sung according to a melodic line that in Ferrandina is traditionally used in laments for the dead: it is articulated on a pentatonic scale descending from *F* to *B:* this gives each verse a sense of falling, indeed of release, accentuated by the frequent portamento of the *F,* which creates a brief initial rising, like a balancing before falling. A second characteristic that dominates the chant is the void in the melodic line of each verse created by the persistent lack of the *D* pitch. Such a void is not accidental with respect to the verbal text, since it always occurs before the emotive refrain invoking the brother. The dynamic of this lamentation, then, presents three distinct forms: the iterative use of conventional phrases, *rubato* and *accelerando.* The first is normal and dominates all lamentation; the *rubato* usually appears in relation to the emotive refrains, as in verses 7 and 19. And acceleration is particularly evident in verses 6 (*'o vuogghie bé*) and 22 (*frate mí*), where the standard iteration is interrupted by two anguished explosions of the voice, so rapid and violent as to trun-

cate the final word (*bé* instead of the usual *bene,* and *mí* instead of *mio*). (p. 91)

In this "organic nexus" between the lament's verbal and melodic strains we come closer to the main topic of this chapter, namely the underlying nexus between grief and human vocalization. Whether such chants are poetry, speech, or song is impossible to say. They are, I would submit, an echo of the recursive matrix from which all three arose. De Martino remarks that the observer of these lamentations in their monotonous iteration and unvaried rhythms often has the impression that the lamenters have become detached, anonymous agents mechanically rehearsing the accents of grief. This impression is both accurate and inaccurate. As ritual lament submits the emotive spontaneity of grief to impersonal forms of expression, it opens the possibility of an interpersonal nexus of participation and thereby gives grief a *voice.* Indeed, it was perhaps through grief that the human voice gained its first articulations.

When it comes to speculations about its early prehistory, we may safely assume, along with Vico and several other theorists ancient and modern, that the human voice sang before it spoke. Vico's claim about the cantatory origins of speech appeals to axioms like this: "Mutes utter formless sounds by singing, and stammerers by singing teach their tongues to pronounce," followed by "Men vent great passions by breaking into song, as we observe in the most grief-stricken and the most joyful" (*New Science,* §228, 229). From such axioms "it follows that the founders of the gentile nations, having wandered about in the wild state of dumb beasts and being therefore sluggish, were inexpressive save under the impulse of violent passions, and formed their first languages by singing" (§230).

Jean-Jacques Rousseau, who had at best only a marginal acquaintance with Vico, certainly shared this assumption when, some three decades after the 1744 edition of the *New Science,* he composed *On the Origin of Language.* "Simple sounds emerge naturally from the throat," writes Rousseau, "but the modification of the tongue and palate, which produce articulation, require attention and practice" (p. 14). This claim sympathizes with Vico's distinction between singing and stammering. The former comes naturally, says Vico, while the latter is learned with difficulty ("vowels are easy to form and the consonants difficult. . . . Stutterers use a syllable which they can more readily utter singing in such a way as to compensate for those they find difficult to pronounce" [*New Science*, §461–62]). Like Vico, Rousseau concludes that "[s]ince sounds, accents and number, which are natural, would leave little to articulation, which is conventional, [the first language] would be sung rather than spoken. Most of the root words would be imitative sounds or accents of passion" (*On the Origin of Language*, pp. 14–15).

Most theories about the origins of language say more about those who promote them than about the empirical beginnings of language as such, and Rousseau's case is no exception. His claim that human language began in nonarticulate, melodic vocalizations of passion, which would have been understood through their musical accents alone, is tied to his doctrine of the originary benevolence of human nature. According to Rousseau the only passion that could have moved the tongue to sing its first songs of accented vowels was that of joy: "In a mild climate with fertile land, it took all the animation of pleasurable feelings to start the people speaking. The first tongues, children of pleasure rather than need, long bore the mark of their father" (p. 46). Since it was not out of any *need* to come together (in a social contract, for example) but rather out of a spontaneous amorous *desire* to unite with the other, *aimez-moi!* was the essential semantic content of these first vowel-based melodies (p. 47).

While Rousseau makes a typically seductive (and typically narcissistic) case for joy as the generative impulse, Vico sees grief and joy as equally plausible candidates for the overwhelming passion that first moved the tongue to sing. The same goes for stammering, to which Vico traces the origins of articulation, yet there is an important difference here. Stammering for Vico is a kind of singing punctuated by consonantal gaps: "since men are shown to be originally mute, they must have uttered vowel sounds by singing, as mutes do; and later, like stammerers, they must have uttered articulate consonantal sounds, still by singing" (*New Science*, §461). This type of punctuation arises under strain—the strain to master an emotion and arrest its spontaneous release. Certainly stammering is more consistent with overwhelming trauma than effusive ecstasy. While the amorous passion drives toward unification and fulfillment, the loss of a loved-one violently interrupts the continuity of a preexistent bond and opens a gaping void of separation. Stammering arises from serial interruption, while the vowel-based melodies of the early human voice were continuous. In the realm of speculation in which we find ourselves here, it would seem that the first human consonants arose as the vocal introjections of this void, or effect of interruption, which the death of a loved one brought about.

To clarify (but certainly not verify) this speculation, let us to turn for a moment to Hegel. In a passage from his 1803–4 Jena course, he speaks about how the "empty voice of the animal" assumes rudimentary articulation and meaning when "the pure sounding of the voice, the vowel . . . gets interrupted by the mute [consonants]." These consonants are "the authentic restrictions of mere sounding," in the sense that they arrest the vowel sounds. Through such an arrest "every tone has a meaning on its own account. For the distinctions of mere tone in a song are not determinate distinctions on their own [i.e, in their own right], but are determined in the first place through the preceding and following tone." In effect Hegel sees (or hears) in consonants the power of the negative at work in the voice. This is the power that initiates the process of mediation and makes abstraction possible. The consonant abstracts the sound of the animal voice—tears the voice away from its immediacy by interrupting its spontaneity and in so doing transforms the "empty voice of the animal" into the voice of consciousness as such. In Hegel's formidable prose: "Speech as articulated sounding is the voice of consciousness, because every tone within it has meaning, i.e., because there exists in it a name, the ideality of an existing thing; [in other words] the immediate non-existence of the thing" (*First Philosophy,* in *System of Ethical Life (1802/3) and First Philosophy of Spirit,* p. 222). By the "immediate non-existence of the thing" Hegel means its mediated, abstract existence in language. The blockage of the breath stream brought on by the consonantal gap is what grants the thing its existence in human language.

Hegel may well be right when he remarks that "every animal discovers a voice in its violent death" and that, through its groans of expiration, "it expresses itself as a sublated self" [als aufgehobnes Selbst] (*Gesammelte Werke,* 8:170). He may also be right that human speech in essence prolongs and articulates the voice of this suffering, dying animal. Yet surely it is a mistake on his part to locate the presence of death exclusively *inside* rather than outside the vocal self. Human beings find their voice not in their own imminent death but in the other's already transpired death. The sublated or removed self of which Hegel speaks is first and foremost the self that has left behind a corpse, that has removed itself from the sphere of presence, that has abandoned the world of the living: "In the voice, meaning turns back into itself; it is negative self, desire. It is lack, or substancelessness in itself" (ibid.). All this applies directly and concretely to the voice of bereavement, for what is it that provokes cries of grief if not this violent "sublation"? The human corpse is the locus of a sublated or removed self. It is where the disappearance takes place or leaves behind its unambiguous evidence. If animals find a voice in their violent death, humans find their voice in the presence of the corpse. This is the voice that calls out to the dead without response, that seeks to say what can no longer be heard, and that turns back into itself only to prolong and articulate its call in words of grief.

In sum, the grieving self *is* the "negative self of desire," and it is from that self's impossible desire to reunite what death has separated that something like the quest for meaning first gets under way. Or perhaps it was the insane intensity of such a desire that first forced articulation on the voice, in a desperate attempt to master that desire and gain distance from the corpse. One way or another, the opening up of that distance is crucial to any attempt to make the dead die within rather than die with the dead.

To summarize, by arresting and articulating the pure resonance of the animal voice, consonants allow for the formation of words, concepts, and the semantics of abstraction. The movement whereby consciousness both annuls the immediacy of things (through the power of the negative) and preserves that which it annuls in mediated form (i.e., in the concept) has its vocal beginning in the muting effect of consonants, which cause the vowel sound to die. The death or measured finitude of the vowel is what turns melodic vocalization into human verbalization. Articulate speech is in the first instance an interruption of the spontaneity of song. It is a kind of reappropriated stammering or stuttering that, as we have seen, has at least analogical associations with traumatic loss. We recall that the primary purpose of ritual lament is not to honor the dead, nor to mechanically discharge emotion, but to master grief by submitting its potentially destructive impulse to objective symbolization. One could say that ritual lament does to "irrelative" grief what speech does to stammering in that it provides it with rules of articulation. There is more here than mere analogical association, however. De Martino's research into the rhythmic and verbal characteristic of the lamentation chant shows that the chant's formal articulation begins, at the most rudimentary level, with the individuation of repetitive sounds—sounds which, in their rhythmic modulation, speak as well as sing the condition of grief. Ululation is also reiterative and rule bound, yet the chant differs from ululation by introducing consonants (hence words and a minimalist semantics) into the latter's "pure resonance."

There is no better way of illustrating this critical transition from cursive vocalization to discursive articulation than by looking at a textual trace of it that is preserved in one of the oldest extant Greek tragedies, Aeschylus's *The Persians*. I am referring to the lament of Xerxes that brings the play to an end:

> XERXES: Weep, weep over our calamity, and depart to your
>   homes.
> CHORUS: Alas, alas, woe, woe!
> XERXES: Cry now aloud in response to me.
> CHORUS: A wretched offering from the wretched to the
>   wretched.
> XERXES: Cry out, tuning thy strain to mine.
> CHORUS: Woe's the day! Grievous indeed is this visitation. Alas,
>   indeed, for this thy woe too I suffer.
> XERXES: Ply your strokes, ply your strokes, and groan for my
>   sake.
> CHORUS: I weep in lamentation!
> XERXES: Cry now aloud in response to me.
> CHORUS: This care, my liege, is mine.
> XERXES: Lift up now thy voice in lamentation.
> CHORUS: Woe's the day! And with our wailing, alas, shall be
>   mingled blackening blows and shrieks of pain,
> XERXES: Beat thy breast, too, and raise the Mysian wail.
> CHORUS: Anguish, anguish!
> XERXES: And tear, I pray thee, the white hair from out thy beard.

CHORUS: With clenched nails, with clenched nails, with loud
  wailing.

XERXES: And utter shrill cries.

CHORUS: This I will do

XERXES: And with thy fingers rend the robe that drapes thee.

CHORUS: Anguish, anguish

XERXES: And pluck out thy locks and lament our host.

CHORUS: With clenched nails, with clenched nails, with loud
  wailing.

XERXES: Let tears moisten thine eyes.

CHORUS: I am steeped in tears.

XERXES: Cry now aloud in response to me.

CHORUS: Alas, alas!

XERXES: With sounds of wailing wend ye to your homes.

CHORUS: Alas, alas!

XERXES: Alas! through the city.

CHORUS: Alas, indeed! Yea, yea.

XERXES: Put forth your wail as ye move on with dainty steps.

CHORUS: Alas, alas, O Persian land, grievous now to tread!

XERXES: Ah me! Those that perished in three tiered galleys, ah
  me!

CHORUS: I will escort thee with dismal sounds of woe.

                    (vv. 1038–76; Grene, *Aeschylus II*, 84–86)

Xerxes here acts as the traditional *princeps planctuum*, or leader of the
lament. With its metrically respondent antiphons and dictation of successive gestures (beating of the breast, tearing of hair, scratching of the
face with clenched nails, rending of clothes, etc.), the exchange between Xerxes and chorus shows just how formal and programmatic
were the ancient threnodies, or funeral laments, which serve as its underlying model.

  David Grene, to whom we owe the English translation cited above,
remarks that in *The Persians* "much that is hard to render in English lies
in an area where thought and expression melt into one another so that
it appears impossible to capture the original, or approach it, in another
tongue" (*The Persians*, General Introduction, p. v). This would certainly
apply to those "words" that in fact are not words at all but brief ejacula-

tory exclamations and ululations. For instance, in English the verse that follows Xerxes' first enjoinder to the chorus reads: "Alas, alas, woe, woe." In the Greek text the verse reads as a series of vowel sounds: "aiai aiai, ea ea." In verse 1043, translated as "Woe's the day," the original records only a stuttered vocalization—"otototototoi" (repeated in verse 1051). Where the English interjects words like "alas," "woe" and "anguish," the Greek features a variety of wailing sounds. In those primitive howls, which translators generally do not know what to do with, we hear echoes of the stammering voice of grief prior to its articulation in discrete words, referential semantics, and regulative grammar. Whether the human voice first developed its consonants under the annihilating threats of grief as a means of withstanding the trauma of loss and mastering its destructive impulse, we'll never know for sure. Yet there is little doubt that those "dismal sounds of woe" with which the chorus escorts Xerxes through the grief-stricken city at the end of *The Persians* contain echoes of the earliest human vocalizations.

At the extreme other end of *The Persians'* antiquity we find a twenty-first-century poem by Susan Stewart which juxtaposes ancient Greek and modern English exclamations of grief. The poem, titled "O," was composed in 2002:

> Toi, toi, toi, said Peleus.
> Grieving, Hecuba
> barked like a dog.
> *O* said the woman
> who spoke only English,
> who cast an English
> zero out, a wreath
> on the battering waves.
> *O* the teeth clenched.
> *O* a fistful of hair.
> (*Columbarium,* p. 68)

There are at least two subtexts here. One has to do with the fact that Susan Stewart recently cotranslated into English Euripides' play *Andromache,* in which Peleus appears as an archetypical figure of parental grief (Stewart, *Andromache*). The aged father of Achilles, who has already been shattered by the death of his son, now suffers the loss of his grandson Neoptolemus at the hands of Orestes' henchmen. As for Hecuba, her pain was so uncontainable after the deaths of Polyxena and Polydorus that, as Ovid tells it, she barked her grief like a dog. What is the proper English equivalent of those wild barks, stutters, or shrieks of Greek sorrow? "*O* said the woman / who spoke only English." This "O" sounds horribly trite by comparison. Long usage has worn it down to a commonplace utterance ("O really?" "O, why not"). Stewart's poem rescues the "O" from its everyday banality by correlating it with its ancient Greek precedents, if not predecessors. Even more subtly—and here is the second subtext—it identifies the "O" with a zero ("the woman . . . cast an English / zero out") and thereby links the exclamation to "ground zero." With the tragedy of September 11 now haunting the occasion, the "O" of the woman who spoke only English becomes not merely an English equivalent of Hecuba's bark and Peleus's terrible stammer, but their natural homology. The "teeth clenched" and "fistful of hair" of the last two verses complete the return of "O" to this primordial, universal source from which human exclamations of grief gain their voice.

To bring this meditation to a provisional conclusion I would like to return to a few phrases in the lament of the Ferrandina sister and consider what I would call the semantics of grief. Certainly the meaning of the sister's words are secondary in importance to their intonation, rhythm, and melodic phrasing, yet in their semantic minimalism they in fact tell us what the chant puts to music. In verse 14 she says, "I must go, o brother." In verse 9 she had already declared, "Now you must go, o brother." Presumably what she means is that while *he* must go to the world of the dead, *she* must return to the world of the living. This is the reality of separation: one must return to the place from which the other must depart. And the brother *must* depart, for the sanity of the community he leaves behind depends on the willingness of the dead to take their leave. So much of the traditional mourning ceremony works to appease the dead, to secure their goodwill, as it were, so that they might go gently, without rage or reluctance, into that good night. Nevertheless, the sister's desire, expressed in verse 18, is in fact to join her brother in death: "I want to die too, o my brother." While "I must go" is a statement of obligation, "I want to die too" is a statement of desire. It is this divide between obligation and desire that the mourning process works to accomplish; it works to reinforce the obligations the living have to one another. The most essential such obligation is to overcome the persistent, contagious, and insane desire to die with the dead.

In verse 15 the sister declares: "I must die too, o brother," which in the original corresponds metrically and syntactically to "I want to die too, o my brother" [Agghia murí pur' ie—Vogghie murí pur' ie]. Despite their respondent meters and parallel constructions, these are two very different semantic utterances. "I must die too" is a statement of obligation, not of desire. It expresses more than an emotive impulse to join the dead, for the death that has claimed the brother has now turned back upon mourner and *mortalized* her, as it were. The declaration reveals a cognizance of the fact that the living share the mortal fate of the dead, hence that a deeper communion underlies their separation—the communion of death itself. If it is true that "in the voice, meaning turns back into itself," as Hegel puts it, then the realization of this obligation—"I must die too"—is where such a turn takes place in the sister's lament. In such an act of reflection meaning in its semantic mode finds the terms of its articulation.

In the final analysis mourning is the work of coping ("O how will I cope, o brother," v. 17)—not merely with the loss of a loved one but with the reality of loss in its irreducible, mortal extensions. Coping does not consist merely in effecting a separation with the dead and "getting on with one's life," as we are so fond of saying in America, but in complying with the ultimate obligation of all, namely the acknowledgment of death as the very condition and ground of life. This is a lesson that only the death of others can teach. The child Margaret in Gerard Manley Hopkins's poem "Spring and Fall" grieves "over Goldengrove unleaving," yet in time she will learn that all grieving has a self-referential dimension and that, in the end, "it is Margaret you mourn for." She will learn this lesson through the pedagogy of grief itself. Mourning rituals would be feckless if they did not provide the means, or language, to cope with one's own mortality even as they help one cope with the death of others. It is because lament always has this element of self-reference that its voice is universal and its rituals are open to the participation of strangers and kin alike. In the other's grief I hear and see my own, for mortality makes brothers and sisters of us all.

It is not simply because one is fated to die that death presents itself as an obligation. The obligation conveyed by grief is that of self-mortalization. To mortalize oneself means to learn how to live as a dying creature, or better, to learn how to make of one's mortality the foundation of one's relations to those who live on, no less than to those who have passed away. To cope with one's mortality means to recognize its kinship with others and to turn this kinship in death into a shared language. The moment I cease to speak to the other as someone who shares my mortal parentage, I become a linguistic orphan. I merely adopt language rather than reappropriate its power to ground my relations with others. Through grief I learn to speak my death to the world, to find the phrasing for it, and to understand that whoever has the capacity to speak is, like me, a creature for whom dying is first and second nature. Where this pedagogy fails, language invariably works against us, grief remains locked in aphasia, and the work of objectification miscarries.

At a certain point in *Morte e pianto rituale* De Martino, who is generally averse to such generalizations, writes: "If we wanted to define human civilization in a single pregnant formulation, we could say that it's the formal power to transform into value that which in nature hastens toward death. This power makes of man the procurer of death at the very heart of natural death, consigning what passes without and against man to the cultural rules of passage" (p. 214). To this we should add that the cultural rules of passage are historical, hence they too succumb to the law of passing. If new ones do not take their place, the transformation into value does not happen, precisely because we are at a loss when it comes to knowing how to mourn. When that happens we find ourselves surrounded by words without knowing how to speak, by death without knowing how to die.

CHAPTER 5

THE ORIGIN OF OUR BASIC WORDS

Even if we take it on faith that in the beginning was the *logos* (John 1:1), no one really knows what the word *logos* meant in the beginning, for by the time our words begin to mean something they already have a past, they already reach us by way of our forebears. Regardless of our dialect, we speak with the words of the dead. That, in a special sense, is how and why we speak at all. Just as humanity begins where there is already an ancestor, language begins where it has already begun.

Linguists tell us that the word *logos* harkens back to the Proto-Indo-European root *leg*, which meant "to gather, to collect, to bind together." Or so they gather, for, like Dante's redolent panther, no one has actually seen or heard this fossil tongue from which all Indo-European languages supposedly derive. Its roots have been reconstructed through conjecture. We hypothesize that such a tongue was once spoken by an aboriginal tribe who, in their dispersion across the earth from a common point of origin, proliferated the various Indo-European language groups known to us today, yet the fact remains that this progenitor exists only in its descendants.

A truly dead language is one that has no dead language at its core—one which was never born in the first place, hence an artificial language, grounded not in the *logos* of legacy but in a merely formal logic. It is only by constantly retrieving the priority from which they arise that our words retain their capacity to bind, gather, collect, and mean. That is why we speak of natural languages. A language is natural to the degree that its native speakers are born into the generative source from which the saying power of its words ultimately springs; which means that the origin of our words lies not so much behind them as *in* them, which in turn means that they contain within them humic underworlds where the dead hold sway over the very means of speech. To descend into those depths philologists need a golden bough.

The Italian poet Giacomo Leopardi, who knew a thing or two about philology, maintained that a plurality of bygone worlds come alive in the mind of a native Italian speaker who hears words like *notturno, oscuro, antico, lontano, irrevocabile, agevole, costringere*—words with Latinate roots that reverberate in deep latent recesses of cultural memory. Leopardi believed that the worlds our words once inhabited reinhabit in turn the words that outlive them. Hence the famous distinction he drew between *parole* and *termini,* words and terms. *Parole* are words that preserve their metaphorical and sensory prehistory, conveying in their etymons and phonemes a host of accessory images, indefinite connotations, and tropological associations. *Termini* are abstract, univocal, often scientific locutions that have no such recessive draw. For all their referential precision, *termini* lack the *parola*'s genetic bond between word, world, memory, and time. They denote but do not, as it were, arouse. "A thing expressed with a technical word is not familiar to us. It arouses none of the infinite memories of life" (Leopardi, *Zibaldone,* p. 128). It is not only the technical word but the *thing* it names that is unfamiliar to us: "If I call a plant or animal by the Linnaean name instead of the usual name, I have aroused none of these [accessory] ideas, even though the thing itself is clearly indicated. . . . These ideas are bound to the word more than to the thing, or bound to both in a manner that should the thing be separated from the word (since the words cannot be separated from the thing), the thing no longer would produce the same ideas" (ibid.). In Leopardi's reflections on the *parola* we have a "history of ideas" that passes through our words, not through things or concepts, unless we prefer to say that every mental idea, Leopardianly understood, is in fact the accretion of a verbal history.

One way to understand the vocation of poetry in the modern era is as an ongoing effort to reparolize our words and prevent them from degenerating into terms. A poem, or at least a certain type of poem, is a kind of entrenchment where words put up a resistance against the denotative machine—the "terminator," as it were—which prosaicizes our natural languages, rendering their words more clear and distinct while silencing their prior speakers. Poems that militate against terminalization must descend into the word's depths with a sound box, as it were, which picks up the "hoarse" voices of the once loquacious dead, who have long remained silent, to speak with Dante ("chi per lungo silenzio parea fioco" [*Inferno* 1.53]). Take the following lyric, "Doria," written by Ezra Pound for his wife Dorothy Shakespear:

> Be in me as the eternal moods
>   of the bleak wind, and not
>   As transient things are—
>   gaiety of flowers.
> Have me in the strong loneliness
>   of sunless cliffs
> And of gray waters.
>   Let the gods speak softly of us
> In days hereafter,
>   The shadowy flowers of Orcus
> Remember thee.
>   (*Collected Early Poems*, p. 193)

Here it is the word *be*—the most washed out of words—that regains its association with the underworld and overflows its copulative function in everyday grammar. From the depths of its dimly remembered lethic history, an ancient semantics comes forth to assert its primordial claims on its modern declensions. Between the heavily stressed "be" and equally stressed "are" falls the formidable "not"—a negation that, in its repudiation of transience, restores to the word *be* its imperative of endurance, perseverance, and weathering. "To be" now means "to last and to outlive"—to persist beyond the regime of transitory presence. Orcus's realm of poetic memory envelopes the "be" in its shadows, from which shadows the word reemerges as an aboriginal copula between husband and wife, the living and the dead, the here and the hereafter. Indeed, the word now transcends the transience of the wedding vow itself—"until death do us part"—and makes of matrimony a bond that continues in and after death. "Until death do us part" is a vow that belongs to the gaiety of flowers, not to the "shadowy flowers of Orcus." Thus the poem's title, "Doria," which is printed in Greek characters, refers Dorothy's name to its ancient antecedent, making that inscription *hers* in an ultimate "gift" of being.

The main heir to Leopardi's poetics of the *parola* in twentieth-century poetry is not Pound, however, but Giuseppe Ungaretti, whose encounter with Leopardi in the 1920s convinced him that his poetry had to descend into the humic underworld of words. According to Ungaretti, "A word that has lived for centuries, that through so much history reflects so many different things, that returns us to the presence of so many people whose bodies have disappeared from the earth but whose spiritual presence remains when their words are operative within us . . . such a word, that Leopardi had seized upon with such truth and beauty of effect, could still suggest to the poet of today the best means of enriching himself both morally and in his lyric expansiveness" (*Saggi e interventi*, p. 745, trans. and cited by Cary, *Three Modern Italian Poets*, p. 175).

It was this Leopardian concept of the *parola* (as well as Leopardi's own enthusiasm for Petrarch) that accounts for Ungaretti's hyperbolic estimation of the Latinate elegance of Petrarch's language. "A language recovered from the grave—such is the miracle of the *Canzoniere*," he writes. "Through Petrarch's merit Italian suddenly became an ancient language, an efficient mode of speech that would serve as model for the tongues of adolescent Europe" (quoted in Cary, *Three Modern Italian Poets*, p. 203). *Make it new!* was Pound's rallying cry for poetry, but what was new about Petrarch's language was precisely its antiquity. Only the source, in its latent futurity, dispenses the power of renewal. By retrieving and purifying its Latin ancestry from out of its future, Petrarch turned Italian into an ancient language and thereby into *the first modern language of Europe*.

One might compare Petrarch to Shakespeare on this score, for certainly Shakespeare (along with Chaucer) did something similar to the English language, although in a contrary sense. Rather than purify its idiom he expanded, to the point of exploding, its genetic legacies by marrying English to its distant Roman cousins. In so doing he helped make of English the legitimate adoptive heir of Latin and the Romance languages that contaminated its Germanic ancestry. One could say that he *claimed* an expansive Romanic-Latin ancestry for English. In that sense Shakespeare was, like Petrarch, a genuine modern. The genuinely modern does not chase after the new; it makes the old new again. As Hölderlin put it in one of his prefaces to *Hyperion:* "On no account do I wish it were original, for originality is novelty to us, and nothing is as dear to me as things as old as the world itself" (p. 235).

Ungaretti's own poetry bears the signatures of Petrarch's "miracle" and Leopardi's mentalism. Take, as a typical instance, these two verses in the first canto of *La morte meditata*, where the speaker is addressing death:

Ti odo nel fluire della mente
Approfondire lontananze,
Emula sofferente dell'eterno
(*Vita d'un uomo*, p. 131)

[I hear you in the flowing of the mind
deepening distances,
suffering emulator of eternity]

Every one of these words is a Leopardian *parola*. Together their cadence produces that distinctly mellifluous Petrarchan effect, dissolving the word *mente* into a stream of indefinite associations. Death ceases to be the termination of life and becomes the sound of existential and historical time in the mind, the deepening of its distances as the latter are heard in the mind's temporal flow. By the power of poetic association this flow can't help but conjure up Leopardi's most famous lyric, "L'infinito," with its "sound of the dead seasons" and the "sweet" shipwreck of the finite mind in a nonfinite sea of time. One could say that in these verses Ungaretti literally hears his predecessor, and in so doing hears again the "sound of the dead seasons" in their gathered relation to the eternal.

"To relegate the animated, vigorous word to the immobility of a univocal, mechanically programmed sequence of signs would mean the death of language and the petrification and devastation of Dasein." This is Heidegger speaking in 1936 (*Nietzsche*, 1:144). Our "basic words," he says, possess a plurality of meanings that derives from the plurality of prior worlds through which they have passed on their way down to us. Thus the word *Bildung* meant something different for Goethe and Hegel than it did for the educated person of the 1890s, not because "the formal content of the utterance is different, but the kind of world encapsulated in the saying is different, though not unrelated" (ibid.). Heidegger goes on to affirm the following about the historical nature of our words: "That does not mean simply that they have various meanings for various ages which, because they are past, we can survey historically; it means that they ground history now and in the time to come in accordance with the interpretation of them that comes to prevail. The historicity of the basic words, understood in this fashion, is one of the things that must be heeded in thinking through these basic words" (ibid.).

I share the widespread belief that Martin Heidegger is the most important philosopher of the twentieth century and that for years to come we will be trying to catch up with his thought; yet it is fair to say that, when it came to heeding his own enjoinder, Heidegger shunned much of the philological effort, by which I mean that he rarely really probed the history of the words he famously etymologized. That is not surprising. In the final analysis Heidegger remains a philosopher, and what Vico affirmed over two and half centuries ago still applies to the Heideggerian corpus today: "the philosophers failed by half in not giving certainty to their reasonings by appeal to the authority of the philologians, and likewise the latter failed by half in not taking care to give their authority the sanction of truth by appeal to the reasoning of philosophers" (*New Science,* § 140). This is perhaps the most radical challenge one can throw not only at philosophy in general but at Heidegger in particular; hence it is worth pondering for a moment its import.

Vico's expansive concept of philology "includes among the philologians all the grammarians, historians, critics, who have occupied themselves with the study of the languages and deeds of people: both at home, as in their customs and laws, and abroad, as in their wars, peaces, alliances, travels and commerce" (§139). (Nowadays this would also include psychology, anthropology, archaeology, and other historical disciplines.) As Vico understood it, philology deals with the "certain" in its particularity, philosophy with the "true" in its universality. When I say that, in his attempts to "think through" the historicity of our basic words, Heidegger shunned much of philological effort, I do not mean that he ignored empirical linguistic philology—he in fact relied on it heavily—but that his philosophical etymologizing relentlessly pushed toward the highest degree of abstraction, emptying words of their sensory as well as secular density. Take as an example his etymology of the word *logos,* which he pursues by way of the verb form *legein,* whose archaic meaning, or so he claims, is both "to lay" and "to gather." Abstracting the concept of laying in its relation to gathering, Heidegger reconceives the word *logos* in these terms: "*O logos:* the Laying: the pure letting-lie-together-before of that which of itself comes to lie before us, in its lying there. In this fashion *logos* occurs essentially as the pure laying which gathers and assembles. *Logos* is the original assemblage of the primordial gathering from the primordial Laying. *O logos* is the Laying that gathers, and only this" (*Early Greek Thinking*, p. 66). Even if this were true, it is far from certain.

Heidegger practically founded a philosophy on his etymologizing of ancient Greek, yet the historical worlds housed by his recursive lexicon of Greek words—*logos, polemos, aletheia, moira, einai*, and so on—were so much noise to a thinker who strove to hear in those words a primal naming of the Being of beings. As Glenn Most has suggested in a recent essay, Heidegger's Greeks were neither statesmen, priests, athletes, wives, daughters, prostitutes, warriors, slave owners, or merchants. They were a select group of philosophers and tragedians who authored a select group of works that contained a select number of discrete sayings or sentences in which Heidegger isolates certain key substantives in whose etymons he finds traces of an aboriginal "Greek" (i.e., Heideggerian) way of thinking (Most, "Heidegger's Greeks"). To put it differently: rarely did Heidegger ever recognize, let alone appeal to, the authority of the philologians.

Heidegger believed that ideas—or "the thought of being"—ultimately determine the course of history. In their priority (or a priority), ideas open, shape, found, and render intelligible the historical worlds we inhabit. Vico neither shared nor rejected this assumption. He simply recuperated its missing half and refounded it on a new basis. In one of the most fundamental axioms of the *New Science*, Vico states: "The order of ideas must proceed from the order of institutions" (§238). The word *institution (cosa)* in Vico's *New Science* refers broadly to whatever serves to *bind* human beings in both the public and private spheres, be it religion, matrimony, customs, laws, the city, the nation, class affiliation, and so on. *Cosa* evokes the Latin *res*, understood by Vico as the place, modes, and laws of human gathering. We might think of it broadly as the historical configuration of determinate human worlds. Such worlds have a "nature" (i.e., they come into being) as well as a pattern of succession.

One of philology's principal tasks, as Vico understood and practiced it, is to excavate the institutional histories (religious, legal, political, etc.) that ground the meanings of our basic words. Vico was guided in his labor by the axiom that follows the one just cited: "This was the order of human institutions: first the forests, after that the huts, then the villages, next the cities, and finally the academies" (§239). Vico calls this axiom "a great principle of etymology" and, in one of the more famous etymologies of the *New Science*, he gives an example of how "this sequence of human institutions sets the pattern for the histories of words in the various native languages" (§240). His example is the Latin word *lex*, which we usually translate as "law" but about which Vico conjectures the following:

> First it must have meant a collection of acorns. Thence we believe is derived *ilex*, as it were *illex*, the [holm] oak (as certainly *aquilex* means collector of waters); for the oak produces the acorns by which the swine are drawn together. *Lex* was next a collection of vegetables, from which the latter were called *legumina*. Later on, at a time when vulgar letters had not yet been invented for writing down the laws, *lex* by a necessity of civil nature must have meant a collection of citizens, or the public parliament; so that the presence of the people was the *lex*, or "law," that solemnized the wills that were made *calatis comitiis*, in the presence of the assembled *comitia*. Finally, collecting letters, and making, as it were, a sheaf of them for each word, was called *legere*, reading. (§240)

This is more than one of those "fanciful" etymologies that tend to amuse today's readers of the *New Science*. To begin with, we know that the Latin word *lex* is distantly related to the Greek word *legein* and that both, if we believe the linguists invoked earlier, derive from the Indo-European root *leg*. Vico was of course unaware of the Indo-European root, but he "gathered" from the linguistic evidence that all the various meanings associated with the word *lex* or its root have to do with gathering, binding, relating, and collecting. What he attempts to think in his conjectural etymology is what exactly the *lex* would have gathered—

what sort of referents its semantics were bound up with—in the various stages of the institutional order. That is the task of philology as Vico understood it. Philology unearths the acorns, swine, vegetables, citizens, and letters, while philosophy abstracts what is common to these different institutional referents—the idea of gathering as such. What is important in Vico's etymology—at least for us—is not so much the empirical exactness of the referential conjecture (which falls under the category of certainty) but the sustained attempt to link the word to the order of institutions, hence to derive its meanings not from ideas but from what Leopardi called the "things"—things which, as I have stressed, come to us through the words themselves.

Vico's Italian reader of course knows that from the Latin *legere,* which ends the genealogy of this dead word, comes the Italian *leggere,* "to read," and with it a whole new lexical afterlife. We may recall that from the Latin *legere* comes a host of basic English words as well: *lectern, lecture, legend, legible, legion, collect, diligent, elect, intelligent, neglect, select, sacrilege,* and so on. Likewise to the word *lex* itself we can trace the words *legal, loyal, legislate, privilege, legitimate, allege, colleague, delegate, relegate,* and others. Yet the purpose of Vico's example is not to provide a historical survey of a word's multiple meanings, nor to show how many different words can be spawned from the same root, nor for that matter to advance a social history of language as such. It is to draw attention to the mysterious genetic logic by which the gathering of the *lex* is gathered within the word itself, in such a way that its accumulations of past meanings perdure, however latently, in its various derivatives. More important, its purpose is to show how word and world copenetrate each other, and how this copenetration engenders the order of institutions and binds it to the order of ideas. For it is the *lex* itself—understood now as the principle of synthesis in general—which holds together and interrelates the order of ideas and institutions. In that sense Vico's genealogy of a dead word does more than simply exemplify the "great principle of etymology"—it uncovers in the word *lex* the principle itself.

Vico affirmed, along with most philosophers, that the human mind is the ultimate source of all synthesis. The act of gathering acorns in the primeval forest is one that speaks of an already instituted world, call it a linguistic or lexical world. If forests form part of the institutional order it is because the sort of gathering that took place in them was a meaningful, and not just a foraging, activity. Heidegger puts it somewhat differently but to the same effect in his "Logos" essay when he declares of the harvests that "gathering is more than mere amassing." There is always "something extra" in the act of gathering that makes it "more than a jumbling together that snatches things up" (*Early Greek Thinking*, p. 61). This "something extra," claims Heidegger, "comes first"; it is that which one has in view whenever one gathers anything. For we never gather blindly but always with some purpose (in mind), which directs the gathering. The question is what exactly is this "something extra" which, by virtue of coming first, gets the order of institutions under way and makes our human worlds, as well as our basic words, historical? Or better, what are the conditions that make this "something extra" possible in the first?

For Heidegger an anthropological answer is not possible here. Only an ontological one will do. I will postpone reviewing the one he advances in *Being and Time* until the next chapter and keep the focus here on Vico's *New Science*. Now Vico does not offer a systematic elaboration of conditions of possibility, to be sure, yet his archaeology of what he calls the "principles of civil society" reveals the following philological certainty, which itself harbors a universal truth: before the order of institutions could even get under way in the forests there had to be human families, which came into being through what Vico calls the three "universal institutions of humanity"—religion, matrimony, and burial of the dead. Each institution has its special role in the founding of civil society, yet all three of them serve to bind the living to the dead and the dead to the unborn through the "certainty" of family genealogy. When Vico speaks of the "certainty" of family genealogy, he means that the giants could now point to the graves of their ancestors and claim descent from their line, whose future resides with the coming generations. In its most primordial human instantiation, the *lex* is what binds the family together as an institution that, perduring through time, opens up the durations of historical time. Through its idea of divine providence (from *providere*, "to look forward"), religion projects the future. Through its piety toward the ancestor and its ritual commemorations, burial institutes the past. Through its injunction to keep the genealogical line between past and future intact, matrimony seals the contract between predecessor and progeny in the present. What Heidegger calls the three temporal "ecstasies" have first and foremost an institutional, not a psychological or noetic, foundation.

The three universal institutions humanize the giants by throwing them into the ecstatic reaches of time and situating them—the giants— in a historical and not merely natural continuum. If gathering acorns in the forests is a meaningful and not just a foraging activity, it is because the gatherer is already directed, is already intentionally oriented in his or her behavior and thinking. Such intentionality is possible only because the gatherer is already humanly related to the predecessor, not merely biologically but institutionally, as it were. The earliest creeds, customs, myths, allegories, poetic characters, and natural languages that philology studies all point to this genealogical law—this being unto the dead, and through them unto the unborn—as the "something extra" that comes first in the gathering of the *lex*. One cannot get back behind the law of legacy. To speak in terms that are in fact alien to the *New Science*, there is no a priori ground of the *lex*. There is at best an a priori underground, too deep under the earth to reach by concept or idea. The injunction to "Know thyself" calls for a veritable undertaking, one that leads through the Stygian Forest into a realm of antecedence receding beyond the Lethe River. Philosophy does not possess the "authority" to penetrate very deeply into that lethic realm. Such authority derives ultimately from the ancestor. For all its truth and analytic abstraction, philosophy comes too late in the historical *corso* for first principles. By the time it flails its way out of the womb of myth, the story is already half over. The way back to the origin passes through other languages and other modes of thought than those that inform its critical reason. It is a way that calls for the golden bough of a poetic philology.

Vico's quest for the principles of civil society led him, he says, into "the night of thick darkness enveloping the earliest antiquity" (*New Science*, §331). He was obliged "to descend from these human and refined natures of ours to those quite wild and savage natures [of the first men], which we cannot at all imagine and comprehend only with great effort" (§338). It was an undertaking in which, as he put it, "we encountered exasperating difficulties which have cost us the research of a good twenty years" (ibid.). Yet for all the darkness of that night enveloping the earliest antiquity, "there shines [in this night] the never failing light of a truth beyond all question: that the world of civil society has certainly been made by men, and that its principles are therefore to be found within the modifications of our own human mind" (§331). I take this axiom to be crucial, not so much for the reason Vico scholars frequently draw attention to it—namely as evidence that the *verum factum* principle (we can know only what we make) remains the epistemological foundation of the *New Science*—but because it postulates that the human mind retains its prior modes of synthesis and carries them over into its subsequent modifications. Were the mind not retentive in this metasynthetic way we could neither share the words of the dead, nor understand the worlds from which those words come down to us, nor decipher the hieroglyphs in the early fossil record of poetic wisdom. Indeed, there would be no such thing as civil society at all, since it is precisely in the human mind's vast reservoirs of retention that we find its principles, or enduring beginnings.

Nothing is more difficult than to get a firm conceptual grasp of the retentive nature of the human mind, since at any given time we find ourselves inside a retaining framework the boundaries of which we can never fully circumscribe. Certainly retention as Vico intends it is not reducible to memory. Memory's diverse powers of recollection have their source in human retention, no doubt, yet the retained is not necessarily remembered. It is carried over, bestowed, put in reserve. One could say that it is buried, if by that one understands its consignment to the humus of humanitas, whose contents are at any given time only partially retrieved or retrievable. A society or individual may in fact retain a host of legacies without ever activating their potential. Nor do most of the legacies that in fact get activated, either in people, societies, or nations, pass through the faculties of personal or collective memory. Much that is pathological and malignant in both individuals and societies, as well as much that is redemptive, springs from this latent, nonremembered endowment. In its selective capacity, memory actually protects us from the overwhelming excess of what we in fact retain.

How now? Does retention then belong to what psychology calls the unconscious? Hardly. The mind's synthetic activity extends well beyond our psychic life in its totality, be it on the conscious or unconscious levels, if for no other reason than the human mind is a self-externalizing phenomenon that *creates* its places of retention outside of its psychic interiorities. Indeed, its creative activity is largely a world-forming, that is, retention-creating, activity. Our institutions, laws, landscapes, cities, statues, scriptures, houses, books, ideologies—these are among the many places in its secular topography where the human mind stores both the past and future of what it retains. To say that all these places where the mind engenders its worlds and transmutes past into future have their true residence in the unconscious is to psychologize the mind—and with it the worlds of its own making—in a manner that Vico had already soundly rejected in his repudiation of Cartesian mentalism. Wallace Stevens's jar does not rise up to the hill in Tennessee from the depths of the unconscious, nor from any mental interiority as such. If anything its presence there is what opens the realm of the mental in the first place. The jar and its placement on the hill are the poetic act of the mind's self-transcending, world-engendering *ingenium.*

It may well be that retention has a genetic component, yet we are still far from understanding the role that genes play in human legacy—to what extent they are neutral agents of transmission, to what extent they promote or inhibit certain aspects of the heritage (ideologies, for instance), to what extent they are more loyal to the forefathers than they are to the unborn, to what extent they think, project, direct, intend, and so forth. It is not at all clear whether they promote the interests of the species or the interests of humanity (the two belong to different orders of being, as we have seen). However vast or narrow their field of operations may turn out to be, genes remain at best only one among countless dwelling places where the ancestor carries on an afterlife. If the dead restricted themselves to our genes history would be a simpler and no doubt saner story, but for better or worse the dead are not content to reside in our genes alone, for genes are not *worlds,* and the dead seek above all to share our worlds.

To the degree that the mind's retentive *ingenium* cannot be reduced to the mnemonic, the psychic, or the genetic, or even to their complex synergies, it remains steeped in the mystery of lexification, which is my word for a kind of synthesis that is neither merely predicative nor merely pragmatic but, as it were, historial and world forming. Lexification is a retentive relating or binding by which the human mind, like our basic words, continuously accesses the priority into and out of which it is born. In its temporal and historical schematizing, it enables human directedness in the verbal, institutional, and cognitive domains through its synthesis of the law of legacy. Certainly gathering acorns in the primeval forest is a primitive activity of the human mind, just as the coming together of citizens to form the *comitia* of human laws is a subsequent historical modification of such activity. Yet the synthesis that binds these modes of gathering as a historical unfolding is of a different ontological order than collecting vegetables, rounding up swine, or tying letters in a sheaf. Indeed, lexification is that which makes of forests, huts, villages, and cities a correlative *order* in the first place, and not just a historical sequence.

What Vico calls the "natural law of the gentes"—a law that relates the generations in cognational, institutional, linguistic, and various other modes—disposes in time what the mind retains in its otherwise anachronic reserve of legacy. Lexification is the creative and relentless agitation of this law. It allows the past to reach out to us from the future and the future to meet us from out of the past, transforming human finitude into a field of historical relations rather than a flow of chronological moments. Temporalizing and historicizing that which it conjoins, it turns sounds into words, time into ages, and humans into heirs. As it binds the living to the ever-receding priority of the dead and the eventuality of the unborn, it is the true "synthetic a priori" of civil society.

Lexification as I understand it is not a transcendent agency that operates in history immanently. It is neither purposeful nor teleological, as far as we know, nor does it dispense the laws of history. At most it occasions the law of legacy through which history gets under way in the first place. In *New Science* the concept that perhaps comes closest to what I intend by the term is "authority," as when Vico speaks of the "certainty of authority" of the preenlightened ages when societies were governed by precedent and custom. We must take the word *authority*, says Vico, "in its original meaning of property." "The term *auctores* was accordingly applied to those from whom we derive the title to property," in other words the ancestors, who were the original title holders of the property they bequeathed as well as the authors of the laws, institutions, and religions that sanctioned the legitimacy of those titles (*New Science*, §386). Thus when Vico says of his *New Science* that one of its "principal aspects" is a "philosophy of authority," he does not mean a philosophy of private property but a philosophy of lexification: the relational law by which the dead maintain their hold on the worlds they have handed down to their descendants. We share with animals our thrownness into gender and into our species-being, but in addition to those determinations we are also thrown into the authority of the past.

By the same token we are thrown into the history as well as historicity of the word. Language is possible only where lexification has already bound the temporal ecstasies humanly. Heidegger calls on us to "think through" the historicity of our basic words. Vico calls on us to restore their historical density. The *New Science* is no ontology à la *Being and Time,* yet Vico was as aware as Heidegger of the difference between a word's history and its historicity. If words have a history it is because they come down to us from former words, former worlds, and former speakers; if they have a historicity, is because they naturally lexify this priority. For Vico the lexification passes through the certainty of philology. For Heidegger it passes over that certainty. Heidegger's avowed objective was to think through the historicity of words in order to hear in them the echoes of some primal naming of lexification itself. Vico's was to think through their history in order to reclaim their secular legacies. Much is at stake in the difference. To think through the historicity of our words without thinking through their history means to depopulate their underworlds, to disjoin them from their antecedent speakers and thereby dispossess the dead of their claims on language. To think through their history, as Vico does, means to reanimate their saying capacity and liberate their lexifying power as such.

Vico believed that the first symptom of the decline of nations into what he called the "barbarism of reflection" was not the corruption of morals but the corruption of language—the failure of words to retain their institutional binding power, to preserve their humic past, and to access their historicity. One could say that in the age of the new barbarism words lose their moral memory. For even our morality—indeed, our morality above all—depends on the historical resonance of its foundational words: *liberty, duty, sacrifice, compassion, equality.* The "false eloquence" of the times exploits the traditional charisma of such words while at the same time emptying them of their historical memory. This loss of historicity (one of whose manifestations is in fact over-historicization) is itself a historical event, a sort of undoing of the historical *corso* as a whole. The binding power of the *lex,* or so Vico believed, has an intrinsic, institutional finitude of its own, such that it eventually exhausts its synthetic capacities and begins to unravel. At certain times and under certain circumstances nations run their course and succumb to disorder—not the productive sort of disorder that accompanies evolutionary shifts in the order of institutions but the degenerative sort that signals the death throes of nations. We could call it the "dislexification" of the order of institutions, the primary symptom of which is a corruption of the word's historical, signifying power.

Many poets in the modern period have given voice to what they believed was an ultimacy of this sort, a sort of darkening of history with its concomitant loss of the word's capacity to mean anything more than its failure to mean. One such poet who situated himself at the extreme end of history, in the night of thick darkness enveloping not the earliest antiquity but the latest modernity, was Giorgio Caproni (d. 1990). Caproni was the direct poetic descendant of Ungaretti and, through him, of Leopardi. He was a modernist who was fully aware that he had outlived the end of modernism, hence the posthumous nature of his voice. In one of his last poems, entitled "Quattro appunti," we hear that voice fall back on all that's left to it—the simple words of a handed-down language:

1.
Son già dove?
        Già quando? . . .
(Chiedo.
        (Non è che mi stia allarmando.)

2.
Son già oltre la morte.
Oltre l'oltre.
        Già oltre
(in queste mie estreme ore corte)
l'oltre dell'oltremorte . . .

3.
Io, già all'infinito distante.

Qui, in questo mio preciso istante.

Dove, morto ormai il bettoliere,
aspetto—"come se" Nulla *fosse*—il solito
(già dileguato) bichiere . . .

4.
(Io già al di là d'ogni attesa . . .
Già scavalcata ogni resa . . .)
(*Tutte le poesie,* pp. 798–801)

[1. I'm already where? / Already when? . . . / (I ask. / It's not that
I'm alarmed.) 2. I'm already beyond death. / Beyond the beyond.
/ Already beyond / (in these my extreme brief hours) / the beyond of death's beyond . . . 3. I, already distant from the distant
infinite. / Here, in this my precise instant. / Where, the inn-
keeper by now dead, / I wait—"as if" it *were* Nothing—the usual
(already diluted) glass . . . 4. (I already beyond all waiting . . . /
Every surrender already done with . . .]

Even more than the word *oltre,* "beyond," I would say that the key
Leopardian *parola* here is *già,* "already." A process or course of events,
founded on an expectation of finality, is already over. The "already" is
beyond this history of anticipation. In the *qui,* or "here," of an already
consummated end, only the words of the poem's utterance have any
further afterlife.

In an earlier poem of 1974, "Parole (dopo l'esodo) dell'ultimo della
Moglia," from which I will quote selectively, Caproni describes the end
beyond which the later poem situates itself:

> Chi sia stato il primo, non
> È certo. Lo seguì un secondo. Un terzo.
> Poi, uno dopo l'altro, tutti
> Han preso la stessa via.
>
> Ora non c'è più nessuno.
>
> La mia
> Casa è la sola
> Abitata
> . . . .
> Il trifoglio
> Della città è troppo
> Fitto. Io son già cieco.
> Ma qui vedo. Parlo.

Qui dialogo. Io
Qui mi rispondo e ho il mio
Interlocutore. Non voglio
Murarlo nel silenzio sordo
D'un frastuono senz'ombra
D'anima. Di parole
Senza più anima.

[Who had been the first is not / certain. He was followed by a second. A third. / Then, one after the other, all / took the same road. / Now there is no longer anybody. / My house is the only / inhabited one. . . . / The clover / of the city is too / thick. I'm already blind. / But here I see. I speak / Here I converse. / Here / I answer myself and have my / interlocutor. I don't want / to immure him in the surd silence / of a din without a shadow / of soul. Of words / with no more soul.]

However much Caproni's poetry in general may strive for and even attain a terminal rhetoric, the fact is that the end, like the beginning, is always beyond us. Just as there are no first words, there are no last words. Already several poets in Italy have inherited Caproni's corpus, continuing in their own ways his quest for an impoverished language of simple and denuded words, much the way Caproni himself inherited Ungaretti's hermetic minimalism, to say nothing of Leopardi's nihilism. The imperative to go on, even when one can't go on, is irresistible. As Molloy says in Beckett's novel, *Molloy,* "I have always been inclined to submit to [imperatives], I don't know why. For they never led me anywhere. . . . Yes, these imperatives were quite explicit and even detailed until, having set me in motion at last, they began to falter, then went silent, leaving me there like a fool who neither knows where he is going nor why he is going there" (p. 117). That ultimate imperative—to keep the story going, however absurd or unredeemed it may be—comes to us from the giant family of the dead, who live on only as long as the story continues.

CHAPTER 6

CHOOSING YOUR ANCESTOR

Why, in a study about the modes of being of the dead, do I appeal to the tumulus philology of Vico—a relatively archaic, not to say eccentric, theorist—rather than to the ontology of Martin Heidegger, the most radical philosopher of death in the history of philosophy? Precisely because *Being and Time* is an ontology of death, not of the dead. In *Being and Time* Heidegger gives back to death the world-disclosive power it rightfully possesses, yet its existential analytic suffers from some essential shortcomings—in particular it fails to show, or even suspect, that Dasein's relation to its death passes by way of its relation to the dead. A great deal is at stake in this claim. To substantiate it I will first review some basic tenets of *Being and Time,* which remains in my view Heidegger's most fundamental work.

We have seen that for Heidegger there is always "something extra" that "comes first" in human gathering, namely that which directs the gathering and orients it toward a future goal (storing the grain, providing for coming needs, legislating laws, etc.). For Heidegger, only Dasein among all creatures is able always to have something in view that directs its actions toward longer term goals. These projections are possible because Dasein is temporally "ecstatic," that is, thrown beyond the immediacy of beings in their actuality into a recessive realm of future possibilities. If it did not stand outside itself in such a manner, transcending its temporal present, it could not have sufficient distance from entities to grasp them in their being or understand them for what they are. Insects or even higher mammals presumably do not see the tree *as* a tree, since they are not existentially distended in such a way as to grasp the tree intelligibly, meaningfully, or what we might call discursively. Dasein, on the other hand, has a native "preunderstanding of Being" thanks to the fact that it runs ahead of itself existentially and temporally.

Heidegger does not stop here, however. The radicality of *Being and Time* consists in its claim that Dasein's projective, future-directed, and gratification-deferring behavior has its basis in Dasein's thrownness into its ultimate future possibility, namely its own death. Time and again Heidegger insists that human death must be understood not as the biological termination of life but as an immanent possibility that claims Dasein's existence before it claims Dasein's life. In Heidegger's most succinct formulation: "Man dies constantly until the moment of his demise." Because it relates to its death as its "ownmost possibility," Dasein is existentially aware of itself as a finite being. Or as Heidegger puts it: "Dasein is essentially disclosed to itself, and disclosed, indeed, as ahead-of-itself" (*Being and Time*, p. 294). This being-at-the-end-before-the-end-comes-about—"being-toward-death" for short—makes of Dasein's finitude the "absymal" foundation of its existence. Finitude generates, rather than puts a limit on, our existential transcendence. It mortalizes and, in so doing, humanizes us. Humans are called mortal "because they can die," Heidegger writes in his essay "The Thing." "Only man dies. The animal perishes. It has death neither ahead of itself nor behind it" (*Poetry, Language and Thought*, p. 178). If Dasein did not have death ahead of and behind itself, it could neither gather together acorns, nor reap the harvests, nor put subjects together with predicates.

Heidegger's existential analytic in *Being and Time* represents a crucial chapter in the history of philosophy, without doubt, and I take nothing away from its philosophical truth when I say that it too fails by half, insofar as it lacks certainty. By this I don't mean that it fails to offer an account of how human beings have conceived, signified, or ritualized their mortality over the ages—we do not ask of Heidegger an anthropology of that sort—but that it fails to interrogate the nature of Dasein's primitive access to the phenomenon of death. Why is this important? It is important because, as Vico declares, "Doctrines must take their beginning from that of the matter of which they treat" (*New Science*, §314). One cannot proceed from truth to certainty, or in this case from the concept of death to the reality of dead, rather the other way around. This is not to say that there are no transhistorical truths. Vico grants philosophers their "ideal" truth, he even pretends to such truth himself when he defines his *New Science* as an "ideal eternal history traversed in time by the history of all nations" (*NS* §393). Truth is not "based" on certainty, rather it "proceeds" from certainty.

Vico reminds us time and again that the primitive human mind did not possess the capacity for abstraction, that it thought concretely, in terms of personifications, anthropomorphisms, and embodied substances. Where we moderns form a concept, our ancestors imagined a god; where we spiritualize, they materialized (and vice versa); where we think with our minds, they thought with their bodies (*New Science*, §402 ff.). We will never fulfill philosophy's injunction—"know thyself!"—if we do not recognize the "poetic" prehistory of our abstract conceptual thought, a prehistory that we have not merely left behind long ago but still carry within us as the ever active matrix of abstract thought. Here one could translate Vico's axiom, "The order of ideas must proceed from the order of institutions," in the following way: the idea of death must proceed from the dead. Indeed, it must proceed from the corpse. For the corpse is one of the most primordial of human institutions.

It is impossible to overestimate how much human culture owes, in principle and in origin, to the corpse—not the animal corpse in its sacrificial generosity but the human corpse in its personification of loss. Heidegger makes a serious blunder in *Being and Time* when he states that the corpse is a mere "thing" which, in its presence-at-hand, gives Dasein no access to its own death as such (pp. 281–82). A corpse is indeed present-at-hand, yet its lifeless mass is what is left of what is no longer there, what is on its way elsewhere. The corpse is the site of something that has disappeared, that has forsaken the sphere of presence, that has passed from the body into . . . into what? Death? The past? Another dimension? We hear these words and understand them abstractly, but faced with the spectacle of a dead body the primitive mind did not think to itself: "My mother has passed away into the dimension of the has-been." It more likely thought to itself (something like): "Here is my mother lying before me. I can see her, touch her, feel her, yet she is not here. How can this be?" How indeed? Only something as resistant as the insensate body of a loved one—the enigma of its expired life and remnant thinghood—could give the anthropomorphic mind its first access to what we abstractly call death, and with it to the ethos of finitude. In its perfect likeness of the person who has passed away, the corpse withholds a presence at the same time as it renders present an absence. The disquieting character of its presence-at-hand comes precisely from the presence of a void where there was once a person. In this void both past and future in their ecstatic reach come into "being," as it were. One could say that the corpse is the aboriginal locus of the temporal ecstasies (past, present, and future) in and through which our thinking, signifying, projecting, and recollecting derive their measure of finite transcendence.

For all its grave stillness there is nothing more dynamic than a corpse. It is the event of passage taking place before our eyes. This phenomenon of passage—from which devolves our abstract idea of the past—makes of the unalive body a relational "thing" which, in its subjection to the power of death, binds past, present, and future. The past (or no-longer-hereness of the person), the present (the corpse in its presence-at-hand), and the future (the fate awaiting those who follow in the footsteps of the deceased) all converge in the dead body, as long, that is, as it remains an object of concern or solicitude for the living. A corpse in itself is neither disquieting nor disclosive. Only in its genealogical, sentimental, or institutional relation to the surviving loved one does it become the personification of transcendence.

There is a substantial difference, therefore, though not necessarily an incommensurate one, between the philosophical truth of death and the philological certainty of the dead. Before it became the ultimate, unrepresentable possibility of my own impossibility of being—indeed, before it became exclusively *mine*—death wore the mask of the dead. Heidegger insists that Dasein cannot relate to its own death by way of the death of others (he calls death "non-relational"), yet this is as philologically inadequate as his reduction of the corpse to mere presence-at-hand. On this score we should listen rather to Freud, who certainly was no philologian in Vico's sense but who nevertheless had excellent reasons to believe that human beings lack any innate notion of their own deaths (Freud, "Thoughts," p. 289). Only the shock of the loved one's death persuades us—against our deepest instinctual convictions—that we will or even *can* die. After many decades of research into the human psyche, Freud's ex-disciple Jung also concluded, for slightly different reasons, that the unconscious has no sense of its own mortality, indeed, that it believes itself—perhaps even rightly so—to be immortal (Jung, "The Soul and Death"). The doctrine of the soul's immortality may well have its source in this complete lack of an innate sense of mortality in the psychic life of the unconscious. All of which confirms that it is essentially the death of others—institutionalized and ritualized in funerals, burial, lamentation practices, and protocols of commemoration—which provokes the eruption of being-toward-death in human existence.

The dead are our progenitors in more ways than one, then, for as they humanized mortality they also mortalized humanity. To say that they personify death in the primitive mind does not mean they personify merely the termination of life, for if that were the case they never would have acquired the sublime authority they enjoy in almost all world cultures; rather, the dead personify the temporal ecstasies themselves. Or better, they *inhabit* those ecstasies. The *New Science* teaches that from the moment human beings began to think humanly they have believed that through their dying the dead return to a realm of origins from which both the living and the unborn draw life. This is the awesome, anachronic realm of the progenitors to whom the living remain beholden for their houses, their harvests, their laws, their customs, their patrimonies, their wisdom, and everything else that keeps their societies from relapsing into an inhuman barbarism. Herein lies the authority of the dead and the charisma of the ancestor. By passing from the realm of the engendered into that of the engendering, the dead become the authors and proprietors of life, personifying all that transcends and yet at the same time generates human society.

Classical literature bequeaths a powerful image of this anachronic matrix of the institutional order. In Virgil's underworld the future generations of Aeneas's lineage coexist alongside his ancestors. Look, there is Silvius, Procas, Numitor, Romulus, and Julius Caesar himself. As they await their turn in the light they share the same ontological status as the dead forefathers. Both those who have yet to enter the world and those who have departed from it figure as disembodied spirits whose pasts and futures are merely provisional, relative concepts. They are masks of each other. In Virgil's vision, born of more ancient visions, the unborn come forth as the projective transcendence of the dead—the same transcendence that carries the living along in its wake, as if Hades were the wellspring of human destiny prior to its temporal unfolding in the world above.

In Hades Aeneas learns that past and future in fact copenetrate and codetermine each other. The downfall of Troy remains an unfinished event whose outcome and consequences have yet to be determined. It all depends on the manner in which Aeneas resolves upon his mission and succeeds in reprojecting the Trojan legacy in the future city of Rome. The purpose of his descent into Hades is to receive from his ancestors what Heidegger calls the "repeatable possibilities of existence," in this case the possibility of repeating Troy's past in Rome's future.

Authentic repetition, as we will see, entails the renewal and redetermination of legacy, rather than merely its pious reproduction. Book 3 of *The Aeneid* offers a pathetic image of the latter, inauthentic repetition. There Aeneas comes across a colony of Trojan refugees, among them Andromache and their leader Helenus, who have reconstructed a "little Troy" in the wilds of southern Italy: "I see a little Troy, a Pergamus that mimes the great one, and a dried up stream / that takes its name from Xanthus" (455). This dried-up stream tells us all we need to know about the sterility of this ghostly place, where the fallen city has been mimetically recast in miniature. Andromache and her fellow Trojans have foreclosed the dynamic transcendence that pushes Aeneas forward on his journey—a transcendence that seeks a Trojan *vita nova* in a *terra nova*, and not merely a recreation of Troy's empty shell. "Your fate is here," says Aeneas to Andromache, who spends her days before a cenotaph erected for Hector, whose body remained behind in Troy. "But we are called from one fate to another" (642–43). The other fate to which Aeneas is called is that of genuine renewal and repetition. His story, as it comes to us through Virgil, gives abundant philological certainty to Heidegger's otherwise abstract claim that the legacies handed down from the past lie not behind us but run out ahead of us. We would do well to examine that claim more in depth, for all the various strands of Heidegger's existential analytic come together around his concept of repetition.

Heidegger discusses *Wiederholung*, or repetition, in section 74 of *Being and Time*, which deals with the ground of Dasein's "authentic historicality." There he defines repetition as a future-directed retrieval of the past that is based on Dasein's resolute embracing of its mortality. The more resolutely we anticipate our death, the more decisively we are *thrust back upon our personal heritage.* As Heidegger notes, "The resoluteness which comes back to itself and hands itself down, then becomes a *repetition* of a possibility of existence that has come down to us" (*Being and Time*, p. 437). Let us unpack this loaded sentence. The German word *Ueberliefern*, translated here as "hand down," has a remote, etymological meaning of "to free up" or "to liberate," while the word *Wiederholung* ("repetition") is better read as "retrieval" (*wieder-holen*, "to haul up again" or "to re-new"). So let us paraphrase: "The decision or existential resolve whereby one returns to and liberates oneself [after having "shattered" against the possibility of one's death] then becomes the retrieval and renewal of an inherited possibility of existence" (see Sheehan, "Choosing One's Fate"). The passage continues: "*Repeating is handing down explicitly*—that is to say, going back into the possibilities of the Dasein that has-been-there. The authentic repetition of a possibility of existence—the possibility that Dasein may choose its hero—is grounded existentially in anticipatory resoluteness; for it is in resoluteness that one first chooses the choice which makes one free for the struggle of loyally following in the footsteps of that which can be repeated" (*Being and Time*, p. 437). What, then, is resoluteness exactly? A few pages later Heidegger writes that resoluteness "constitutes the *loyalty* of existence to its own Self . . . this loyalty is at the same time a possible way of revering the sole authority which a free existing can have—of revering the repeatable possibilities of existence" (p. 443). Resoluteness is an active decision to embrace one's finitude and, through that embrace, to take over the repeatable possibilities of existence.

What is interesting here, among other things, is the way Heidegger fuses two different meanings of the phrase that most succinctly sums up the concept of authenticity in *Being and Time*: "become who you already are." On the one hand, to become who I already am means to become my dying, to take over my mortality lucidly and resolutely, through anticipation of my death. On the other hand, it means to resolve upon a set of handed-down possibilities that I am thrown back upon when I reach out toward and shatter against my death. Yet Heidegger never adequately clarifies the (causal?) relation between becoming my dying and becoming an heir, between reaching out to the nullity of death and retrieving legacies in my heritage. Instead he affirms the following: "history has its roots so essentially in the future that death . . . throws anticipatory existence back upon its *factical* thrownness, and so for the first time imparts to *having-been* its peculiarly privileged position in the historical" (p. 438). This is a radical account of the connection between futurity and historicity, to be sure, yet it hardly explains why or how being-toward-death throws Dasein back upon the law of legacy, or why in my "moment of vision" I reclaim a heritage that comes down to me (though I free it up for myself) from my predecessors.

Only when we realize that what Heidegger means by the word *future* in such statements as "history has its roots . . . essentially in the future," or "[f]rom the phenomena of handing down and repeating, which are rooted in the future. . . ."—only when we realize that this existential futurity is in fact thoroughly populated by the dead as well as the unborn, only then can we fully make sense of this connection. This underworld of futurity may lie beyond the bounds of Oceanos or deep in the Avernus Woods, yet it remains always *in* Dasein, insofar as Dasein stands outside of itself, held out into the nothing. ("Da-sein means: being held out into the nothing. . . . Holding itself out into the nothing, Dasein is in each case already beyond beings as a whole. This being beyond beings we call 'transcendence'" ["What Is Metaphysics" in *Basic Writings*, p. 105]).

For Heidegger it is because no one else can die for me that my resolute being-toward-death individuates me. But death, understood in these abstract terms, is a universal possibility common to every Dasein. It is purely generic. Yet if in my confrontation with my death I am in fact confronted by my dead, and if it is from *them* (my personal, cultural, or freely chosen traditions) that I receive the sum of those repeatable possibilities that I am thrown back upon in anticipatory resoluteness—in other words, if my being-toward-death is in fact a being-toward-the-dead—then authenticity individuates me in a culturally specific, even genealogical way. It makes of my mortality a coffer of legacies consigned to me from my forebears, awaiting retrieval and renewal. In his entire corpus this is as close as Heidegger comes to thinking what I have called lexification.

Before we turn to the question of Dasein's freedom to choose its hero, a word about the key Heideggerian concepts of guilt and conscience. In division 2 of *Being and Time* Heidegger goes to considerable lengths to demoralize the concept of existential guilt and redefine it in terms of the primary meaning of the German word *Schuld*, namely "debt." Guilt now refers to the debt I owe to my future. As long as my life has not reached an end I remain existentially insolvent, burdened with a debt, guilty with respect to my "outstanding end," as Heidegger calls it, alluding to an outstanding debt. Such guilt is the very stuff of finitude.

The "call of conscience" that Heidegger discusses in section 57 is a "silent call" that issues forth from this finitude, calling Dasein back to its primordial guilt. The call has no specific content. It says nothing. It merely "points *forward* to Dasein's potentiality-for-Being, and it does this as a call which comes from *uncanniness* . . . the 'whence' of the calling is the 'wither' to which we are called back" (*Being and Time*, pp. 325–26). It is a call, we might say, from the temporal ecstasies themselves. Yet could we not say, by appeal to the authority of the philologians, that the call of conscience, which reaches us from the nullity of our being's ground, in fact comes from—or comes in the guise of—the dead? Is it not *they*—the dead—who, in their uncanny modes, indwell in the temporal ecstasies and come out to meet us in our self-overreaching? Are we not constitutionally guilty in *their* regard, indebted to *their* sacrifice and labor, subject to *their* authority insofar as they, not we, authored the institutions that ensure our future? Certainly in most world cultures the dead are hounders, harassing the living with guilt, reminding them of their debts to the forefathers, calling on them to meet their obligations. ("Uniform ideas originating among entire peoples unknown to each other must have a common ground of truth"; *New Science*, §144). They trouble our sleep, colonize our moods, whisper in the dark, insinuate themselves into our imagination, urge us to continue their work on behalf of the unborn. It is for a reason, in any case, that cultures the world over have imagined the dead as unreconciled and in need of periodic appeasement. To demoralize the call of conscience, as Heidegger does in *Being and Time,* means to veil the more proximate source of our anxieties, the most basic of which stem from our compulsion to justify our ancestors, or, when this is not possible, to free ourselves from their overbearing demands. More often than not we fail in those tasks and take our unresolved anxieties with us to our graves, from which abode we in turn hound those who come after us.

Let me, by way of pursuing the certainty of example, open a parenthesis here about the strange career of Arthur Rimbaud, who was raised by his peasant mother in the provincial French town of Charlesville after the premature death of his father. During his early youth Rimbaud's drunken boat drifted far and wide in the great Poem of the Sea, free from obligation, free from the law of the father, free from the institutional bindings of the *lex*. Then one day the young man caught a glimpse of another boat—the riverboat in "Mémoire," perhaps, with its old man calmly waiting at the helm ("Un vieux, dragueur, dans sa barque immobile"), like Charon biding his time. Shortly thereafter, finding himself back in Charleville after years of errant wanderings, Rimbaud's season in hell began. Composed at his mother's house between April and August of 1873, *A Season in Hell* descends into the *mauvais sang* of ancestry: "From my Gallic ancestors I have blue-white eyes, a narrow skull, and clumsiness in wrestling. . . . From them I inherit: idolatry and love of sacrilege, oh! All the vices" (p. 175). The poet of *Illuminations*, who had "tried to invent new flowers, new stars, new flesh, new tongues," ends up having to "bury" his imagination ("je dois enterrer mon imagination et mes souvenirs," p. 206) and confront the residents of his bad blood.

The difference between *A Season in Hell* and *Illuminations* is that the former has depth while the latter are miraculous poetic levitations more at home among angels than ancestral demons. *Illuminations* contains some of the most perfect poems ever written and one day we may be able to inherit them properly, but for now they still lie beyond our capacity for appropriation. *A Season in Hell*, by contrast, speaks a more human, call it a humic, language—a language of frustration, lament, rage, self-pity, accusation, exculpation, missed opportunities, and failure. Are these not the dominant passions of the dead? In this hell of self-accusation from which *A Season in Hell* fetches its words the poet, after ignoring if not defying them, finds himself face to face with his dismal ancestors. Ancestors are a patient bunch. In any case they did not have to wait very long before this strange son of theirs fell to earth: "I who called myself magus or angel, exempt from all morality, I am thrown back to the earth. . . . Peasant! I will ask forgiveness for having fed on lies" (p. 209).

It amazes us that at nineteen years of age Rimbaud gave up poetry to devote himself grimly to the task of making money, that his letters from

Africa are filled only with the merchant's prose of profit and parsimony, and that from one moment to the next he turned his back on his genius (the *genie* "who has known us all and loved us all") without ever once looking back. But we should not be amazed. A descent into hell is serious business. It exposes you to the risk that the dead may reclaim you as one of their own, that they may have their way with you. This is what happened in the case of Rimbaud. Aeneas descended into Hades in a spirit of piety, Rimbaud in a spirit of despair, yet the result in both cases was similar. In both cases the descendant received instruction from the ancestor. Rimbaud's peasant forefathers looked him squarely in the eye and ordered him to put an end to his nonsense, instructed him to render his labor productive. Work, work, work! Work, earn, save, and suffer—that is your lot and obligation. In one of his few remarks about poetry in his later years, Rimbaud is reported to have said, "La poesie c'est de la merde." This from the poet who, in his infernal tribunal, confessed: "It is very clear to me that I have always belonged to an inferior race. I am unable to understand revolt. My race never rose up except to loot: like wolves over the animal they did not kill" (p. 175). At nineteen years of age Rimbaud's dead caught up with him, and that was that.

Before closing this parenthesis I would remark that, in retrospect, it seems inevitable that the ancestral dead would eventually have won out over Rimbaud's adoptive angels, for the simple reason that, from the very beginning of his remarkable career, Rimbaud's strongest allegiance was to the earth and all that rises up through its depths. One of his earliest poems, composed at the age of fourteen, speaks of this allegiance:

> *Sensations*
>
> Par les soirs bleus d'été, j'irai dans les sentiers,
> Picoté par les blés, fouler l'herbe menue:
> Reveur, j'en sentirai la fraicheur à mes pieds.
> Je laisserai le vent baigner ma tête nue.
>
> Je ne parlerai pas, je ne penserai rien:
> Mais l'amour infini me montera dans l'âme,
> Et j'irai loin, bien loin, comme un bohémien,
> Par la nature—heureux comme avec une femme.
>
> (*Ouevres*, p. 41)

[In the blue summer evenings, I will go along the paths,
And walk over the short grass, as I'm pricked by the wheat:
Daydreamer, I will feel the coolness at my feet.
I will let the wind bathe my bare head.

I will not speak, I will not think:
But infinite love will rise up in my soul,
And I will go far, far off, like a gypsy,
Through the countryside—happy as if I were with a woman.]

This juvenile poem describes the upwelling of infinite love as no more than a sensation, yet it was only a matter of time before that love's more atavistic and humic contents would work their way up through the earth and into Rimbaud's unsuspecting soul, drawing him down eventually to its underground source. Without knowing it, his love of the earth was calling up the dead. "Do I know nature yet? Do I know myself? *No more words.* I bury the dead in my belly" (*A Season in Hell*, p. 181).

It is precisely because the dead are able to exercise such tenacious, subterranean authority over our lives, mentalities, behavior, motivations, psyches, and who knows what else—our genes, personalities, dispositions—that freedom is linked so intimately to authenticity. Authenticity consists neither in a blind rebellion against, nor a slavish submission to, the dead's authority. We have seen that authentic retrieval is not mimetic repetition. It does not take the form of Andromache's "little Troy" by a dried-up stream named after the river Xanthus, but more the form of Aeneas's creative or futuristic reprojection of the Trojan legacy (I leave aside here Aeneas's killing of Turnus at the end of *The Aeneid*, a gesture that can be seen to "repeat" in a tragic sense the cycle of retributive vengeance).

Let us return now to *Being and Time* and ponder a critical passage from section 74: "The repeating of that which is possible does not bring again *[Wiederbringen]* something that is 'past,' nor does it bind the Present back to that which has already been 'outstripped' [i.e., whose life is over]. Arising as it does from a resolute projection of oneself, repetition does not let itself be persuaded of something by what is 'past,' just in order that this, as something which was formerly actual, may recur" (pp. 437–38). A crucial affirmation lies at the heart of this string of negatives, which distinguish authentic repetition from a deferential piety toward tradition—an affirmation that, in some cases, authenticity consists in resolutely *refusing* to repeat the past. Yet here too only an authentic anticipatory resolve puts us in a position to effectively refuse repetition. Heidegger writes that authentic repetition frees up the possibility of a *"disavowal* of that which in the 'today,' is working itself out as the 'past'"* (p. 438). This disavowal entails what he calls a "reciprocative rejoinder" to the past. Macquarrie and Robinson, the English translators of *Being and Time,* offer the following note of clarification on the term "reciprocative rejoinder": "The idea seems to be that in resolute repetition one is having, as it were, a conversation with the past, in which the past proposes certain possibilities for adoption, but in which one makes a rejoinder to this proposal by 'reciprocating' with the proposal of other possibilities as a sort of rebuke to the past, which one now disavows" (ibid.). Our negotiations with the dead are rarely so genteel, to be sure, and the mutual rebukes can take the form of an outright aggravated conflict. Be that as it may, authenticity does not only free up repeatable possibilities of existence, it also frees up the possibility of an effective disavowal of those possibilities. Nothing is more essential to modern freedom than the possibility of an authentic, as opposed to inauthentic, disavowal.

The difference lies precisely in the "reciprocative rejoinder" through which one engages and converses with the dead. This becomes possible only if one has first heard and understood the proposals to which a rejoinder is made. An inauthentic disavowal either fails to hear the proposals or does not understand the language in which they reach us. That is why our intercourse with the dead must be frank and ongoing: so that we may keep open the possibility of a "reciprocative rejoinder" that never simply denies but freely avows or disavows the will of the ancestors—and not only of the ancestors but also of those around us who, with sanctimonious piety, seek to make the historical present conform to an "outstripped" past. Thus Heidegger speaks of disavowing that which "in the 'today,' is working itself out as the past." There is much in any "today"—but perhaps in ours more than others—that works itself out as the past without a genuine retrieval. The problem with inauthentic repetition, whether on an existential or communal level, is that it almost always means allowing the dead to choose our inherited possibilities for us. When their legacies are not retrieved from the margins of our existential and historical future, when they are not freely transfigured and renewed, when their intent is literalized by dullness of mind or failure of nerve or simple dyslexia, then more often than not the dead have their way with us. How many nihilistic wars, pathological conniptions, and murderous passions stem from the failure to give the ancestor a "reciprocative rejoinder"?

To Heidegger's remarkable analysis of repetition I would simply add the following by way of expansion: authenticity liberates the possibility of choosing one's own ancestors. To some of our ancestors we are condemned by blood, race, and cultural history. We can hardly avoid their claims on us, or make as if such claims didn't exist, for we are always—whoever we are—thrown into our biocultural ancestry. While it does not dispense us from the claims of our tribe, authenticity opens up the freedom of ancestral adoption, as it were, in and through which we turn ourselves into the elective heirs of non-consanguine predecessors. An adopted ancestor is more than a hero whom one aspires to emulate, more than a forerunner whom one has read, studied, admired, or been influenced by. He or she is someone who fosters the becoming of who one already is, someone whom one "makes one's own" through elective affiliation and unconditional allegiance.

In one of the last notes of *Mon coeur mis à nu*, Baudelaire writes of his resolve to pray every morning to the souls of his father, his governess, and Edgar Allan Poe—to pray to them as intercessors, so that they may "communicate to me the strength necessary to fulfill all my duties" and to work to the full extent of his powers (*Oeuvres complètes*, p. 642). Clearly Baudelaire did not pray to Edgar Allan Poe merely as a disciple or enthusiast but rather as a veritable adoptive heir, as one of Poe's own, as it were, the way he prays to his governess as one of her own, and vice versa. In this note scribbled near the end of Baudelaire's abbreviated life, we find an elective ancestor (Poe) side by side with a biological ancestor (Baudelaire's father) who for all practical purposes has nothing more in common with his counterpart than this shared filial connection.

To gain an affiliation of this sort it does not suffice to imitate or translate or admire Poe; one must meet him, retrieve him, and inherit him in that place where the fate of the past has yet to be decided by the descendants. Baudelaire sought Poe out at the very edge of his finite transcendence, in some deep recess of his selfhood; or perhaps it was Poe who lured him there in the first place, in order to offer up a legacy for repetition. It is not clear to what extent authenticity allows us to choose or in effect allows us to be chosen for adoption. Personal choice, spiritual kinship, and the fate of circumstance all conspire to bring about unpredictable lines of descent. In effect one never knows who one's descendants will turn out to be once one is dead, for to be dead means to give oneself up to the possibility of ancestral adoption. Could anyone have imagined, before it happened, that the elective affiliation of a poet like Baudelaire would turn Poe into the father of French modernism and give him an afterlife in France—and in French—the likes of which he has never enjoyed in his own native country?

It is tempting to believe that history would be less of a nightmare if all our ancestors were chosen rather than genealogically determined, or if the natural authority of the biological ancestor were done away with altogether. Polybius once stated that if there were more philosophers in the world there would be no need of religions, to which Vico rejoined, "without religions no commonwealths can be born, and if there were no commonwealths in the world there would be no philosophers in it" (*New Science*, §179). Likewise one could say that if there were no biological ancestors there would be no elective ancestors—not because our lives depend on biological reproduction but because it is at the genealogical level that lexification first opens up the possibilities of affiliation. If lexification did not begin with the authority of genetic ancestors, Dasein would have no historicality and consequently no freedom to retrieve legacies at all. The freedom in question arises only where Dasein has already been historicized by the law of genealogy. The institutional expansion of that law is what creates the conditions for ancestral adoption.

What is true of individuals is true of societies and nations as well. Where and what would Rome be without the free adoption, or adoptive freedom, which comes from repetition? Look at the great mythic line that leads from Priam's Troy to Augustan Rome, the past and future extensions of which are on procession in Virgil's underworld—look at how it all falls on the shoulders of Aeneas, the great adopted ancestor of the Roman race. Aeneas became an ancestor relatively late, adopted by the Romans during their conquest of the Greeks. Does that make him any less genuine? Hardly. It makes him all the more Roman, if we understand Rome as the city of retrieval and repetition.

And who knows? Perhaps if one goes back far enough all our ancestors are adopted, including the great ancestor of them all: God the Father. Would Christianity have been remotely possible without what Paul called the spirit of adoption? "For you did not receive a spirit of slavery, but you have received a spirit of adoption. When we cry 'Abba! Father!' it is that very Spirit bearing witness with our spirit that we are the children of God, and if children, then heirs, heirs of God and joint heirs with Christ" (Rom. 8:15–17). We know that in Christianity's case it was not so much the Father who adopted his Gentile heirs as the heirs who adopted the Father, through faith in his human Son and a readiness to "suffer with him [the son] so that we may also be glorified with him" (ibid.). The spirit of adoption went well beyond that, however. We shall see in the next chapter that, just as Rome adopted Christianity, so too Christianity adopted Rome—all through the power of an empty tomb in Jerusalem.

CHAPTER 7

HIC NON EST

In the days leading up to her martyrdom in the Carthage arena in AD 203, Saint Perpetua kept a meticulous written record of her dreams, known to us today as the *Passio Perpetuae*. The diary describes two visions of her brother Dinocrates, who had died years earlier from a skin cancer at the age of seven. In the first he comes forth from a triste multitude of souls and approaches a basin of water that is too high for him to drink from. Wretched and thirsty, he bears the same wound on his face as when he had died. Distraught by her vision, Perpetua "day and night prayed for Dinocrates, groaning and weeping that my prayer be granted" (Dronke, *Women Writers of the Middle Ages*, p. 3). A few days later he appears to her again in her dreams, this time healed, radiant, and joyful. The rim of the basin has been lowered to the level of his navel and he drinks from it to his heart's content, splashing the water the way young boys are wont to do. "I realized then that he'd been freed from pain" (p. 4). Many of her editors take Perpetua's remark to mean that through the power of her prayer her brother had been "translated" to the realm of the blessed.

These pages from Perpetua's diary show just how much Christianity did to expand and alter the medium of relation between a living person and a dead soul. Wherever may be the place where the departed live on (and we have seen many such places by now), a Christian believer has intimate access to it, either in spirit, dream, or private petition. Likewise from their side the departed may, when summoned, freely enter the abode of the Christian soul. Through such communion—based on the Christian belief in the afterlife, the efficacy of prayer, and the intercession of saints—the living may influence the fate of the dead, and vice versa. The permeability of that boundary is not specific to Christianity, by any means, yet with respect to the pagan traditions of societies like the one Perpetua was born into at the end of the second century AD, the

Christian soul figures as a locus for the afterlife of the dead in a new and distinct sense. Grief, mourning, and remembrance, once the dominant modalities of relating to the dead, now become preludes to hope, expectation, and anticipation. One might say that Christianity rendered the souls of the living and those of the dead continuous in a new way, as if the living soul were in some sense already dead, while the dead soul, in that very same sense, were still alive. Certainly Perpetua's soul was not of this life, if we understand "life" in strictly secular terms.

When it comes to the nature and the causes of this expansive spiritual transformation that Christianity brought about in the ancient world, there are any number of approaches one could adopt. The ones I will follow in this chapter revolve around the meaning of Christ's tomb in Christian doctrine. If one can come to terms with this article of faith, one goes a long way in understanding the ground of the Christian revolution, for it is from out of Christ's empty sepulcher that the new religion, as we know it, was born. Whether the historical Jesus was ever laid in a tomb is of little concern here. It is the *meaning* of the Easter story as it comes to us through the Gospels, and mediated through our own interpretation, that is of primary interest. For life and death, the dead and the living, come together in the Resurrection—whatever that may *mean*. Let us turn to the Gospel narratives, then, and try to gain some clarity about the events surrounding Easter Sunday.

The earliest written account of that first Easter morning comes to us from Mark's Gospel, composed about AD 70 (almost four full decades after the death of Jesus of Nazareth). Mark relates that when Mary Magdalene, Salome, and Mary the mother of James arrive at Jesus' tomb on the first day after the Sabbath to anoint his body and complete the rites of burial, they discover that the stone has been rolled away from its entrance. From within the tomb a young man dressed in white tells them: "Do not be alarmed; you are looking for Jesus of Nazareth, who was crucified. He has been raised: he is not here [*hic non est* (Vulgate)]. Look, there is the place they laid him" (Mark 16:5–6). The angel alludes to a future appearance of Jesus, although the original Gospel of Mark does not describe any such epiphanies: "But go, tell his disciples and Peter that he is going ahead of you to Galilee; there you will see him just as he told you." The original Gospel of Mark ends abruptly, with the women running away in fear: "So they went out and fled from the tomb, for terror and amazement had seized them; and they said nothing to anyone, for they were afraid" (vv. 7–8). The remaining ten verses, which describe Jesus' post-Resurrection appearances to the disciples, are later additions to the original text. As for the much more elaborate appearance-narratives in the Gospels of Matthew, Luke, and John, they were composed anywhere from fifteen to thirty years after Mark's.

While Mark's is the oldest written account, biblical scholars, using form and redaction techniques, have been able to isolate the lineaments of an earlier Easter narrative that circulated orally among Christian believers in Jerusalem. This pre-Marcan legend of the Easter event was presumably identical to Mark's version except for the fact that it contained no mention of Jesus' future appearance in Galilee. Some scholars have speculated that the story was told as part of a liturgical celebration that took place annually, or perhaps even more frequently, at Jesus' tomb. Here is how Thomas Sheehan summarizes their theory in *The First Coming:*

> In the first decades after Jesus' death, the theory claims, believers made pilgrimages to Jesus' grave "very early in the morning on the first day of the week," presumably on what we now call Easter, but perhaps even more frequently. At the tomb they would hear a story about women who came there after the crucifixion, found the tomb open, and encountered an apocalyptic messenger, who announced that Jesus had been assumed into God's eschatological future. The pilgrimage reached its climax when the liturgical storyteller proclaimed, "He has been raised," and then pointed to the tomb: "He is not here; see the place where they laid him." The pilgrims' trip to the tomb to "seek Jesus of Nazareth, who was crucified" was meant to end with the insight that the journey had in a sense been fruitless—for why should they seek the living among the dead? (p. 138)

However plausible the theory may be, we will never know for sure whether this is in fact how the Easter story first originated, nor whether the events it describes correspond to real occurrences in Jerusalem in the decades after Jesus' death. Even if we could, it would not get us much closer to the meaning of Christ's death for Christians. What historical investigation can establish as matters of fact, and what faith believes about the Resurrection, belong to different, noncoincidental orders of truth. I am interested here in the foundations of the latter, not the empirical grounds of the former. No amount of empirical probing can penetrate the Gospels' tomb, whose emptiness remains the crux and crucible of Christian faith. It is an emptiness that reveals its contents, or lack thereof, only to those who have already entered the crypt of its *sema* by way of the sacraments.

Paul never mentions the empty tomb and seems to know nothing about the Easter morning events described decades later in the Gospels, yet one could say that the famous Pauline definition of faith as "the substance of things hoped for and the evidence of things unseen" (Heb. 11:1) has its narrative correlate in the Easter morning story. In all its different versions the emphasis in the Gospels falls on what the women and disciples *don't* see when they look inside the tomb, namely Jesus' dead body. "Look, there is where they laid him." This *there* is the site of a disappearance whose void in effect engenders the appearance narratives, all of which are subsequent expansions—some would say misunderstandings—of the story of the empty tomb. If the tomb offers evidence only of what it does not contain, one must look for Jesus elsewhere: in Galilee, in one's heart, in the community of those who believe in him, in heaven itself. Wherever Christ *is,* and in whatever *mode* he exists after the Crucifixion, there is nothing left of him *here* except the sign of his elsewhereness. "Blessed are those who have not seen and yet have come to believe." These words of Jesus from the Gospel of John (20:29), directed against the skepticism of the disciple Thomas, hark back to the scene of the empty tomb and proclaim that Christian faith does not, or *should* not, rely on empirical evidence of the Resurrection, such as Jesus' post-mortem appearances to Mary and the disciples. The empty tomb is evidence enough of things unseen.

There is a fundamental analogy, then, between the tomb and the scene of history, both of which Jesus has disappeared from, leaving behind a sepulchral promise that belongs to the futurity of hope rather than to the aftermath of grief. Just as the tomb is full of meaning in its emptiness, so too history is full of that same meaning. While the vocation of faith is to hold fast to the unseen in history, the vocation of the Gospels is to inspire, nourish, and sustain that faith. As Christ passes from the sphere of the seen into that of the unseen, his spirit is consigned primarily to the word and his presence to the sacraments. The Gospels, written both retrospectively and proleptically—looking backward to Jesus' first coming and forward to his second—speak of this consignment. Indeed, they *receive* this consignment and, in so doing, point to the evidence of things unseen. One could say that the Christian Scriptures in general—all of which testify to a Christ who has abandoned the scene of history and yet remains operative within it—are written in or under the sign of the empty tomb. On the one hand they are like the angelic messenger who points to Jesus' disappearance and glosses its meaning (seek not the living among the dead); on the other, given that they were composed anywhere between twenty and seventy years after the death of Christ, the Scriptures are like Mary and the disciples, who arrive at the tomb after the fact. They speak retrospectively of events whose historical traces are found only in their own belated testaments.

The tomb of the Gospels transmutes from within the foundational power of the sepulcher. *Hic non est* is a deixis that points away from *hic jacet;* away, that is, from a site marked by its resident dead. If early believers sought out the tomb of Jesus as the site of their commemoration, it was not in order to sacralize the ground of burial but to recall its ultimate vanity. No one underlies this *hic.* In this sense Christ's empty tomb distinguishes itself from those "white-washed tombs, which on the outside look beautiful, but inside they are all full of the bones of the dead and of all kinds of filth" (Matt. 23:27). Indeed, it distinguishes itself even from "the tombs of the prophets" and "graves of the righteous" which the Pharisees hypocritically "decorate" and make a show of honoring (v. 28). In Luke's Gospel Jesus compares such Pharisees to "unmarked graves, and people walk over them without realizing" (Luke 11:44). The empty tomb is not such a grave. It is the sign or *sema* of what escapes its containment.

It is hardly an exaggeration to say that, theologically speaking, the whole earth becomes, for the person of faith, the empty tomb of Easter morning—a place rendered sacred, not because it is swollen with the bones of those who have died, but because its law of death has been overturned by Christ during his residence in the tomb. The three women who arrive at the tomb with spices and oils come to anoint his dead body and fulfill traditional obligations to the corpse of the dead, yet Jesus' corpse, if ever there was one, has become the new mystical body of Christ. In its resurrected and sacramental plenitude, it does not receive but now dispenses anointment, blessing the earth and giving new life to its otherwise dead matter. In and through that resurrected body, the earth and the cosmos are transfigured. Christ is not *here* because he is now everywhere—or at least everywhere the church institutes its sacraments. And henceforth there is no place on earth to which those sacraments, and with them Christ's presence, cannot be brought. Filled with the promise of a new life, the earth as a whole becomes not a conglomerate of places but *one* new place: the place of Easter morning.

Hence the so-called universalism of the church. The transcultural and transgeographical dissemination of the Christian kerygma, which is potentially at home anywhere, has its theological basis in the utopic transitivity of the *hic non est*. Instead of being bound to a sacred place, with all the localization and partisan particularity that heroic sepulchers tend to sponsor, the church extends its proclamation to the uttermost ends of the earth. The empty tomb becomes present in its *sema* wherever the church performs its sacraments. As the institutional correlate of Christ's triumph over the grave, the church can lay its spiritual foundations anywhere.

Alas, if it were only that simple! On the one hand Christian faith marks a repudiation and transcendence of sepulchral foundationalism; on the other hand, its institutional history shows very clearly that its church retrieved or fell back upon precisely such foundationalism. Rome became its *hic*. On Peter's tomb it built its house. While Peter's bones may in fact be missing from the central crypt, the Basilica of Saint Peter today is nonetheless a veritable "porch at the entrance of a burrow," to recall Thoreau's definition of the house. A vast necropolis of tombs—of popes, cardinals, bishops, and dignitaries—underlies its lofty edifice. Not only the Basilica of Saint Peter, but every consecrated Holy Roman church contains the tombs, relics, or bones of dead saints. How is one to account for this apparent contradiction between a theology of resurrection, of which the empty tomb is the sign, and an institutional history that visibly reappropriates the foundational power of the sepulcher? Are we dealing here with a contradiction or instead, a transformation of the meaning of the sepulcher?

Clearly it is the latter thesis that I have been promoting, and in the remainder of this chapter I intend to push that thesis further, not by reviewing the foundational history of the Roman church but by bringing to bear on that history certain perspectives that strategically recast and recapitulate some of the basic themes that I have isolated in this study so far. These themes include: the sanctity of the earth as the elemental correlative of history (chapter 1); the founding power of the grave (chapter 2); the house as a place of cohabitation between the living and the dead (chapter 3); grief in its traumatic and restorative modalities (chapter 4); the institutional ground of the *logos* (chapter 5); and finally, "repetition" as the free retrieval and renewal of legacy (chapter 6).

To that end I propose to enlist the hermeneutic help of an unlikely book, *Marius the Epicurian,* written by Walter Pater in 1885. Pater was no theologian or church historian, to be sure; yet in his unusual narrative, which is not so much a novel as a poetic history of the Roman Empire in the third century AD, he offers a singular description of how the early Roman church was in every respect "a porch at the entrance of a burrow." Painting an unforgettable picture of Cecilia's house of worship on the outskirts of Rome, *Marius the Epicurian* probes in impressionistic fashion the deep ritualistic continuities between the Christian Mass and the aboriginal Latin domestic religions, to which I alluded in the second and third chapters of this book. Pater's fictional representation yields an important insight into the way early Roman Christianity renewed or "sublated" the spirit of those antecedent religions. Thus rather than submit his narrative to a textual analysis I will use its poetic reflections on the founding of the Roman church as another point of entry into the topics that my discussion of the empty tomb has thus far opened up to reconsideration.

But let us start from the beginning. In the first chapter of *Marius the Epicurian* we are introduced to the book's protagonist, Marius, who came of age in Latium at the beginning of the reign of Marcus Aurelius. Pater describes how, in his youth, Marius would devoutly observe the pieties of the earliest, autochthonous religion of the Romans, the "Religion of Numa," which revolved around the worship of ancestral deities in their sepulchral abodes:

> The urns of the dead in the family chapel received their due service. They also were now becoming something divine, a goodly

company of friendly and protecting spirits, encamped about the place of their former abode—above all others, the father, dead ten years before, of whom, remembering but a tall, grave figure above him in early childhood, Marius habitually thought as a *genius* a little cold and severe. . . . The dead *genii* were satisfied with little—a few violets, a cake dipped in wine, or a morsel of honeycomb. Daily from the time when his childish footsteps were still uncertain, had Marius taken them their portion of the family meal, at the second course, amidst the silence of the company. They loved those who brought them their sustenance; but, deprived of these services, would be heard wandering through the house, crying sorrowfully in the stillness of the night. (p. 41)

Pater's reconstruction of the religion of Numa in the first chapter of his fictional biography probably owed more than a little to Fustel de Coulanges's *Ancient City* (1860), a book one would expect him to have known well. But against the French scholar, who argued in his conclusion that the rise of Christianity represented a decisive ideological and religious break with the archaic Latin religions, Pater saw in the Christian ritual a profound rescue of what had been most genuinely spiritual and devotional in them. The passage cited above continues as follows:

And those simple gifts, like other objects as trivial—bread, oil, wine, milk—had regained for him, by their use in such religious service, that poetic and as it were moral significance, which surely belongs to all the means of daily life, could we but break through the veil of our familiarity with things by no means vulgar in themselves. (ibid.)

Compare this to Marius's reaction some two hundred pages later when he witnesses for the first time the "divine service" of the Christian Mass, which takes place in Cecilia's house, or more precisely in "the vast *Lararium,* or domestic sanctuary of the Cecilian family." Here a fascinated Marius recognizes an astonishing analogy between the Christian service and the domestic worship that had instilled an indelible piety in him during his childhood:

A sacrifice also,—a sacrifice, it might seem, like the most primitive, the most natural and enduringly significant of old pagan sacrifices, of the simplest fruits of the earth. And in connection with this circumstance again, as in the actual stones of the building so in the rite itself, *what Marius observed was not so much new matter as a new spirit, moulding, informing, with a new intention, many obser-vances not witnessed for the first time today.* Men and women came to the altar successively, in perfect order, and deposited below the lattice-work on pierced white marble, their baskets of wheat and grapes, incense, oil for the sanctuary lamps, bread and wine espe-cially—pure wheaten bread, the pure white wine of the Tusculan vineyards. *There was here a veritable consecration, hopeful and animat-ing, of the earth's gifts, of old dead and dark matter itself,* now in some way redeemed at last, of all that we can touch or see, in the midst of a jaded world that had lost the true sense of such things, and in strong contrast to the wise emperor's renunciant and impassive attitude towards them. (p. 250, my emphasis)

By the time Marius was introduced to the Christian ceremonies he had become an Epicurian devoted to the sanctity of the visible world, though he was still searching (more or less in vain) for the secret of its noumenal origin. He was not yet ready to become a Christian, and even on his deathbed his conversion remains suspended in ambiguity; nev-ertheless, as a spiritual sensualist he was both captivated and enchanted by Christian sacraments, which seemed to him to respond to, or to arise from, or in any case ceremoniously to acknowledge, the presence of that noumenal mystery that envelops the visible world, lending earthly things their aura of sacrality. Here at last was a religion that reconse-crated the earth and "all we can see or touch," that blessed the same bread, wine, and oil that the Numa religion, now superannuated, had once blessed within the confines of the family house. Just as the Chris-tian Mass reanimated the "old dead and dark matter" of the earth's "simple fruits," so too it seemed to retrieve and expand the sacramental core of a primitive religion that had since died out in the "jaded world" of late paganism:

Such were the commonplaces of this new people [the Chris-tians], among whom so much of what Marius had valued most in the old world seemed to be under renewal and further promo-tion. Some transforming spirit was at work [in Christianity] to harmonize contrasts, to deepen expression—a spirit which, in its dealing with the elements of ancient life, was guided by a wonderful tact of selection, exclusion, juxtaposition, begetting thereby a unique effect of freshness, a grave yet wholesome beauty, because the world of sense, the whole outward world was understood to set forth the veritable unction and royalty of a certain priesthood and kingship of the soul within, among the prerogatives of which was a delightful sense of freedom. (p. 239)

If nothing else this is an excellent example of what Heidegger means by "repetition"—a transfiguration based not on a recycling of the past but on "a wonderful tact of selection, exclusion, juxtaposition" that gives new life to the legacies of a given heritage. Pater's vision of the "transforming spirit" of early Christianity gives body to Heidegger's otherwise abstract concept of "liberating one's inherited possibilities" in repetition. We recall that for Heidegger freedom is the essential element of the anticipatory resolve through which "one first chooses the choice which makes one free" for repetition (*Being and Time*, p. 437). In a similar vein Pater speaks of the "delightful sense of freedom" with which Christianity "deepened [the] expression" of ancient pieties.

In Pater's vision the success of the Christian retrieval was due to the fact that the Roman church, like the Roman religion of Numa before it, built its house on and around the tombs of the dead, not only figuratively but literally. He insists on these necrological foundations time and again, but nowhere as compellingly as in the several pages he devotes to describing the vast underworld of catacombs beneath Cecilia's house, where the early Christian prayer services in Rome took place. This underworld, it turns out, was nothing less than a *lararium*, or extended family grave, the description of which parallels the earlier description of the *lares* of the family house at the beginning of the narrative:

> A narrow opening cut in [the hill's] steep side, like a solid blackness there, admitted Marius and his gleaming leader into a hollow cavern or crypt, neither more nor less in fact than the family burial place of the Cecilii, to whom this residence belonged, brought thus, after an arrangement then becoming not unusual, into immediate connection with the abode of the living, in bold

assertion of that instinct of family life, which the sanction of the *Holy Family* was, hereafter, more and more to reinforce. Here, in truth, was the centre of the peculiar religious expressiveness, of the sanctity, of the entire scene. That "any person may, at his own election, constitute the place which belongs to him a *religious* place, by the carrying of his dead into it":—had been a maxim of old Roman law, which it was reserved for the early Christian societies, like that established here by the piety of a wealthy Roman matron, to realize in all its consequences. Yet this was unlike any cemetery Marius had ever before seen: most obviously in this, that these people had returned to the older fashion of disposing of their dead by burial instead of burning. Originally a family sepulchre, it was growing to a vast *necropolis,* a whole township of the deceased, by means of some free expansion of the family interest beyond its amplest natural limits. (*Marius the Epicurean,* p. 229)

Here too we see how third-century Roman Christianity, in Pater's retelling, had more in common with the older Latin religions than with subsequent, adulterated forms of pagan worship. It even reinstituted the archaic practice of inhumation. As the family *lararium* became an entire "township of the deceased," the Christian house (its church) "freely expanded" the concept of family beyond its "natural limits," in other words beyond the genetic bloodlines that linked the *lares* to their descendants. It made of all Christians an extended family through their consanguinity with Christ, linked by their shared faith in his redemptive death and Resurrection. This free expansion was the expression of that "spirit of adoption" that Paul speaks about in the Book of Romans and which I referred to at the end of the previous chapter. What is expanded here, in Pater's portrayal, is the core of the earlier domestic religions. In that sense the early Roman church did far more than merely revive certain of its elements. It resurrected their enduring "moral significance" and gave their understanding of the family institution and their veneration of the dead a new expansive spirit.

Pater's statement that the Christian Mass was "before all else, from first to last, a commemoration of the dead" (p. 249) should be understood in the historical context of the pre-Constantine period, when

many of the Christian prayer services in Rome were held in the catacombs. The statement affirms, however, that there was far more to that
catacomb scene than clandestinity. In effect, even after the persecu-
tions had ended, the Eucharist continued to be celebrated over the
tombs of the martyrs. Later the commemoration took the form of a full-
fledged cult of relics. This cult, so maligned by the Protestant Reform-
ers, was certainly no secondary or ancillary phenomenon of church
history; it was a crucial element in the foundational history of the
church. The martyrs' deaths were understood as participating in, or repeating, the Savior's death. Their relics served to ground Christian
faith in the putative *reason* for that death, namely salvation. But how are
we to reconcile the cult of saintly bodies and body parts with a faith that
believes Christ left no such relics of his own body behind?

The theology on this issue is not entirely satisfying. Preoccupied as
they were with securing the institutional foundations of the church, fathers like Jerome and Augustine brought out the heavy artillery against
Vigilantius, who in the fifth century opposed the cult of relics on the
grounds that it amounted to a form of pagan idolatry. Against the
charge of idolatry Jerome argued that by adoring the martyrs' relics
Christians were in fact adoring the Lord on whose behalf they were
martyred. Augustine, who saw in the Christ event a radical break with all
forms of paganism, went even further and declared the saints' bodies to
be the holy limbs and organs of the Holy Spirit. (It was on the basis of
Augustine's pronouncement that scholastics like Aquinas would later
lay the strictly theological arguments for the cult of relics.) In AD 787
the Second Council of Nicea protected and even reinforced the cult by
explicitly condemning the contempt of relics and by proclaiming that
only churches that possessed them could be consecrated. These relics were
and still are often enclosed in the "altar stones" of Roman Catholic
churches. When the priest kisses the *mensa* at the beginning of the Mass
he is in effect acknowledging the presence of the dead in the altar
stone. Thus does the saint's body, or part thereof, nourish Christian
faith in an afterlife.

The apparent contradiction between a theology of the empty tomb
and the Christian cult of relics is resolved only if one conceives of the
saints' bodies as somehow "alive" with expectation and animated by futurity. It was after all in a spirit of affirmation that the prayer services of

the early Roman church took place in the catacombs. In this space, which Pater sees as the womb of the Roman church, the living joined destinies with the dead in the promise of the Kingdom of God. Like Christ's empty tomb, the graves of the martyrs were no more than a sign of what escaped their grasp. The tombs held their relics, to be sure, yet the relics were adored as the evidence of things unseen, namely the promise of resurrection. The saints' dead bones were the skeletal preludes to a glorified body. This transformation of death into life—this "seek not the living among the dead"—made of the martyr's tomb a monument of projective hope. One could say that, in some mystical way, the saint's body or parts thereof brought forth into the church the empty tomb of Jerusalem—or at least its *sema*.

I argued in the preceding chapter that repetition can be conceived of as a mode of relating to the dead, of retrieving their legacies from our existential and historical futures. What Pater saw as the essence of the Christian Mass—its commemoration of the dead—was indeed an expansion of life "beyond its amplest natural limits," that is, beyond the finality of the grave. "But go," says the messenger at Christ's tomb, "tell his disciples and Peter that he goes before you to Galilee; there you will see him, as he told you." Whether this verse in Mark's Gospel means that Christ was literally raised from the dead and would appear shortly in person to his disciples in Galilee, or whether it alludes to Christ's universal appearance at the end of time, the crux of Christian faith lies in the notion that Christ "goes before" us—that the *meaning* of his death, if not the death itself, lies in our future, to be fulfilled either at the end of time or in our own passage beyond the threshold that separates the living from the dead. Likewise the meaning of the martyrs' deaths lies not with the victimized bodies but with the infinite expectation to which and for which they resolutely gave up their lives.

The Christian commemoration, in sum, was anything but mournful in nature. Grief grieves over separation, whereas Christian repetition (which Kierkegaard defined as a "recollection forward") saw in death a reaching out into the eschatological future—a future in which and to which the living and the dead remain bound. It is because the *logos* became flesh in Christ that the living and the dead reestablish their bond in that event, with all its promise. Grief despairs of that promise. In the

Old Testament Isaiah prophesizes a time when the Lord will create new skies and a new earth, and when in Jerusalem "the voice of weeping shall no more be heard in her, nor the voice of crying" (Isa. 65:17–19). In Revelation we are told that "God shall wipe away all tears from their eyes; and there shall be no more death, neither sorrow nor crying" (4:1). These future tenses refer to an eventuality *rendered present* in the moment of commemoration. For the commemorators the dead already belonged to the ever-present futurity of the Kingdom, and so too did the souls of the believers in the moment of commemoration. Just as the martyrs' deaths repeated the Crucifixion, so too those who stayed behind repeated, or petitioned again, the Kingdom to come. As they recollected it forward on the tombs of the martyrs they brought the Kingdom forth in the ever-present prospect of their expectation.

It is against this background that we must understand the Christian polemic against immoderate grief and the severity of those legislative proscriptions of excessive public lamentation in the early Christian era. Those proscriptions harked back to Isaiah, Revelation, and the Gospel of Luke, where Jesus denounces the loud ululations that accompanied his climb at Calvary: "And there followed him a great company of people, and of women, which also bewailed and lamented him. But Jesus turning unto them said, Daughters of Jerusalem, weep not for me, but weep for yourselves, and for your children" (Luke 23:27–28). They should weep for themselves because they weep in the first place, hence they despair. With Christ's coming it is no longer death but sin that calls for grieving. It was certainly in this vein that Paul preached against our natural impulse to grieve for the dead: "But I would not have you be ignorant, brethren, concerning them who are asleep, that you sorrow not, even as others who have no hope. For if we believe that Jesus died and rose again, even so them which sleep in Jesus will God bring with him" (1 Thess. 4:13–14). Paul goes on to stress that those who will be alive at the second coming "shall not prevent them which are asleep," in other words they will not "come before" the dead; rather "the dead in Christ shall rise first." This priority of the dead, stressed time and again by Paul, is what the Christian sacraments commemorate, recalling once again that the dead run ahead of us; hence for the true believer they neither need nor solicit our grief.

Augustine speaks eloquently for this fundamental change in the Christian attitude toward grief in book 9 of *The Confessions,* which describes the death of his mother, Monica:

> I closed her eyes, and a great flood of sorrow swept into my heart and would have overflowed in tears. But my eyes obeyed the forcible dictate of my mind and seemed to drink that fountain dry. Terrible indeed was my state as I struggled so. And then, when she had breathed her last, the boy Adeodatus burst out into loud cries until all the rest of us checked him, and he became silent. In the same way something childish in me which was bringing me to the brink of tears was, when I heard the young man's voice, the voice of the heart, brought under control and silenced. For we did not think it right that a funeral such as hers should be celebrated with tears and groans and lamentations. These are ways in which people grieve for an utter wretchedness in death or a kind of total extinction. But she did not die in misery, nor was she altogether dead. Of this we had good reason to be certain from the evidence of her character and from a faith that was not feigned. (9.12)

As for our *Marius the Epicurian,* its narrative reinscribes in a powerful way the Christian transmutation of natural sorrow into commemorative celebration. Culling and paraphrasing sentences from the *Shepherd of Hermas,* Pater records a sermon on the perversity of grief. Here is a sample:

> "Take from thyself grief, for (as Hamlet will one day discover) 'tis the sister of doubt and ill-temper. Grief is more evil than any other spirit of evil, and is most dreadful to the servants of God, and beyond all spirits destroyeth man. . . . Put on therefore gladness that hath always favour before God and is acceptable unto Him, and delight thyself in it; for every man that is glad doeth the things that are good, and thinketh good thoughts, despising grief." (p. 239)

One must assume that the sermon alludes to Pater's contemporaries, for whom a certain type of grief had become an endemic, perhaps even interminable cultural condition (hence the anachronistic reference to Hamlet). In the immediate context of the book, however, it is implicitly directed against the emperor Marcus Aurelius, who saw in death the ultimate vanity of all earthly things and adopted a merely stoical resignation to its fatality. Aurelius refused to grieve, to be sure, for he held the dread of death a worse evil than death itself; yet at the core of his imperial melancholy lurked an incurable despair, manifest, among other things, in his "renunciant and impassive attitude" towards those earthly gifts which the Christians meanwhile were reanimating in their liturgies and sacraments. In *Marius the Epicurean* the emperor embodies the highest wisdom and virtue of which paganism was capable at that point in its long and by now exhausted history. Marcus Aurelius may well have been "one of the best men that ever lived," as a recent admirer has claimed (Brodsky, *On Grief and Reason*, p. 291); yet that does not mean that the emperor, at least from Marius's point of view, was not inwardly wretched and full of dread, or that he did not suffer from a spiritual wound for which neither he nor his physicians nor his philosophers nor the Roman society he presided over in its totality had a cure.

The *Meditations* were authored by a man who despaired of life, precisely because he despaired of death. For all his attempts to live in accordance with cosmic law Marcus Aurelius had no such "delightful sense of freedom," which, in Marius's perception, emanated from the Christian ritual. It was this freedom, or sense of it, that for Marius marked the soul's true attunement to the order of Creation. Creation is by nature free, yet Marcus Aurelius and his fellow stoics were stoically stifled and shackled. What so many of us in the modern era admire about the emperor is the fortitude with which he suffered his wound, as well as the fact that he was sensitive enough to suffer from it in the first place. He looked through the veil of worldly appearances and saw the underlying absurdity of life. In that respect he remains seductively Hamletian, without ceasing to be Roman. His melancholy, which leaves its subtle imprint on almost every page of the *Meditations,* not only prefigures Hamlet's depression but lends it an august authority. That is why we moderns love him so much—he flatters us.

It is astonishing to think that while Pater was writing *Marius the Epicurian* his fellow (ex-)classicist Nietzsche was on the verge of composing *The Antichrist.* Nothing could be further removed from Nietzsche's rant about Christianity's slave rebellion, with its life-denying, earth-loathing impulses, than Pater's vision of early Roman Christianity as the spiritual flower of epicureanism. The appeal of Christianity to an Epicurean like Marius lay in the fact that it seemed to reconsecrate the earth, reanimate the senses, and reaffirm the sacrality of life in the face of late paganism's gloom and desperation. Passages such as the following seem like a direct response, even though they were not intended as such, to Nietzsche's frontal attack on Christianity as a religion of resentment and denial:

> With her full, fresh faith in the *Evangele*—in a veritable regeneration of the earth and the body, in the dignity of man's entire personal being—for a season, at least, at that critical period in the development of Christianity, she [the church] was for reason, for common sense, for fairness to human nature, and generally for what may be called the naturalness of Christianity.—As also for its comely order: she would also be "brought to her king in raiment of needlework." It was by the bishops of Rome, diligently transforming themselves, in the true catholic sense, into universal pastors, that the path of what we must call humanism was thus defined. (*Marius the Epicurian*, p. 242)

The main difference between their understandings of the historical conditions that allowed Christianity to triumph throughout the empire, and above all in Rome itself, is that Nietzsche refuses to address the reality of Roman nihilism, while Pater never loses sight of it. By Roman nihilism I mean Rome's failure to counter the death drive that had taken hold of the spiritual life of the empire, denigrating the earth and the visible world as a whole. Pater's central chapters on Roman bloodlust put in sentimental relief the fact that, as death began to lose its sanctity, so too did life, leading gradually but inexorably to a lust for the daily spectacle of murder—of animals, gladiators, criminals, or Christians. Nothing reveals the spiritual exhaustion of the Romans more than their need to incessantly reproduce and inflate the scene of senseless death, a scene which, for those who sponsored or watched it, confirmed that life was as senseless as the immolations in which it found its end.

Where Nietzsche saw the Christian afterlife as a fiction generated by life-denying forces of resentment and vengeance, Pater saw it as the source from which came a new power of blessing, one that possessed the means to resanctify life and bring the dead back into its impover-ished sphere. One might say that the afterlife erupted into the midst of the here and now, transfiguring the earth and animating its "old dead and dark matter," including the bones of saints. Like the old religions whose legacies it retrieved from the futurity of expectation, the church grounded its affirmation of the visible and invisible worlds on its com-memoration of the dead, because any consecration of life—be it pagan, Christian, or otherwise—depends first and foremost on regenerating the forces of copenetration, of liberating the past and future reaches of time itself, and of opening the world to what Paul called the evidence of things unseen. Where the dead are simply dead, the living are in some sense already dead as well. Conversely, where the afterlife of the dead receives new life, the earth as a whole receives a new blessing.

CHAPTER 8

THE NAMES OF THE DEAD

Ernesto De Martino, whose work on ritual lament I discussed in chapter 4, speaks of "the formal power to transform into value that which in nature hastens toward death," adding that "this power makes of man the procurer of death at the very heart of natural death, consigning what passes without and against man to the cultural rules of passage" (*Morte e pianto rituale*, p. 214). Citing those sentences, I remarked that the cultural rules of passage are themselves historical, hence they too pass away in time, to be replaced by others. Yet it is not simply a question of new forms taking the place of old ones. It is also a question of retrieving the latent possibilities in what is replaced and in so doing giving the latter a new, transformed life. We have seen how not only the forms but also the very *meaning* of mourning underwent a transformation in the Christian era, thanks in part to Christianity's sacramental retrieval of select elements in the pre-Christian cults of the dead. Creative retrieval has a way of liberating latent possibilities in the heritage by reprojecting them in new frameworks, be they religious, cultural, or even political. We have seen various instances of this retrieval-reprojection syndrome at work, for example in the refounding of the American republic through the Gettysburg Address and Lincoln's martyrdom; in Rilke's internalization of the *lares* of the traditional house; in Petrarch's Latinization of modern Italian; and in modernism's recapitulations of antecedent literary traditions.

In this chapter I propose to look at how certain elements of both the Christian and pre-Christian heritages are brought to bear on a contemporary monument: the Vietnam Veterans Memorial wall in Washington, D.C. This monument is so distinctive in its own right that it is hazardous to base any general claims on its example; yet in its singularity it offers insights into the transformation of cultural rules of passage in our own time. My analysis will proceed in two phases. In the first I will trace the genealogy of a literary image as it runs through the Greek, Roman, and Christian traditions, with several modern declensions as well. In the second I will relate this image, with its variegated history, to the memorial wall. The chapter as a whole, in its more specific focus, sets up the terms for the more general reflections that inform the next and final chapter of this book.

Before getting under way, however, let me state that I neither fought in the Vietnam War nor lost anyone in it who was close to me. I do not presume to share the grief of those who did. Yet grief is by nature transitive, as long as it finds what Croce calls its forms of objectification. That the Vietnam Veterans Memorial represents a powerful formal objectification is confirmed by the fact that it is the most visited and, some would say, most stirring monument in America. My intention here is not to "explain" its emotive power, only to provide a particular perspective on it—a perspective that sees it as recapitulating, if only implicitly, the various instantiations of the image whose genealogy I trace here. Among other of its features, this makes it one of the most humic, hence human, of monuments. As they say in Latin: "homo sum; humani nil a me alienum puto." The memorial, insofar as it is human, is not alien to any of us.

Genealogy of an Image

While he was fighting in the trenches of World War I, Giuseppe Ungaretti composed the following poem, entitled "Soldati," or "Soldiers":

Si sta come
d'autunno
sugli alberi
le foglie
(*Vita d'un uomo*, p. 87)

Literally translated:

One is as
in autumn
on the trees
the leaves.

There is something quintessentially lyrical about the suspended image and elegiac tone, yet the use of the impersonal "One is" rather than the first person singular evokes the epic prehistory of the poem's simile, a prehistory of which Ungaretti was no doubt aware when he compared soldiers to leaves on the verge of falling to the ground in autumn. Lyric poetry is traditionally understood as a universalized first-person-singular voice, hence as an individuation of the universal, while the epic represents a different type of universality: one that synthesizes a plurality of voices and speaks for a given collective in its public concerns and passions. By recalling its epic genealogy, Ungaretti's poem gives a lyric inflection to the collectivity that the image of the autumn leaves has traditionally figured; for in the epic poems in which it occurs the image appears as a simile for the appurtenance of the individual to his family, race, class, or species. In that sense one could say that it registers the divergent claims of the lyric and epic vocations, not by pitting them against each other but by figuratively thematizing, or poetically intensifying, the tension that in any epoch defines the relation between the individual and the community. This relation has a long and vexed history in Western culture, so much so that one could say that what is most distinctively Western about Western culture is the history of how that relation has been conceived and represented.

The genealogy of Ungaretti's image takes us all the way back to book 6 of *The Iliad,* where two armies on the fields of Troy have come together to do battle. A warrior from the Trojan side detaches himself from the throng, moves out ahead of the others to confront the awesome Diomedes. This bold gesture of separation provokes the demand for identification. As the two horsemen approach each other, Diomedes inquires after his opponent's identity:

> Who among mortal men are you, good friend? Since never
> before have I seen you in the fighting where men win glory,
> yet now you have come striding far out in front of all others
> in your great heart, who have dared stand up to my spear
>   far-shadowing.
> Yet unhappy are those whose sons match warcraft against me.
>
> (4.123–27)

In essence Diomedes wants to be sure that his foe is a mortal and not a god in disguise. By asking him to identify himself he is asking not only about his family lineage but also about his "generation," in the sense of his genesis or genus (mortal or immortal). The reply he receives suggests that his antagonist is not only human but knows what it means not to be a god:

High-hearted son of Tydeus, why ask of my generation?
As is the generation of leaves, so is that of humanity.
The wind scatters the leaves on the ground, but the live timber
burgeons with leaves again in the season of spring returning.
So one generation of men will grow while another dies.

$$(145-49)$$

This warrior may have bravely separated himself off from the crowd, yet he speaks here as an indifferent member of his species, aware of the futility of distinctions among men, all of whom share a common mortal fate, precisely by virtue of their "generation." Why ask of my generation when my generation is human?

The answer to that question is to be sought perhaps in the question itself. Ludwig Feuerbach, for example, in the opening paragraphs of *The Essence of Christianity,* claims that what distinguishes humans from animals is that we take cognizance of ourselves not merely as individuals but as a species. We ask of our generation because it is our nature to take cognizance of our nature: "Consciousness in the strictest sense is present only in a being to whom his species, his essential nature, is an object of thought. . . . The brute is indeed conscious of himself as an individual—and he has accordingly the feeling of self as the common center of successive sensations—but not as a species. . . . Science [knowledge] is the cognisance of the species" (Feuerbach, *The Essence of Christianity,* pp. 1–2). For Diomedes' interlocutor, whose name is Glaukos, the ultimate cognizance of the species is the cognizance of death, which renders us all equal and indistinguishable. Death is the nature, or coming-to-be, of the generationality that subsumes all specific human genealogies, be they lofty or humble.

This sober wisdom, however, does not prevent Glaukos from going on to divulge his lineage to Diomedes in great, even boastful detail. In the next sixty verses we learn that in Argos there lived Aiolos's son Sisyphos, who had a son named Glaukos, who in turned sired Bellerophontes the blameless ("blameless" because he was unjustly accused and exiled by the Argive king to Lykia), and that Bellerophontes' wife bore him three children—Isandros, Hippolochos, and Laodameia. Laodameia lay with Zeus and gave birth to Sarpedon, king of the Lykians.

> But Hippolochos begot me, and I claim that he is my father;
> he sent me to Troy, and urged upon me repeated injunctions,
> to be always among the bravest, and hold my head above others,
> not shaming the generation of my fathers, who were
> the greatest men in Ephyre and again in wide Lykia.
> Such is my generation and the blood I claim to be born from.
>
> (*Iliad*, 4.206–11)

Never once does the Lykian disclose his name to Diomedes. To the query: "Who among mortal men are you?" the answer is: "Such is my generation and the blood I claim to be born from." Glaukos's identity is proudly reducible to his descendancy. This goes for his so-called moral selfhood as well, for here is a man whose principal motivation is not to shame "the generation of my fathers." His act of "coming out ahead of the others" on the battlefield fulfills his father's injunctions to "hold my head above others." In that sense Glaukos is happy and even eager to derive his identity from family and kin, his *genea* and *genos*.

Listening to Glaukos retrace his ancestry, Diomedes realizes to his delight that there exists a connection between them, for Bellerophontes was once a guest in the house of Diomedes' grandfather Oineus. The two of them had exchanged gifts of friendship. Diomedes proposes to Glaukos that they venerate this legacy, embrace each other as friends, and vow to avoid each other henceforth on the field of war. He even proposes that they exchange their armor, "so that others may know / how we claim to be guests and friends from the days of our fathers" (ibid.). Recognition gets the better of anonymity as two strangers on opposite sides of the war's divide discover a bond that runs deeper than the circumstance that pits them against each other. Thus in a sublimely ironic fashion the episode as a whole belies Glaukos's preamble about the impersonality of the human generations. Here it is precisely their "generations," or genealogies, that turn foes into friends.

Or so it would seem. We will never know if Diomedes was telling the truth about the connection between Bellerophontes and Oineus, or whether he had all the while been eyeing Glaukos's splendid armor and plotting a strategy by which to possess himself of it:

but Zeus the son of Kronos stole away the wits of Glaukos
who exchanged with Diomedes the son of Tydeus armor
of gold for bronze, for nine oxen's worth the worth of a
    hundred.

                                                    (234–366)

Diomedes was, after all, a Greek—no more to be trusted than the wife of the king of Argos, Anteia, who, spurned by Bellerophontes the blameless, falsely accused him of attempting to lie with her.

Glaukos's simile—"As is the generation of leaves, so is that of humanity"—is one of the most poignant and lyrical in all of Homer, evoking not only the general caducity of the human condition but also an analogy between the falling of leaves and the falling of soldiers on the battlefield, condensed and intensified in Ungaretti's "Soldati." Yet let us not assume that Glaukos proclaims such wisdom wistfully, as if to imply the vanity of earthly glory (or golden armor). That the generations succeed one another like leaves on a tree—such is the order of things. It is natural, it is good, it is as it should be. Despite the lyricism of the passage, therefore, the simile of the leaves is essentially epic in its import, by which I mean that it speaks not for or as the single individual but for or as the collective. It speaks, in other words, of a communal destiny—what Heidegger calls Dasein's *Geschick* as opposed to its *Schicksal* (*Being and Time*, p. 436).

When Virgil takes up the Homeric image of the generation of leaves in book 6 of *The Aeneid*, the context is at once more ominous and more rueful than in *The Iliad*, for we are now no longer among the living but among the dead. Aeneas has just begun his descent into the gloomy depths of Hades. One of the first scenes he witnesses is that of a "multitude" of recently arrived shades swarming toward the shores of the Styx, which they must cross in order to gain their designated place in the underworld. Those who have been properly buried and mourned will be ferried across by old man Charon. The others must wait.

And here a multitude was rushing, swarming
shoreward, with men and mothers, bodies of

high-hearted heroes stripped of life, and boys
and unwed girls, and young men set upon
the pyre of death before their fathers' eyes:
thick as the leaves that with the early frost
of autumn drop and fall within the forest.

(*Aeneid* 6.401–7)

By drawing attention primarily to those who died prematurely, Virgil strains the very simile of autumn leaves, since these souls presumably never made it into the autumn of their years. One has a sense here of an underworld congested with the dead, an unnatural excess made up mostly of innocent victims cut down in their prime. There is something in Virgil's version which is lacking in its Homeric counterpart, namely the scandal of death. In Homer the simile serves to naturalize the human generations. In Virgil, the correspondence between humanity and the natural order seems troubled and compromised, as if to suggest that the injustice by which death takes its toll among the living is hardly "natural," or that, if this be nature's justice, human justice remains unreconciled to it. In both Homer and Virgil the simile speaks of the generic nature of human generations, but by elaborating on the image—what with the thickness of the leaves, the autumnal forest, and the early frost—Virgil almost overdetermines it. While Homer emphasizes the successive nature of the seasons, namely the succession of death by life ("So one generation of men will grow while another dies"), Virgil dwells only on the season of death. These leaves do not grow and die. They only fall in the autumn's "early frost." It is almost as if Virgil makes of the dead the genus of which we the living are only a species.

The notion that life is a form of living death is not foreign to Virgil. Think of the famous *pietas* of Aeneas, alluded to frequently in the foregoing pages. That piety is sacrificial and oppressive, a mark of the servitude that enslaves the living to the commandments of the dead. Homer's Glaukos is pious toward his fathers, to be sure, but with an exuberance not to be found in the sullen, necrocratic universe of Virgil, where the burden of the generations weighs heavily upon the individual, interring him prematurely. One could even argue that it is only because Aeneas is in some sense already dead—that his piety in fact subjects his life to the will of the ancestors—that he is able to descend into the underworld and commune with the shades of the deceased. That descent, and Aeneas's mission to found the future city of Rome, are the matter of Virgil's *Aeneid,* whose epic vocation is to exalt and commemorate Rome's grandiose destiny. But Virgil knew, and his poem registers the fact, that Rome's destiny exacted a horrible price: untold innocent victims, only some of whose countless unredeemed shades Aeneas encounters on the shores of the Styx. It was not without reason that the medievals—Dante foremost among them—believed that Virgil was at bottom a proto-Christian who despaired of the earthly city but was born too early to find rescue in the doctrine of the city of God, the only truly eternal and universal city, according to Saint Augustine. ("That Rome whereof Christ is a Roman," Dante calls it in *Purgatory* 32.102–3.)

As is the generation of leaves, so too is that of this simile. It seems forever destined to be reborn. From Virgil it is passed on to Dante. We come across it in *Inferno* 3, on the banks of the Acheron, where a multitude of souls, as in book 6 of *The Aeneid,* waits to be ferried across the river by Charon. Dante describes the scene as follows:

> As, in the autumn, leaves detach themselves,
> first one and then the other, till the bough
> sees all its fallen garmets on the ground,
> similarly, the evil seed of Adam
> descended from the shoreline one by one,
> when signaled, as a falcon—called—will come.
>
> (*Inferno* 3.112–17)

In Homer the leaves are likened to the human generations in their succession; in Virgil, they are likened to the shades of the dead; in Dante, they are likened to the damned. Damnation explains the agglutination of descent imagery in the two tercets: autumn, the detaching of leaves, the "fallen garmets," the seed of Adam (i.e., the Fall from Eden as well as the descendancy of humankind from that first ancestor), the descent of the souls from the shoreline, and finally the image of the falcon descending from the air at the call of the falconer. Yet surely the most conspicuous aspect of Dante's version is his *individuation* of the falling leaves—"first one and then the other"—corresponding to the shades, who "descended from the shoreline one by one." By insisting on the singularity of each leaf (or sinner) Dante in effect reminds us that every individual who comes of age in the Christian era chooses, and does not merely suffer, his or her posthumous fate. Whereas Virgil evokes a multitude of "innocent" dead on the banks of the Styx—boys, unwed girls, and high-hearted heroes—the shades on Dante's riverbank are the engineers of their own damnation, for each is (or in life was) endowed with individual free will.

In other words, in God's providential dispensation there is no more tragedy. The Christian era is that of comedy, in the sense of a story (or history) that ends happily for those who choose to accept God's free grace. The legacy of original sin is still with us, our nature is still corrupt, and we still have an inborn tendency to sin, yet the event of the Incarnation has opened the possibility of expiation in and through the person of Jesus Christ. This redemption, however, is not general. As Augustine declares in his *City of God*, expiation can take place only in the individual, not in the race as a whole: "That offense [original sin] was committed when all mankind existed in one man, and it brought universal ruin on mankind; and no one can be rescued from the toils of that offense, which was punished by God's justice, unless the sin is expiated *in each man singly* by the grace of God" (p. 582). When it comes to expiation, each man is all mankind existing in one man. Each man is Adam. The individual has become a universal. This is the providential meaning of Christ's incarnate personhood.

It has been remarked that the *Inferno* is full of damned souls whose powerful portraits as individuals show that Dante's theology is frequently at odds with his all-too-human passions (Auerbach, "Farinata and Cavlacante"). I believe, on the contrary, that the dramatic individuation, if not individualism, of his infernal characters accords well with a theology that puts so much of the burden on the individual's free will. Again, this is not to say that human beings are liberated from a common genealogy that links them all to Adam's seed; it means that the advent of Christ has liberated a space of freedom in the interiority of the individual. Whether one calls it the soul, the conscience, the moral self—it is in each case as singular as the leaves that fall "first one and then the other," or the shades who descend to the river "one by one."

No one would approve more of Dante's gesture of singularizing the falling leaves of autumn than the Christian philosopher Leibniz, whose entire metaphysics represents a sustained attempt to think the notion of identity in terms of singularities. His "principle of the identity of indiscernables" holds that no two things in the universe can be exactly alike, since identity excludes a priori the possibility of being identical to anything but itself, not only because two or more things cannot occupy the same spatiotemporal position but because in God's rational universe there is no sufficient reason for them to be identical. Identity is in each case singular. To illustrate his point, Leibniz offers an example reminiscent of Dante's simile in *Inferno* 3, though that canto was certainly the last thing Leibniz had in mind when he recounts the following anecdote in *New Essays concerning Human Understanding:* "I remember that a great princess [Sophie Charlotte (1668–1705), the first queen of Prussia], who is of a pre-eminently excellent mind, said one day while walking in her garden that she did not believe there were two leaves perfectly alike. A gentleman of distinction who was walking with her, thought he would easily find some. But although he searched long, he was convinced by his eyes that he could always note the difference" (pp. 239–40).

One of the preferred examples of my science teachers in grade school for such generic diversity was not leaves but snowflakes. If it was true then, I presume it is still true now that no two snowflakes have ever fallen to earth which are exactly alike. The crystal form of each flake is unique. This yearly generation of infinite singularities is a wonder to contemplate, lending credence to more than Leibniz's principle of the identity of indiscernables (the hypothesis of God, for instance, which becomes less and less absurd the more one learns about the everyday miracles of natural world). In any case it is in terms of this relation between the individuality of the flakes and the generic blanket of snow which they form when they accumulate on the ground that I have always been tempted to make sense of the epiphanic ending of James Joyce's story, "The Dead." Let us turn for a moment to that ending, one of the most famous in modern fiction.

Upon returning with his wife, Gretta, to their hotel room after the dinner party at his aunts' house, Gabriel Conroy is chilled to the bone to learn that in her youth Gretta was loved by a boy who had "died for her." (The boy, leaving his sickbed one cold and rainy night, had come to her window to tell her he did not want to live without her, and died shortly thereafter.) The ghostly resurrection of Michael Furey in his wife's memory that evening (thanks to a song) opens an unbridgeable distance between her and Gabriel, precisely at the moment when he feels an urge to draw close to her. After she falls asleep in the grief of her memory, Gabriel lies awake thinking about the boy who died in his seventeenth year, and about his wife, himself, his aunts, and all the people he knows and does not know who slowly but surely are on their way toward becoming dead. The story ends with a vision:

> A few light taps upon the pane made him turn to the window. It had begun to snow again. He watched sleepily the flakes, silver and dark, falling obliquely against the lamplight. The time had come for him to set out on his journey westward. Yes, the newspapers were right: snow was general all over Ireland. It was falling on every part of the dark central plain, on the treeless hills, falling softly upon the Bog of Allen and, farther westward, softly falling into the dark mutinous Shannon waves. It was falling, too, upon every part of the lonely churchyard on the hill where Michael Furey lay buried. It lay thickly drifted on the crooked crosses and headstones, on the spars of the little gate, on the barren thorns. His soul swooned slowly as he heard the snow falling faintly through the universe and faintly falling, like the descent of their last end, upon all the living and the dead. (Joyce, "The Dead," in *Dubliners,* pp. 223–24)

Unlike the images of autumn leaves I have reviewed so far, the snow here is not a simile but a symbol. A phrase in the last sentence—"like the descent of their last end"—invites us to associate it with the condition of human mortality. This snow, "falling faintly through the universe," evokes, among other things, an idea of the vast accumulation of the dead over untold human generations—an accumulation to which the living, in their own time-bound falling, will add their heavy numbers. Both the living and the dead are symbolically subsumed under the snow's implacable descent, which falls on both. The snow is "general." It falls *all over* Ireland, on *every* part of the plain, on *every* part of the churchyard, upon *all* the living and the dead. In sum, it is more reminiscent of Glaukos's generic generations of humanity than of Dante's individuated leaves.

Yet in their own way these snowflakes are implicitly individuated as well, for Gabriel's vision is generated by a prior image of a shivering boy standing under a tree in the nocturnal rain, telling a girl named Gretta that he no longer wants to live. The lonely, lyrical image of Michael Furey gives the countless flakes falling silently to the ground their sublime, almost unbearable palpability. The spirit of Michael Furey not only animates the snow but in some subtle yet powerful sense is the symbol of that which the snow as such symbolizes—the drift of life toward inevitable death. It is as if all the snow over Ireland falls in a medium haunted by the soul of this boy, who died for a passion his society would not permit him to live.

Michael Furey is dead, but as a ghost he is more alive than any of the Dubliners of which Gabriel is the everyman. Or so Gabriel imagines in his moment of self-examination. Gabriel embodies the rule of his class, his people, his society. Michael Furey remains an exception to that rule. That is why the presence of his ghost is able to carry Gabriel outside of himself that night and inspire in him the epiphanic vision of a universal snow. Only after this symbolic breakthrough into the realm of the universal does "The Dead" assume a meaning which seemed painfully lacking in the prolonged, excruciatingly boring account of the dinner party at the Morkans'. Suddenly all of those unexceptional, eminently forgettable characters at the party become translucent. They now appear to us as individual snowflakes in their common descent toward oblivion, and their dinner party figures as a last supper of sorts. Yet through their portraits as individuals shines the light of something more generic and epic, so to speak—something like types of the Irish people as a whole, and, more universally, of humanity as such. The falling snow of the last paragraph gathers them all into its drift and renders their caducity at once singular and generic, specific and universal, Irish and human.

I am tempted to say that the snow "repeats" in its symbolism the genealogy of the image I have traced from Homer to Virgil to Dante. It evokes Homer's genericism of the human generations; its shares with Virgil an emphasis on the early, sacrificial, unredeemed death; and with Dante it shares the Christological enigma of individuation. Joyce certainly did not have this prehistory in mind when he wrote "The Dead," but somehow I suspect that the author of *Ulysses* would not have objected to the notion that in his earlier story he intuitively or inadvertently recapitulated it.

To conclude the first phase of this meditation, then, I would remark that if it is true, as Feuerbach claimed, that our distinction as a species is that our species becomes an object of thought for us, this means that human beings have access to a measure outside of (a human life) time—call it death, eternity, the afterlife of the dead, or the posterity of the unborn—by which we take cognizance of our being in time, like leaves on a branch in the autumn, or snow falling faintly through the universe. It is also true, however, that this cognizance of our species-being, pervaded as it is by the tension between our being in and out of everyday time, has a history (of conception and representation) of its own. This history, of which we have caught only a glimpse in this genealogy of a literary image, consists of what I would call the fitful personalization of our species-being. The more our species-being is thus personalized, the more universal do the claims (or "rights") of personhood appear. What Saint Thomas said of the angels—"Omne individuum sit species infima" [Every individual is a species unto itself]—becomes more and more true of humans, at least in our cultural conceptions of ourselves, as we continue in the drive to angelicize our nature.

In short, that our species becomes an object of thought for us is only the beginning of humanization, the beginning, that is, of a process by which personal identity seeks its absolute and impossible absolution (Western culture is the cultural and even political history of this impulse). If such absolution is impossible, at least among the living, it is because of the incontrovertibility of personal death. Death assures that this process by which personal identity seeks its absolute absolution can never reach an end, never attain its goal. It can only continue to symbolize, ritualize, elegize, or memorialize the finitude the cognizance of which is, in the final analysis, the true mark of our species. It is this mark that the poets inscribed in their epics and that we also find inscribed on the Vietnam Veterans Memorial.

The Wall

November 13, 1982, was an unforgettable day in America. Over 150,000 people, many of them Vietnam veterans, descended on Washington, D.C., for the opening of the Vietnam Veterans Memorial.

Wheelchairs, fatigues, old Army jackets and a sea of decorations followed the brass parade toward the park between the Lincoln Memorial and the Washington Monument. After the sundry speeches, when the fences guarding the memorial finally came down, there was a prolonged, uneasy silence as people surveyed the wall, approached it, touched it, walked along it, searched it for the names of fallen kin or comrades. One by one veterans began to break down. Strangers embraced, weeping in each other's arms. Mothers, fathers, wives, daughters, sons, relatives, and friends of the dead also broke down, and before long the scene of spontaneous grief moved reporters and broadcasters to tears as well.

Since that day the Vietnam Veterans Memorial has become the most visited monument in the United States, along with the Lincoln Memorial. On any given day, in the crushing heat of summer or in the dead of winter, one can witness the same cathartic scene taking place in front of the wall. Much of it has to do with the unresolved tensions associated with the Vietnam War and the long-overdue need for a public mourning process, no doubt; but there is also something symbolic about the solemn gravity of the wall—the encrypted presence of its dead—which seems to turn the deaths of those memorialized into a stubborn question. The silence with which it responds to this question gives the wall's inscribed black granite panels an almost overwhelming power of withholding. The irresistible need many visitors feel to touch a chiseled name, kiss it, talk to it, offer it flowers or gifts, leave it notes or letters, is evidence enough of the dead's privative presence in the stone—a presence at once given and denied.

To the depths of silence with which the wall responds to its own question correspond the depths of its symbolic underworld. In structure and form the wall evokes an implacable descent, built as it is below the ground level of the park. A highly charged irony pervades its structural simplicity. The wall is boldly finite in its spatial dimensions, yet its triangulated plane extends to infinity. It has a clear beginning, middle, and end, yet every name in the chronological sequence has an absolute end point. Maybe that is why all the names seem to gravitate toward or explode out of the corner where the wall forms a sharp angle. This highest part of the wall is also the lowest point of the descending pathway and marks the height of the Vietnam war. Here, where the wall peaks and forms a sharp angle, drawing all the lateral names into its somber recess, the names of the dead seem to rain down from a sublime height. Even those at the very bottom of the slabs seem to have fallen to the ground from on high. As it reaches a peak and then begins to descend, the line of the wall evokes the "natural" progress of a human life, from growth to maturity to decline. The average age of the combat soldier in Vietnam was nineteen.

One's initial impression of the memorial wall from a distance is that of its dramatic horizontal extension, yet as one descends along the pathway toward the highest part of the wall, the anxiety of the vertical gradually wins out over that of the horizontal stretch to infinity. Joyce's image of the snow, by contrast, works the other way around. The verticality of the snow's descent gives way, by the end of the last paragraph of "The Dead," to a more sublime impression of its vast horizontal extension over all of Ireland. Yet the effect in both cases is similar. The tense relationship between extension and descension gives both symbols their sublime epic reach.

By that I mean the reach into collectivity and generationality. As in Homer, Virgil, Dante, and Joyce, the wall evokes a generic multitude of the dead, an entire generation of sacrificed Americans. From a distance the thousands of small markings in the granite appear as part of the stone's texture. When one realizes that they are not texture but the names of the dead inscribed along the entire stretch of the wall, one is struck by the sheer profusion that makes up this class of veterans who met their death in Vietnam. One gets an impression of Virgil's vast hosts of the dead in their incalculable numbers, or of the legions of shades which inspired in Dante's pilgrim the famous line: "I had not thought death had undone so many." When we speak of 59,000 dead, that is a crushing figure even in its abstraction. But allow their names to occupy space and suddenly the "so many" undone by the war find an immoderate measure for their excess.

The epic's vocation, as well as its burden, is to contain such excess in its narrative, ideological drive toward synthesis. We have seen, if only briefly and in passing, what moral strains and pressures this put on Virgil as well as Dante when it came to representing or accounting for the fates of history's plethora of victims. In the case of the memorial wall, the excess of names is uncontainable, not because the wall cannot accommodate them—it does—but because in its mute commemoration of the Vietnam War it proclaims, or seems to, that each one of its inscriptions is one too many. The excess lies in the moral doubt raised in and by every name. The wall, in its conception and its material presence, is pervaded with the pathos of an early, sacrificial death reminiscent of Virgil's infernal scene of "high-hearted heroes stripped of life, and boys / and unwed girls, and young men set upon / the pyre of death before their fathers' eyes." Yet Rome—that "eternal idea in the mind of God" which would honor or redeem these deaths—is missing.

If the wall sympathizes with the Virgilian pathos, it sympathizes even more with Dante's conspicuous insistence on the singularity of each damned soul. The genius of the monument lies in the way it particularizes the general at the same time as it reflects the general back upon the particular by simply listing the names of every man and woman who never made it back from Vietnam. The chronological order of the listing, according to the dates on which these soldiers met their deaths, drives home the reality that they fell one by one, first one and then the other, like Dante's autumn leaves that "detach themselves, / first one and then the other, till the bough / sees all its fallen garmets on the ground." The intersection of time, identity, and death in the dolorite stone makes of its names a seasonal accumulation of dead leaves, each one "identical" in Leibniz's sense of identical only to itself.

While it is clearly symbolic, the wall defies the most traditional definition of the symbol. In *The Statesman's Manual* Coleridge famously affirms that the symbol is characterized by "a translucence of the special in the individual, or of the general in the special, or the universal in the general" (p. 30). This is a compelling definition, and one that works well in the case of the generic Tomb of the Unknown Soldier. The (unidentified) soldier buried in such a tomb "symbolizes" all the known and unknown soldiers who died in a given war; and, more generally, all the soldiers who died in battle on behalf of a particular nation; and more universally, the soldiers of all nations who have lost—and who in the future will lose—their lives in war. The symbolism of the Vietnam Veterans Memorial works the other way around. We see on its wall an almost endless list of names of "known" soldiers who make up a (special or general) class. But in this case it is the individual that shines in and through the generic multitude of names. The epic ambition to monumentalize the Vietnam War in the memorial wall comes to grief in the lyric singularity of each and every name. This failure of the epic gesture is deliberate, and it accounts for the wall's astonishing solemnity. The translucence of the individual in the general, embodied in the reflective surface of the stone itself, makes of the wall a contrarian symbol, or a symbol of contrariness. In that sense it is an appropriate memorial for a war which, at bottom, was a civil war—a war at odds with its own concept.

When the project for the memorial wall was first announced, many veterans protested its conception and considered it yet another insult to their dignity. They called it "the black gash of shame." They had expected something more in keeping with other war memorials. They expected and demanded to be honored the way their fathers and grandfathers had been honored in previous wars. These were the Glaukos types, eager to follow their fathers' injunctions, eager for a patriotic monument that would finally authorize their pride for having served in the Vietnam War. To placate them, a bronze statue of three anonymous soldiers was commissioned and placed near the wall. These three soldiers, in their generic status, are evidence of just how pathetic a conventional symbolism appears in this context. The suggestion of heroic patriotism and camaraderie rings, if not false, then fatuous—an idol that Nietzsche's hammer would have found hollow and deceiving. For the Vietnam War was not like other patriotic wars. On the contrary, it shattered the very concept of a patriotic war. How do you memorialize that?

The names on the Vietnam Veterans Memorial wall are the signatures of a generation that many believe was betrayed by its fathers, fathers who had asked of their sons—as Hippolochos had asked of Glaukos—not to shame them. But the shame in this case fell on the fathers, who enlisted a generation and sent it off to a war that had little to do with the abstract concepts in which the war sought its justification: freedom, democracy, honor, patriotism. These universals proved to be, if not meaningless, then at least devoid of content when it came to the reality of the war's conflagrations. Just as the Vietnam War remains unsubsumable under the general reasons for which it was engaged, so too its dead remain unsubsumable under the general symbolism of honored veterans. To honor someone means to affirm the moral basis from which one presumes to honor, and no one in America has the moral authority to honor the Vietnam veterans. Their honor is above and beyond us.

In its silent refusal to honor those who died in the Vietnam War, the wall's countersymbolism proclaims its thousands of names (morally) unaccounted for, even as it accounts for every last one of them. Each name stands out, in excess of the reasons for its signature. In that sense the memorial constitutes an ecstasy of individuals which the wall cannot contain, or cannot absolve, since their deaths are fundamentally absurd—as is death in general. After all, the wall is not a grave, which for better or worse can presume to contain "all that was mortal" of the dead whose name its headstone registers. The bodies of those nearly sixty thousand names lie scattered all over the nation. In some cases there were no bodies left to bury or cremate. The wall's purpose is not to bury the soldiers, nor even to mourn them. Its purpose is to mark their absolution as mortal individuals.

If the Vietnam Veterans Memorial belongs authentically to its time—a time when De Martino's concept of a "formal power" that transforms death into value too often falls short of its public task—it is because its wall throws into relief the nugatory character of the traditional war memorial, not by an overt or latent critique but by a deliberate refusal of the honoring, call it sepulchering, gesture. Such a refusal is not merely captious or derogatory. It arises from a deeper affirmation of the absolute mortality of the individuals it names. As it absolves that mortality in its formal objectification of their identities—their identities as soldiers in a war that in itself cannot redeem their deaths—the wall reconfigures the rules by which death, at least in this case, is transformed into value. In so doing the memorial rediscovers the humic ground of a human mortality. Such an achievement confirms that our humanity is never turned over to us once and for all but must regain or resecure its ground ever anew in the mad vortexes of history. This is no easy task. It is difficult enough to "consign what passes . . . to the cultural rules of passage" and thereby redeem the guilt of what passes away humanly; it is even more difficult, once they are scrambled, lost, or trivialized, to retrieve the powers of human absolution.

CHAPTER 9

THE AFTERLIFE OF THE IMAGE

To whom does the corpse belong? Who has jurisdiction over its fate? It is fair to say that nowadays we children of enlightenment expect our right to self-determination to extend beyond life to the dead body—where and if it will be buried, where and if its ashes will be strewn, whether or not its organs will be donated, under what conditions its DNA may be cloned, whether to have it plastinated; in short, we expect or demand freedom of personal decision regarding body disposal. Such a demand rests on the assumption of the self's posthumous ownership of its cadaver, as if the latter were of the same ontological order as property or patrimony. But is the corpse really assumable under the concept of personal property? Does it belong, by testamentary right, to the person who has (who will have) evacuated its biomass, or does the deceased person belong in fact to the corpse? And what do we mean when we say "belong," in either case? The answers to such questions all depend on what one believes—for it is finally a matter of belief—about the bond between self and corpse.

Let us return for a moment to Heidegger's claim in *Being and Time* that what belongs to Dasein most properly or authentically is its death, understood not as its "perishing" but as its "ownmost possibility for Being." My death, says Heidegger, is in each case mine (no one else can die for me) and my being-in-the-world, properly understood, is a being-toward-death, which I may either resolve upon authentically or flee in the face of inauthentically. As long as I have not yet redeemed whatever time is left for me to live, I am "indebted" to its terminal future. To the degree that I owe myself or belong to its still outstanding potential, I am "guilty" (the German word *schuld*, we recall, means both "debt" and "guilt"). Authenticity is not a question of "settling" my debt to time—there is nothing I can do in the moral or existential sphere to attenuate this guilt—it consists rather in assuming responsibility for it. Since death is the ultimate creditor of Dasein's existence, it is only by finishing my life, or by dying in the biological sense, that I can redeem the guilt of finitude.

From the point of view of Heidegger's existential analytic there is not much one can say about the bond between self and corpse, given that Dasein's "who" ceases to exist at the moment of its biological extinction. Are things so clear-cut, though? Is the sword of biological death so sharp that there is no lingering association between corpse and person? Are there no eddies or countercurrents in the flow of finitude such that the flow transcends or crosses over into Dasein's demise? It is precisely because human dying does *not* coincide with perishing, as Heidegger himself claims, that we could answer all these questions in the affirmative and say that Dasein's "who" continues to inhabit the corpse until the link gets severed by those who have been left behind. If human dying is a mode of being mortal and of transforming mortality into history, then we could say that Dasein's death, understood as the final redemption of its guilt, is an event that takes place in the aftermath of perishing, in and through the participatory care of the caretakers. To put it propositionally: *Dasein does not die until its remains are disposed of.*

The truth of this proposition proceeds from considerable certainty. Everywhere one looks across the spectrum of human culture one finds what we might call an *obligation* to the corpse, or the remains thereof (I leave aside, for the moment, distinctions between corpse, bones, remains, relics, and the like, which are otherwise crucial to an anthropology of perishing, if not an ontology of dying). The obligation usually takes the form of a traditionally mandated duty, in the name of which Antigone, for instance, will risk her life, yet it has its basis in a human imperative to dispose of the dead deliberately and ceremonially. Consider the cruel and, from our point of view, unusual punishment that awaited those Greek generals who had won a major victory at sea but who had neglected, due to bad weather, to retrieve the bodies of some of their soldiers. They were tried in Athens upon their return and sentenced to hang. To deprive the grief-stricken of the loved one's remains was a calamity worse than the one that brought on their grief, for it denied them the means by which to meet their obligation. Elpenor in *The Odyssey* and Palinurus in *The Aeneid* are archetypes of the post-mortem misery of the unburied as the Greeks and Romans imagined it. One could say that the torments suffered by the souls of the unburied in Hades are imaginary projections of the torments and guilt suffered by their loved ones under the sun. In the absence of a body the latter were at a catastrophic loss, their grief could not find its proper object; hence the work of mourning, by which the dead are made to die, was destined to fail. The missing body meant that the deceased person was fated to remain, in effect, *undead*—a condition, once again, that speaks above all of the open-ended, unreconciled psychic state of the grievers.

The distress of those who, for whatever reason, are deprived of mortal remains is not reducible to the religious or superstitious creeds of bygone societies. We witness it today in the relatives of the kidnapped, of soldiers missing in action, of the victims of airplane accidents, of those who perished in death camps or in the attacks of September 11 with no recoverable remains. The cruelest act of those regimes in Latin America that sponsored the "disappearance" of so many of their citizens during the seventies and early eighties was to withhold information about their victims' fate and above all to withhold their dead bodies. This led to an interminable anguish, especially for the *desaparecidos'* mothers, who in Argentina were the first to protest publicly against the disappearances. By internalizing the fate of their missing children, many of them neither lived nor died, but succumbed themselves to a condition of the undead. "At that point, my life ended," declared one Argentine mother, referring to the day her son was kidnapped. According to her testimony in a newspaper interview she remained in this catatonic state for several years, until the remains of her son were finally exhumed, identified, and returned to her. Her reaction upon receiving them indicates to what extent the bodies of the dead belong by natural right to those who cannot go on living without laying them to rest: "I became very moved because I had found my son. I began to kiss him, kiss all of his bones, touch him, and caress him. But the feeling was mixed with pain, because now that I had found him, I knew that he was dead. . . . I lived the wake and burial as if he had died only yesterday" (quoted in Crossland, "Buried Lives," p. 154). Several other testimonies of this sort stress how crucial was the reunification of the disappeared person with his or her remains if the living were to get on with their lives.

The extent to which this was the case is revealed by the seemingly incongruous reaction of many Argentine mothers to the postjunta government's efforts to excavate the mass graves left behind by the state-sponsored murders during Argentina's "dirty war." The purpose of these exhumations was ostensibly to uncover material evidence of the crimes as well as to return the remains to the relatives, yet The Association of the Mothers of the Plaza de Mayo as well as other human rights groups denounced the policy for its putative complicity with the previous regime. In 1989 an advertisement placed in a Buenos Aires newspaper by The Association of Mothers read: "The compromise reached by the government to pardon the genocists is the same as that authorized by the judges who exhume human remains. . . . With these tactics they implement the forgetting and reconciliation required by the murderers" (Crossland, "Buried Lives," p. 149).

This objection—apparently incongruous but in fact perfectly logical—was motivated by the mothers' demand that the people responsible for the disappearances be punished. They did not want the nation to forgive and forget what had taken place until justice had been done, but reconciliation is what they rightly feared from the return of the remains. In the words of one activist: "It's very difficult for a mother who has received the remains of her child to go on fighting" (p. 154). Why? Because as Zoë Crossland puts it in her stirring article on the politics of exhumation in postjunta Argentina, "The funerary ritual surrounding the remains of the disappeared has the effect of remaking the world, as the dead take their 'proper' place in individual and collective memory—becoming of the past, rather than the present; of the dead rather than the living" (ibid.). It was precisely this burying of the past along with the dead that the Association of Mothers objected to. As long as the disappeared remained undead, they remained politically alive, and there could be neither a forgiving nor a premature forgetting of the perpetrators' guilt.

Let us move back in time for a moment into other kinds of archives—the Homeric epics. Until he returns home, Odysseus belongs in effect to the undead, although in body he remains alive, for exile is a kind of unrealized death both for him and his kin. During their colloquy in the underworld Antiklea tells her son that she died of grief waiting for his homecoming: "it was my longing for you . . . that took the sweet spirit of life from me" (*Odyssey* 11.202–4). Until his corpse offered evidence of his death and gave her the object of his funeral rites, there was no peace for her. Since she could neither bury him nor embrace him, she died in spirit before she died in body. As for her husband, Laertes, she informs Odysseus that he remains alive in Ithaka, reduced to a pathological condition. He sleeps in his slaves' quarters, "in the dirt next to the fire, and with foul clothing upon him," groveling in thick beds of leaves "as he longs for your homecoming" (ibid.). Laertes' behavior is that of a father under the compulsion to bury himself in the earth, as if out of identification with a son whom he fears lies unburied in a strange land or in the depths of the sea. It is similar in nature to the bizarre behavior of Priam during the ten-day period when Achilles withholds the body of the slain Hector. Like Laertes, Priam turns the impulse to bury his son back upon his own person: "Dung lay thick on the head and neck of the aged man, for he had been rolling in it, he had gathered and smeared it on with his hands" (*The Iliad* 24.163–65).

The retrieval of Hector's corpse is in fact crucial to the psychic survival of Troy as a whole. While Achilles withholds the body of its dead hero the city remains in a state of chaos and hysteria ("It was most like what would have happened, if all lowering / Ilion had been burning from top to bottom" (22.410–11). In vain do Hecuba and Andromache raise a lament and perform their ululations upon learning of the death of Hector: without his body to organize its articulation, their grief remains dysfunctional and ineffective. So miserable are any and all attempts to mourn in the absence of a body that some ten days after Hector's death Troy is on the brink of disaster.

Nothing could be more unlike the chaotic grief that grips the house of Priam during this period than the solemn, highly ritualized funeral ceremony that follows upon the repatriation of Hector's body. It is with this ceremony that the epic comes to its somber conclusion. Given the tragic irony that pervades *The Iliad,* one could speak here of a happy ending of sorts, in the sense that Hector enjoyed the benefit of a funeral at all. Many warriors on both sides will be denied this blessing, so much so that one could affirm, without exaggeration, that this dreaded fate is the underlying "matter" of the epic as a whole. The first verses of the poem name the matter directly:

> Sing, goddess, the anger of Peleus' son Achilleus
> And its devastation, which put pains thousandfold upon the
> Achaians,

Hurled in their multitudes to the house of Hades strong souls
Of heroes, but gave their bodies to be the delicate feasting
Of dogs, and all birds.

$$(1.1-5)$$

Ancient commentators declared of these opening verses that Homer "devised a tragic prologue for his tragedies" (see Griffin, *Homer on Life and Death*, pp. 118–19). One should add that modern wars are no less tragic when it comes to the unrecoverable remains of the slain. Indeed, when the destructive potential of modern weapons is unleashed there are frequently no remains to gather up or identify at all. Be that as it may, it is by comparison to the fate of the unburied, the missing, the unidentified, and the abandoned that Hector's funeral represents a "happy ending" of sorts, albeit one that only adds to the poem's tragic vision of war.

What do such testaments tell us about the human obligation to the corpse? To begin with, they tell us that the corpse, or remains thereof, possesses a kind of charisma, and that in many cases the event of death remains unfinished or unrealized until person and remains have been reunified (in the case of the disappeared) and the latter disposed of ceremonially (as in the case of Hector). I speak of death here as the completion, not extinction, of life, for we have seen that a person can perish yet not die in the full human sense. This does not mean that the missing or unburied are doomed, necessarily and universally, to remain undead in the psyches of their loved ones. It means that the work of getting the dead to die in us, as opposed to dying with our dead, is all the more arduous if not impossible when the dead body goes missing, given the almost universal association between corpse and person among human beings and the fact that mortal remains are never a matter of indifference where bonds of love and kinship exist.

We must not conclude from these various body biographies, however, that the purpose of funeral rites is in fact to reunify person and remains so as to perpetuate their bond. On the contrary, the obligation consists in an imperative to dispose of the corpse so as *liberate* the person from its tenacious embrace. Funeral rites serve to effect a ritual separation between the living and the dead, to be sure, yet first and foremost they serve to separate the *image* of the deceased from the corpse to which it remains bound up at the moment of demise. Before the living can detach themselves from them the dead must be detached from their remains so that their images may find their place in the afterlife of the imagination. For what is a corpse if not the connatural image, or afterimage, of the person who has vanished, leaving behind a lifeless likeness of him- or herself? If the corpse embodies or holds on to the person's image at the moment of demise, funeral rites serve to disentangle that nexus and separate them into discrete entities with independent fates—the corpse consigned to earth or air, and the image assigned to its afterlife, whatever form that imaginary afterlife may take in this or that cultural framework. Between the dead and the undead the essential difference lies in the release of the image.

I speak of the image for several reasons. It is not by chance that the Romans called the ancestor's death mask the *imago*. The wax *imagines* that typically adorned aristocratic households were literally relinquished, or left behind, by the dead, such that the first image to emerge from the deliverance process was the likeness of a person taken directly from the corpse. Family members would sometimes don these masks during burial ceremonies so that the dead ancestors could welcome a newcomer into their midst. This was personification in its primary dramatic mode, the word *persona* in Latin meaning precisely the actor's mask. It was as an image of this sort that the dead person lived on once the disembodiment process was realized.

This ancient practice has its modern counterparts. To this day the photograph retains essential links to its ancestral origins in the death mask, if only because it allows a person's likeness to survive his or her demise, to say nothing of the photograph's similar ceremonial role as ancestral portrait in the family album or domestic interior. In this respect the photograph follows in the footsteps of its immediate predecessor, the painted portrait, itself a modern descendant of the death mask. Whether cast in wax, painted in oil, or exposed on celluloid film, the image is essentially mortuary.

In the ancient Greek imagination Hades (from *Aides*, "the Invisible") was the place where the shadow images of the dead lived on. Released from the body at death—either through the breath or through an open wound of the body—the *psyche* of the person became, precisely, an *eidôlon*, or image. Odysseus discovers the phantomatic, insubstantial nature of the *eidôlon* when he tries to embrace his mother in the underworld. Three times he grasps at her image and "three times she fluttered out of my hands like a shadow / or a dream" (*Odyssey* 11.213). When Odysseus wonders whether she is "nothing but an image that proud Persephone / sent my way, to make me grieve all the more for sorrow," Antiklea answers:

Oh my child, ill-fated beyond all other mortals,
this is not Persephone, daughter of Zeus, beguiling you,
but it is only what happens, when they die, to all mortals.
The sinews no longer hold the flesh and the bones together,
And once the spirit has left the white bones, all the rest
Of the body is made subject to the fire's strong fury,
But the soul flitters out like a dream and flies away.

(216–22)

Once the sinews no longer hold the flesh and the bones together, the dead can no longer be held in our arms. No matter how tightly Achilles in his wild grief clasps the dead body of Patroklos, his friend is now untenable. Only Hades can now hold his image. One need not believe in an afterlife in a religious or doctrinal sense in order to affirm the "reality" of Hades, or to acknowledge the multitude of recesses where the shadow images of the dead maintain a privative presence: dreams, books, portraits, houses, art, and so on. We dispose of what is inanimate in the dead so that they may find their way into realms of the spirit—realms to which the living, by virtue of their existential self-overreaching, have native access. To be mortal means to *be* the place of this imaginary afterlife. What Antiklea describes as the soul's flight from the body once the fire liberates its spirit or *psyche* is a process that takes place in those who, metaphorically speaking, light the fire.

And yet who is Antiklea that she should be so eloquent when it comes to describing the soul's flight from the stricken body? She is an image, an *eidôlon*, that appears to us in the poem. She belongs to Hades because, whatever else it may be, Hades is poetry's topological image of its own poetic imagination—of its chorus of speaking shadows and disembodied characters. All of literature's characters, as well as their voices, belong to the order of the posthumous image. Odysseus's visit to the underworld is, in that respect, a descent into the womb of poetic vision from which such images, conjured and nourished by the human imagination, come alive in the poet's representation. But again, who are these loquacious masks in the theater of literature—Antiklea, Achilles, Odysseus, but also Aeneas, Farinata, Lear, Quixote, Bovary— and where do they speak from? Where and above all *how*? They are all untenably dead, yet they are also alive to the degree that, through the poem, they can be seen and heard by us. The son who visits the dead in book 11 of *The Odyssey* is of the same ontological order as the mother's ghost he seeks to clasp. Both speak through the same medium of poetic personification. Between the living and the dead in literature the difference is strictly "fictional." Be they invented or historical, contemporary or bygone, dead or alive, the persons who speak in and through the literary work belong to the afterlife.

When Vico speaks of the poetic wisdom of the ancients he is speaking also of the tropes of reanimation and personification by which the voices, commandments, laws, and authority of the dead are carried beyond the boundary that separates them from the living. Poetic figuration renders the shadow images of Hades—the realm of the Invisible— visible and audible. The trope (from the Greek *tropos*, "a turn") refuses to stay on this side of the Lethe but "turns" itself to the dead. Whether or not one agrees with Joseph Brodsky's statement that "art 'imitates' death rather than life; i.e., it imitates that realm of which life supplies no notion," or his statement that "what distinguishes art from life is the ability of the former to produce a higher degree of lyricism than is possible within any human interplay," it is hard to disagree with his conclusion: "Hence poetry's affinity with—if not the very invention of—the afterlife" (*Less than One*, p. 104).

Certainly it was his "higher lyricism"—his ability to put grief to music—that won Orpheus his privileged access to the underworld, where, with his *cassa armonica*, he moved the resident *fasma* on behalf of his mournful desire. How could those *fasma* fail to be moved when it was a tropological desire or solicitation of that sort on which their very existence as images depended? Just as Orpheus needed the *eidôla* to nourish his higher lyricism, the *eidôla* needed him to give them voice and visibility. As lord of the underworld Pluto no doubt knew that Orpheus would never resist the temptation to turn back and gaze on Eurydice before she had gained the light. It was not so much a question of Orpheus's anxiety or excessive desire to be reunited with his wife but of his allegiance to his art, or to the image, that made him turn around. Perhaps Pluto was merely putting Orpheus's allegiance to the test. If so, in that fateful moment of looking back Orpheus remained true to his poetic if not marital vow, wedding his voice again—and once and for all—to the afterlife. Certainly all human interplay would hold little interest for someone with such a vocation—an indifference that in fact cost him his life at the hands of those spurned Thracian women who could not entice his Hades-wedded desire.

Orpheus's allegiance to the image represents not so much the lyric poet's mournful desire as his or her devotion to the animating power of the voice. In chapter 5 I claimed that, be it in a mother or father tongue, we always speak with words preinhabited and passed on by the predecessor. Yet that is only half the story. While it is true that we speak with the words of the dead, it is equally true that the dead speak in and through the voices of the living. We inherit their words so as to lend them voice. If lexification binds the generations, institutionalizes authority, and historicizes the law of legacy—if it in fact grounds human historicity as such—then certainly the verbal communion between the living and the dead figures as one of its synthesizing agencies. The living do not have a constitutive need to speak as much as to hear themselves spoken to, above all by the ancestor. We lend voice to the dead so that they may speak to us from their underworld—address us, instruct us, reprove us, bless us, enlighten us, and in general alleviate the historical terror and loneliness of being in the world. Holding fast to this ancient call of language, the poet labors to give birth to the voice's afterlife, either in its lyric singularity or epic multiplicity.

With the invention of gramophones, radio, and other voice-recording technologies, the dead were able to speak posthumously in their own phonetic voices for the first time. Yet lyric poets sang from beyond the grave in their own voices long before that, even if the phonetic voice did not survive the song. While lyric poets tend to animate a voice that is proleptically posthumous, epic poets tend to speak on behalf of those who have already crossed the Lethe and taken up their abode in the underworld. These latter gain their voice through epic prosopopeia. In technical rhetorical terms, prosopopeia is a type of personification, a giving of face and voice to that which, properly speaking, possesses neither, as in the following lyric by Antoine-Vincent Arnault, entitled "La Feuille":

De ta tige détachée,
Pauvre feuille desséchée,
Où vas-tu?—Je n'en sais rien.
L'orage a frappé la chene
Qui seul était mon soutien:
De son inconstante haleine,
Le zéphyr ou l'aquilon
Dupuis ce jour me promène
De la forêt à la plaine,
De la montagne au vallon.
Je vais où le vent me mène
Sans me plaindre ou m'effrayer;
Je vais où va toute chose,
Où va la feuille de rose
Et la feuille de laurier.

> (*Anthologie*, pp. 411–12)

[Detached from your stem,
Poor desiccated leaf,
Where go you?—I know not.
The storm battered the oak
That was my sole support:
With its inconstant breath
The zephyr or north wind
Has led me since that day
From the forest to the plain,
From the mountain to the valley.
I go where the wind takes me,
Without complaint or fear;
I go where all things go:
Where goes the petal of the rose
And the laurel leaf.]

Prosopopeia figures as the rhetorical means, or better the medium, through which the *eidôlon* in Hades becomes loquacious. Even the silence of Ajax in Hades—the most sublime silence in all of literature, Longinus called it—is a form of reticence made possible by the transfer of the voice. Such a transfer is always at work in the epic poem, so much so that we could say that the epic voice is both lent and borrowed—lent in that the dead borrow it to speak, borrowed in that the dead, through their speech, lend poetry the authority of its pronouncements. The epic, which speaks to the degree that it is spoken, comes into its own by losing its voice in a multitude of speaking masks, as Plato understood only too well.

Where the souls in Hades come forth to drink the sacrificial blood that Odysseus pours into the pit we see a poetic image—a "poetic character," Vico would say—of the dead's reliance on the living to nourish their voices. The dead speak from beyond the grave as long as we lend them the means of locution; they take up their abode in books, dreams, houses, portraits, legends, monuments, and graves as long as we keep open the places of their indwelling. This is a collective "we," for it is not only poets who lend and borrow voice through the medium of prosopopeia. It takes listeners and readers to reanimate the words of which our poems, novels, and literatures are composed, to say nothing of our sacred scriptures and founding constitutions. Every reader or listener who reactivates the semantic content of the literary work performs an act of prosopopeia, that is, a reverbalization of the text through a transfer of his or her voice to its otherwise dead letter.

Whether it depicts a descent into the underworld dramatically or not, the epic poem is always in some sense on assignment to and from the precursor. Dante received his assignment from Virgil, who in turn received it from Homer. In the twentieth century a poet like Ezra Pound sought to revive the epic imperative when he embarked upon the *Cantos* with a rewriting of book 11 of *The Odyssey*. Earlier in his career, before he gave up on his lyric vocation, Pound had donned the masks of various predecessors in order to speak in their imaginary voices (see *Personae,* for instance), hence we can't say that his turn to the epic represented a decision to speak on behalf of the dead, rather than on behalf of the lyric self as such. Nevertheless, we can say that the epic drive of the *Cantos* was bound up with Pound's need to give back a voice not only to his literary predecessors but also to the untold dead who were cut down in their youth in the First World War. The primal "and" that opens the first *Canto* ("And then went down to the ship") signals Pound's attempt to conjoin his modern epic enterprise with those of his classical precursors, yet in the same copulative opening gesture it seeks to turn the poet's living voice into a medium for the speechless heroes of his own generation—to turn it into a trans-Lethean voice, as it were, so that his dead contemporaries could use it to speak out to— and *against*—the world.

To survive a war in which so many of your generation perished is the source of a hounding guilt, which the *Cantos* sought to turn into a redemptive poetry. This is not the place to speculate about how Pound's aggravated sense of debt might relate to his hysterical denunciation of usury, or how his epic lending of voice might relate to his epic polemic against money-lending institutions. Suffice it to say that Pound's sense of indebtedness ended up aggravating its cause by seeking to balance its deficits. Poets do not balance deficits. They give voice to loss. We have as much to learn about the modern era from the *Cantos'* abortions as we do from its achievements; and what we have to learn is this: that our debt to the dead has by now become essentially insoluble, just as our guilt with regard to the victims of modern history has become essentially inexpiable.

This brief odyssey among the archives has put us in a position to appreciate more fully what is at stake in what I have called the human obligation to the corpse. Ritual disposal serves to detach the image from the corpse and thereby free the image for its repersonifcations and reverbalizations in various culturally determined guises. To transform natural death into human death means in effect to give birth to the dead in their afterlife. Perhaps this is one reason why women have traditionally played such crucial roles in ritualized mourning and lamentation in general. For dying in the full human sense is a kind of birth, while the afterlife—understood phenomenologically and not necessarily religiously or doctrinally—is the new and altered condition the dead are born into (as souls, images, voices, masks, heroes, ancestors, founders, and the like). Eventually this afterlife will itself expire, at which point human dying gives way to the remorseless oblivion of natural death. Yet as long as the living "care" for the dead, the place of that persistence remains open.

From this philological certainty (namely, that it takes a sustained effort on the part of the living to turn perishing into dying, and vice versa) proceed the following philosophical truths: that Dasein is not the author of its death, to say nothing of its afterlife. Since human death is always handed over to the care of others, Dasein's corpse belongs by natural right to the caretakers. To say that Dasein cannot own its human death means that Dasein's potentiality for being is *not* consummated in its biological demise. While Dasein's afterlife belongs to that potentiality, the potentiality itself does not belong to Dasein as such but to those to whom Dasein's death has been turned over in the aftermath of its perishing. To resolve upon my mortality means first and foremost to acknowledge that its fate belongs as much to others as theirs belongs to me.

If this much is true, then we must rethink the basis of Heidegger's concept of "primordial guilt," which he defines as a condition of *responsibility*. What Dasein owes its finite future does not have the character lack, he says; rather, guilt calls on Dasein to become responsible for its death by responding to the silent call of conscience that arises from the nullity lurking at the heart of its finitude. Yet we have seen that Dasein cannot assume such a responsibility, in the broader sense of accomplishing the transfiguration of biological extinction into human death. At most Dasein can—indeed, it must—assume responsibility for the death of others. The human obligation to the corpse is only one, albeit primordial, manifestation of this responsibility. Guilt is the measure of Dasein's dependence on others to "finish" the death that puts an end to its life, as well as of its obligations to the death of others. What is Dasein's finitude all about, in the end, if not this intrinsic powerlessness to accomplish its own death and, conversely, its responsibility for the mortality of those who share its condition? Where does my mortality end and the other's begin? Precisely because I am mortal my mortality crosses over into my neighbor's, just as his or hers crosses over into mine.

Dasein is under obligation to the Dasein that lives and the Dasein that dies. Its guilt grounds both the bonds of community among the living and the bonds of community with the dead. It is what opens the place of the afterlife at the heart of the *Da*. Here I am simply recasting Heidegger's formal definition of guilt, which reads as follows: "we define formally the existential idea of the 'Guilty!' as 'Being-the-basis for a Being which has been defined by a 'not'—that is to say, as *Being-the-basis of a nullity*" (*Being and Time*, p. 329). Recast in a transitive mode, Heidegger's statement can be taken to declare—against its explicit intention, to be sure—that Dasein's guilt is the sustaining basis of those who are "not," of those whose mode of being is defined by a "not" insofar as they have perished. If to be responsible in the mode of guilt means to "be-the-basis for," Dasein is responsible for whatever is of the order of human dying, and not simply of its own "constant" dying. To the degree that the (non)being of the dead has been handed over to its care, Dasein is indeed the basis of a nullity. Because it is primordially guilty in this personal way Dasein has the power to personify the masks of the dead and throw its voice beyond the barrier of natural death. Or as Heidegger coldly puts it: "Being guilty does not first result from an indebtedness [*Verschuldung*], but . . . on the contrary, indebtedness becomes possible only 'on the basis' of a primordial Being-guilty" (ibid.).

What this means, in simple terms, is that guilt breaks through the nonrelational barriers that Heidegger erected around it. It is no longer simply a question of owing-myself-to-my-death but of owing myself to the death of others and turning my death over to their care. Heidegger of course never denied that the death of others "is an object of 'concern' in the ways of funeral rites, interment, and the cult of graves" (p. 282), yet his strong claim to the effect that "[t]he dying of Others is not something which we experience in a genuine sense; at most we are always just 'there alongside'" (ibid.)—this strong claim has no certainty to recommend its truth. Who would wish to proclaim to a Christian who believes that Christ died on her behalf, and who may be willing to die on behalf of that belief (Perpetua, for instance), that Christ's death "is not something which we experience in a genuine sense"? When the Argentine mother declares that the day her son was kidnapped her "life ended," who would presume to tell her that she is deceived, that death is intransitive and nonrelational? Priam's grief-stricken behavior shows with epic sublimity that a father may die along with his son, if not biologically then existentially. My purpose here is not to confute or correct Heidegger's ontology of guilt but to reconceive its truth in light of such certainties. My death pertains to others before it pertains to me. We hand our deaths over to one another, not because we are inauthentic but because we are mortal; not because of conventional obligations the fulfillment of which cost Antigone her life, but because our bonds and obligations draw their life from primordial guilt, understood now as the mortality of needs, or needs of mortality, that relate me both to neighbor and predecessor.

Whether one is a Christian believer or not, Christ's death on the cross offers an image of what it means to be primordially guilty in this reconceived sense. That so many people over the past two millennia have believed that they live and die through Christ's life and death is evidence enough that his death belonged to anyone but himself. Christ's death was handed over to others, not in the form of a corpse but, as we have seen, in the form of an opening onto the afterlife. To be a Christian means first and foremost to become the caretaker of that afterlife. While the transhumanity of Christ remains a matter of faith, his humanity is a matter of record. Christ was not human because he owed himself to his death. He was human because he owed his death to the world.

If guilt is radically relational—if it in fact underlies the relations I maintain with both neighbor and predecessor—it is because it throws me into, and keeps me bound by, my need for help. The need both to give and receive help belongs to Dasein's essence, as it were. To speak with Vico (who was no Hobbesian), the need for help is the basic condition without which families, cities, and commonwealths would not have come into being. That need does *not* devolve from some intrinsic privation or lack in human nature. On the contrary, it devolves from the generosity of humanity itself—a generosity that puts us at the disposal of others and that, through the *ingenium* of the human mind, generates the social world. Humanity means mortality. Mortality in turn means that we repossess ourselves only in giving ourselves. For even receiving help is a mode of self-giving, just as the refusal of help is, or can be, a failure of generosity. Whether we receive help or give help, we share in the world-engendering generosity that flows from the sources of primordial guilt.

Whereas Heidegger focused on the existential grounds of guilt, Vico approached the generosity in question through its historical and institutional manifestations. Vico's merit, at least as far as this study is concerned, is that he reminds us how that generosity is above all a transgenerational giving and receiving between the dead and the living. The dead, who in effect set up their dominion in human guilt, do not only need our help to sustain their afterlives, they also provide us with help from beyond the grave. The contract between the living and the dead has traditionally been one of mutual indebtedness, for reasons that Vico probes and that I, in his wake, have sought to clarify. The dead depend on the living to preserve their authority, heed their concerns, and keep them going in their afterlives. In return, they help us to know ourselves, give form to our lives, organize our social relations, and restrain our destructive impulses. They provide us with the counsel needed to maintain the institutional order, of which they remain the authors, and prevent it from degenerating into a bestial barbarism. The dead are our guardians. We give them a future so that they may give us a past. We help them live on so that they may help us go forward.

Dante came to understand this mutual reliance when, at the midpoint of his life, he found himself in an aggravated state of guilt, in need of help. We know that the midpoint crisis of one's life, or of one's history, or of one's nation, can occur anywhere along the way. It is when one goes astray, reaches an impasse, or succumbs to an immobilizing despair. There are moments of helplessness that cannot be overcome on one's own, nor through the succor of one's friends and neighbors, whether one be an individual or an entire community. They are moments that call for help from the dead. In Dante's case help came in the guise of Virgil, an adopted ancestor whose afterlife he had sustained through devotion and long study. It was Virgil's guidance, by Dante's admission, that led him back into the light, and beyond.

Whether one shares Dante's belief that the dead all finally belong to God's jurisdiction, the fact remains that in such moments, when all possible paths seem blocked off, it is the dead, if they are well disposed, who come forward to show a way. At times such aid is not forthcoming from them, to be sure; at other times it is rejected, polemically and angrily; sometimes it is passed over by its intended beneficiaries, unrecognized for what it is; at yet other times, the help offered calls for a reciprocative rejoinder. Yet one way or another, we cannot do with it. The primary reason why the dead have an afterlife in so many human cultures is because it falls upon them—the dead—to come to the rescue and provide counsel when that debilitating darkness falls. Why this special authority? Because the dead possess a nocturnal vision that the living cannot acquire. The light in which we carry on our secular lives blinds us to certain insights. Some truths are glimpsed only in the dark. That is why in moments of extreme need one must turn to those who can see through the gloom.

NOTES

For each chapter there is a separate bibliographical entry. The secondary works cited here represent only a portion of the relevant bibliography, to be sure, yet I have included only those that were directly pertinent, useful, or inspiring to me during the course of my research. Unless otherwise indicated, all translations in the chapters and notes are mine.

1. The Earth and Its Dead

What we have learned recently about the antiquity of the earth and of the universe itself has so dwarfed the temporal life span of the human species, to say nothing of the span of human history, that we can no longer speak here of adjusting our scales of duration. We must speak instead of the crisis of scale as a whole, of the ultimate impossibility of fathoming, from a human point of view, the depths of geological time as such. This is what I take Stephen Jay Gould to be saying when he argues for the revolutionary importance of the discovery of geological or "deep" time, and of the mind's need for extravagant metaphors of comparison to comprehend its vastness (see *Time's Arrow, Time's Cycle*). While the imagination finds metaphors that help us approximate the fractional nature of humanity's duration, it also reveals the ultimate inadequacy—or, better, unreality—of those same metaphors. It is precisely such a tension (and interchangeability) between the real and unreal that informs the poetic testaments discussed in this chapter. For a broader historical survey of changing conceptions of geological time, see Claude C. Albritton Jr., *The Abyss of Time*. For a detailed study of the scientific process leading to the discovery of geological time, see Joe D. Burchfield, *Lord Kelvin and the Age of the Earth*. For an analysis of the impact of the discovery of geological time on human conceptions of the earth's solidity and changelessness, see James Lawrence Powell, *Mysteries of Terra Firma*.

The Wordsworth verses come from the poem "A Slumber Did My Spirit Seal," in *Selected Poetry of William Wordsworth*, p. 150.

For a broad historical discussion of the changing status of ruins in the Western imagination as a privileged site for examining the relationship between art, or human intention, and nature, or forces of disintegration, see Paul Zucker, *Fascination of Decay*. For an overview of Western apocalyptic theories, see Eugene Weber, *Apocalypses: Prophecies, Cults, and Millennial Beliefs through the Ages*. For a wide range of global apocalyptic visions, see *Imagining the End*, ed. Abbas Amanat and Magnus T. Bernhardsson. For an excellent survey of the apocalypse as represented in its various guises in Western art, see Nancy Grubb, *Revelations*.

Quotations from the Bible, in this chapter and others, are mostly from *The New Oxford Annotated Bible*, although every now and then, for strategic or historical purposes (as for example the famous Pauline definition of faith as the "substance of things hoped for and the evidence of things unseen"), I cite from the King James Version.

For a treatment of nature and death in Swinburne's "A Forsaken Garden," see Michael A. Joyner, "Of Time and the Garden." Murray G. H. Pittock discusses Swinburne's use of the sea as an agent of transience symbolizing the changes wrought by time in "Swinburne and the 'Nineties" (see esp. p. 127 on "A Forsaken Garden"). In *Swinburne*, David G. Riede analyzes the apocalyptic tone of "A Forsaken Garden" as counterbalanced by some of the more optimistic verses in *Poems and Ballads* (see pp. 134–35). Swinburne's own poetics and especially his desire to translate the rhythms and music of nature in his lyric poetry is discussed in Thomas E. Connolly, *Swinburne's Theory of Poetry*, esp. pp. 64–80. Yopie Prins relates Swinburne's frequent use of anapest to the poet's self-flagellation (*Victorian Sappho*, pp. 112–73).

For brief discussions of the role of the sea in Moore's poetry, see Bonnie Costello, *Marianne Moore* (p. 74); Bernard F. Engle, *Marianne Moore* (67); and George W. Nitchie, *Marianne Moore: An Introduction to the Poetry* (104). Pamela White Hadas gives a more extensive analysis of the multiple valences of the sea for Moore in *Marianne Moore: Poet of Affection*. For an interesting attempt to read "A Grave" as rhythmically scanning Moore's experience of the sea, see Jerrald Ranta, "Marianne Moore's Sea and the Sentence." For a discussion of the importance of religion in Moore's vision of nature, see Guy Rotella, *Reading and Writing Nature*, pp. 141–86.

The best commentary on Eleanor Wilner's poem "Reading the Bible Backwards" comes from the author herself. Shortly before *The Dominion of the Dead* went to press I sent this chapter to Wilner (whom I have never met) and received a remarkable response, too long to cite in its entirety but reproduced in part here with her permission:

> I found your discussion of my poem revelatory, especially where you say that it "describes . . . a redemption, not of history but of nature," making of human history (I loved this) "a natural disaster," and exposing, too, the inevitable contradiction of human words being the medium of such a message. . . . Above all, bless you for saying (what for me is an accurate saying, insofar as I am aware of the poem's deepest intention and implicit admonition) that the poem's sympathy with the flood's elemental, planetary will "is of course deeply human in its impulse insofar as it turns against the impulse of history." I thought of something you said early in the chapter, in relation to the discussion of spatialization vs. temporal flow—"unlike music and poetry, whose rhythms participate in, arise out of, or echo the flow itself." I wonder if this imaginative sympathy with the dissolving waves of the ocean, this rise and fall so like the systole and diastole of our living beings, is not at the heart of the poetic imagination's formalism, and whether there is not a subversively anti-inscriptional power at work in the very forms of our inscription. So that we can feel, with Conrad (what a chilling and memorable piece that is!) the "Behold!" of the captain as the sea claims his ship in one "overwhelming heave of its silky surface." "And then the effort subsided. It was all over, and the smooth swell ran on as before from the horizon in uninterrupted cadence of motion." And yet I think, and wonder, as I share the dread and horror he expresses here, of how many lines of my own depict these obliterations as positively sweet, like my celebration of Charlotte Brontë's friend, the free-spirited Mary Taylor, who left no oeuvre, no plaque in Westminster Abbey—"no trace but a wide wake closing"; or Miriam, "who watched the Nile gape and shudder, / then heal its own green skin," and I wonder how far is the imagination on both sides of this: author of inscription, yet insistent on the sand in which that in-

scription takes place, a faculty connected to both the act of inscribing and the wind that blows the inscription away.

For Wilner's celebration of Mary Taylor, see the poem "Emigration" in *Reversing the Spell* (p. 215); for her celebration of Miriam, see "Miriam's Song" in the same volume (pp. 158–59).

Freud discusses the death drive in *Beyond the Pleasure Principle* as well as *Civilization and Its Discontents*. Lacan powerfully expands the Freudian concept in various of his writings, in particular *The Ethics of Psychoanalysis*, pp. 87–100 and 166–216; and *The Four Fundamental Concepts of Psychoanalysis*, pp. 161–202. For a thorough explanation and discussion of the death drive in psychoanalytic theory, see Dominique Poissonier, *La Pulsion de mort de Freud à Lacan*. For an interesting analysis of psychoanalytic theory as itself proof of the power of the death drive in its continuing existence despite, or because of, predictions of its death, see Todd Dufresne, *Tales from the Freudian Crypt*.

On Conrad's sea career, see Jerry Allen, *The Sea Years of Joseph Conrad*. On the possible genesis of Conrad's interest in the sea as inspired by his father's translation of Hugo's *Travailleurs de la mer*, see John Batchelor, *The Life of Joseph Conrad*, p. 6. Batchelor also discusses at length Conrad's memorializing process in his life as a writer subsequent to his sea years.

The exact source of Keats's epitaph has been much discussed (even in the London *Times* of June and July 1972), and no final conclusion has been reached or agreed on by scholars. The notion of "writing in water" or "on water" is found in Beaumont and Fletcher's *Philaster*, in Shakespeare's *Henry VIII* (4.2), in Donne's Elegy XV, lines 9–11, and elsewhere. The expression *graphein eis (h)udor* or *graphein en (h)udati* appears to be a proverbial expression in ancient Greek, handed down to English literature by way of the *Phaedrus* (276c) or as quoted in Catullus (70). The parallel Greek phrase, *graphein eis tephran*, "to write in ashes or dust," has significantly not found as wide a resonance. See Hyder Rollins, *The Keats Circle*, 2:91 n. 72; Jack Stillinger, ed., *The Letters of Charles Armitage Brown*, p. 91, n. 5; Oonagh Lahr, "Greek Sources of 'Writ in Water'"; and A. J. Woodman, "Greek Sources of 'Writ in Water': A Further Note."

2. Hic Jacet

An earlier version of this chapter appeared as "Hic Jacet" in *Critical Inquiry* 27 (spring 2001): 393–407, reprinted in *Landscape and Power*, ed. W. T. Mitchell, 349–64. Copyright © 2001 by The University of Chicago. All rights reserved. Many thanks to the university for permission to reprint it.

An English translation of Heidegger's interview with *Der Spiegel* can be found in Thomas Sheehan, ed., *Heidegger*, pp. 42–57.

The full quotation from Frank Lloyd Wright alluded to in the first paragraph of the chapter reads: "When *unfolding* architecture as distinguished from *enfolding* architecture comes to America there will be truth of feature related to truth of being" (*An American Architecture*, p. 256). I discuss unfolding and enfolding architecture, as Wright conceived of that difference, in *Forests*, pp. 232–38.

The following titles represent only a small portion of the literature on place, but they are the ones that I have consulted and benefited from the most: Karsten Harries, *The Ethical Function of Architecture;* Edward S. Casey, *The Fate of Place;* David Kolb, *Postmodern Sophistications;* Kenneth Frampton, "Toward a Critical Regionalism"; Massimo Cacciari, *Architecture and Nihilism;* and Manfredo Tafuri, *The Sphere and the Labyrinth*.

The Adolf Loos quotation comes from "Architektur" (1910), cited in Ludwig Münz and Gustave Künstler, *Adolf Loos*, p. 192.

The standard Greek etymological reference, *Dictionnaire étymologique de la langue grecque* by Pierre Chantraine, defines *sema* as "tout ce qui constitue un signe, un signal, une marque, un signe de reconnaissance, un signe envoyé par les dieux, emblème d'un bouclier, ce qui indique la présence de la mort, tumulus, monument funéraire (Hom., ion-att., etc.)." Its etymology, Chantraine remarks, remains obscure. Etymologists do not typically see a parentage between the words *sema* and *soma*, yet as far back as the Orphic poets and the Pythagorean philosophers the near homophony was played on in the classic dictum "soma/sema," or "the body is a grave." Plato mentions it in the *Gorgias* (493a), and in the *Cratylus* (400bc) Socrates plays on the phonic similarity, as well as on the ambiguity between "sign" and "grave" in the word *sema* (see Plato, *Complete Works*, pp. 836 and 118–19). The consonance has been remarked and expounded by many others, notably Jacques Derrida (see esp. "Speech and Writing according to Hegel," pp. 455–77). Chantraine notes that in the Homeric epics *soma* is only used for a dead body, a corpse. It is not until later that the word becomes generally used to indicate a body, either dead or living.

For an extended discussion of A. R. Ammons's remarkable poem, "Tombstones," from his collection *Sumerian Vistas*, see my essay "Tombstones."

When I declare that Stevens's jar "embodies the mortality of whoever forged it," I place the word *embodies* within quotation marks by way of allusion to the short essay by Heidegger, "Art and Space," in which Heidegger claims that sculpture, even more primordially than architecture, "embodies" places *(Verkörperung)* by "localizing" space and "figuring" the site of human habitation. Heidegger's remarks are typically abstract, however, with little anthropological grounding. By contrast, Michel Serres offers a powerful philosophical anthropology of the ancient statue's embodying power in *Statues*.

For an extensive philological reconstruction of the early domestic religions of the Indo-Europeans, see Numa Denis Fustel de Coulanges, *The Ancient City*. Fustel de Coulanges, who boasted of having read every word of every Greek and Latin text that had reached his age from antiquity, based his reconstruction on the textual traces of antecedent religious practices preserved in those ancient texts—most of which postdate by several centuries, if not millennia, the time when the primitive religions reconstructed by him came into being. Nietzsche once remarked that humankind rarely produces a good book. While I do not share that view—on the contrary, it is astonishing just how many good books humankind produces year in and year out, including one or two by Nietzsche himself—there is no doubt whatsoever that *The Ancient City* is a good book.

The question of why Oedipus's burial at Colonus should be a blessing for Athens remains a conundrum among scholars. For those who are interested in the issue, I offer the following extended review of what I managed to learn from my research. The standard view, as expressed, for instance, in Grene's introduction to the *Theban Plays* is that *Oedipus at Colonus* emphasizes Oedipus's innocence of intention with regard to the crimes he committed. His posthumous assistance to the keeper of his grave would then be a kind of reward from the gods for the suffering he had to endure in his lifetime. This is unsatisfying on a number of levels. First, there are indications even in *Oedipus at Colonus* and certainly in *Oedipus the King* that Oedipus was not entirely free from guilt in the parricide or incest. Second, it doesn't address the question of why the gods would choose this specific "reward" for him. Most commentators stress the importance of the timing of the play. It was probably written in 406 BC, toward the end of the Peloponnesian War and after the democratic experiment in Athens had been significantly undermined by the oligarchic regime imposed by the League, and so forth. Making Oedipus a kind of warrior-hero for Athens would thus be a way of foregrounding or bolstering the city's importance at a time when it seemed likely to be going under. If the play is doing such a thing, however, it is only very obliquely. Hence commentators do not agree on whether it is an apology for democratic Athens just by boosting that city's image (Edmunds); a critique of democracy in the authoritarian figure of Theseus (Mills); or a general lament for the lost greatness of Athens (Knox).

The issue becomes more interesting when one looks at the history of the Oedipus legend. The earliest epic versions have Oedipus dying in Thebes. Soon thereafter follow local versions in which he is exiled. Sophocles appears to have been the first to have him buried at Colonus, and to have that burial be a source of blessing (although Euripides' *Phoenissae* of 409 does have him exiled and buried at Colonus, it appears that the burial at Colonus, if not indeed the exile, is the work of a later interpolator). There is slight evidence in a fragment of Androtion, a fourth-century Atthidographer, of a variant in which Oedipus ended his days in Attica and was buried there, but his resting place was kept secret because he was afraid that the Thebans would mistreat his corpse if they knew where to find it. None of these traditions give his grave as a source of benefit.

Directly relevant to the reflections put forward in this chapter is the widespread tradition of the hero cult, very ancient in nature, in which the bones of a hero were thought to confer power on an enemy if he managed to carry them off. In order to prevent such raids, heroes' graves were often guarded or their actual locations kept secret. (Spartans brought home bones of Orestes from Tegea; the graves of Sisyphus and Neleus were secret and the location known only to a single hipparch.) Still, this does not explain why Oedipus receives a hero's welcome, as it were, from the Athenians.

The most interesting possibility involves a different local tradition in which Oedipus was buried at Eteonos. The Alexandrian Lysimachus writes:

> When Oedipus died, his friends thought to bury him in Thebes. But the Thebans, holding that he was an impious person on account of the misfortunes which had befallen him in earlier times, prevented them from so doing. They carried him therefore to a certain place in Boeotia called Keos and buried him there. But the inhabitants of this village, being visited with sundry misfortunes, attributed them to the burying of Oedipus and bade his friends remove him from their land. The friends, perplexed by these occurrences, took him up and brought him to Eteonos. Wishing to bury him secretly, they interred him by night in the sanctuary of Demeter—for they did not know the locality. When the facts transpired, the inhabitants of Eteonos asked the god what they should do. The god bade them not to move the suppliant of the goddess. So Oedipus is buried there and the sanctuary is called Oeidipodeion. (FGrH 382F2)

In other words, Oedipus's grave would have become sacred only because of his accidental burial in sacred ground. This seems like a likely parallel to the suppliant Oedipus in *Oedipus at Colonus*. Sophocles would then have recoded this newly beneficial grave into a fundamental aspect of the Oedipus myth in order to confer a kind of aura on Athens. (All of the above from Lowell Edmunds, *Theatrical Space and Historical Place in Sophocles's "Oedipus at Colonus."*)

The suppliant to the Eumenides aspect is important for other critics as well. For Roger Travis (*Allegory and the Tragic Chorus in Sophocles' "Oedipus at Colonus"*) their "chthonic power" changes Oedipus's *phusis* and puts him in a new relationship to his family and to the earth. Travis's thesis is that *Oedipus at Colonus* fuses the hero cult with religion and politics, and that the Eumenides provide the nexus for this to happen.

For Sophie Mills, on the other hand (*Theseus, Tragedy and the Athenian Empire*), the Eumenides personify what Sophocles is trying to emphasize in his encomium to Athens. She writes:

> In his frightening aspect, combined with the ability to reward respect and acceptance by the community with protection for the community, [Oedipus] resembles the Erinyes, who were welcomed into Aeschylus' Athens as Eumenides over fifty years earlier. In Aeschylus' *Eumenides,* the virtue and courage of Athens turned the potentially dangerous powers of the Erinyes to keeping Athens safe: they may have retained this function in Sophocles, and it may be that Sophocles had Aeschylus' play in mid as a background for the reception of Oedipus. (p. 167)

In short, the Eumenides are also obviously associated with a kind of terrible justice, which could well be a way of transmogrifying Oedipus's awfulness into a positive feature.

Finally, Joseph P. Wilson (*The Hero and the City*) focuses on Oedipus's stature as a hero. For him, the gods have singled Oedipus out, and therefore he gets to be special even though he commits terrible crimes—and so retains that heroic power with a positive valence after death. However, he can never approximate normal humanity, so he must always be associated with liminality. Thus Colonus, as a sacred site contingent to but not actually in Athens. Wilson also points out that Colonus is the site of entry into the underworld (liminal again), where Theseus and Peirithous went in their botched attempt at the rape of Persephone. (Sophocles notes this at 1593–94.) And with that I conclude this extended review, the result of which, I think it is fair to say, is that we still have no clear or compelling idea why Oedipus's burial at Colonus should provide a source of blessing for the city of Athens. It is only fitting perhaps that it should remain a riddle.

The Pirandello novella about the Sicilian baron who refuses to allow his peasants to bury their dead on his land is "Requiem aeternam dona eis, Domine!" in *Novelle per un anno*, pp. 559–66.

About Bedouin burial practices, Shirley Kay, in her study *The Bedouin*, declares:

> Those who . . . die in the desert, are buried the day they die in shallow graves marked by a stone at head and foot. Children's graves are marked by a small oval of stones. . . . The bedouin are buried in a shirt or a white shroud, and laid in the grave with their faces towards Mecca. Women are buried in deeper graves than men so that, should they ever rise in the grave, their breasts would still be covered by the earth. If there are hyenas about, rocks may be piled over the grave. Only the closest women relatives may weep for the dead. That evening, or on the evening of the third day after, a sheep may be sacrificed. The grave will probably not be visited again. (pp. 31–32)

The numerals in my citations from Vico's *New Science,* here and elsewhere, refer to paragraph sections, not page numbers. I discuss §531 of the *New Science* from another point of view in my *Forests*, pp. 7–8.

For a directly relevant discussion of how the intersections of geography, ideology, and history give rise to what he calls "holy landscapes," see W. J. T. Mitchell's "Holy Landscape." At the end of his essay Mitchell refers to the "fantasies of the destiny of Judaism as the possession of a physical place, rather than as an ideal of universal human value. This fantasy has now been realized in an idolatry of place, a territorial mysticism enforced by bullets and bulldozers. The charge is to sound out this idolatry, to unbind its fascination" (p. 223). From the point of view of this chapter, the challenge is to avoid the idolatry of place, wherever it may occur, while at the same time holding on to the placehood of place. It is to be hoped that these two objectives are not incompatible.

In *Heidegger's Confrontation with Modernity* Michael E. Zimmerman sets out a nuanced view of Heidegger's position against technology as a "mode of understanding or disclosing things," sympathetically tracing through Heidegger's writings the systematic opposition to a technological, or modern, worldview, while at the same time showing how Heidegger was himself influenced by the reactionary German cultural criticism of his times.

In certain superficial ways this chapter as a whole sympathizes with Ugo Foscolo's apology for the memorial power of the grave in his famous poem "Dei Sepolcri" (in *Opere*, pp. 25–32). In more profound ways, however, its concerns have little to do with Foscolo's meditations in that poem. In general I am less interested in the sepulcher's relation to, its activation of, or its inspirational effects on, social and cultural memory than I am in its place-founding and world-creating power—a power that, if I am right, operates at a level that is at once below and beyond the reach of the memorializing gesture. Foscolo's modern-Romantic exaltation of the grave's heroic testamental value in the public sphere cannot help us when it comes to Oedipus's grave, for example, whose location remains a secret yet whose blessing continues to operate within its immediate and near vicinity. It is the *sema*'s power of mortalization, not the posthumous sepulchral or semiotic "immortality" it may provide in the memory of those who live on, which engages me above all in this chapter. For an English version of Foscolo's poem see Foscolo, *On Sepulchres.* Foscolo's poem has been the object of many critical studies, among them Spartaco Gamberini, *Analisi dei "Sepolcri" foscoliani;* Tom O'Neill, *Of Virgin Muses and of Love;* Oreste Macrì, *Semantica e metrica dei Sepolcri del Foscolo;* and Gioacchino Paparelli, *Ugo Foscolo.*

3. What Is a House?

An earlier version of this chapter appeared as "What Is a House?" in *Terra Nova* 1, no. 2 (spring 1996): 17–26. Copyright © 1996 by the Massachusetts Institute of Technology. Many thanks to MIT Press Journals for permission to reprint it.

For a synthetic critical discussion of Heidegger's presumably nonmetaphorical characterization of language as the "house of Being," see Robert Henri Cousineau, *Humanism and Ethics;* see also Joseph J. Kockelmans, ed., *On Heidegger and Language,* esp. Otto Pöggler, "Heidegger's Topology of Being," pp. 107–46. For a recent study covering broad questions of language and human existence in Heidegger, see Abraham Mansbach, *Beyond Subjectivism.* For a probing analysis of Heidegger's views on modern homelessness, see Julian Young, "What Is Dwelling?"

A full description of how the *lares* and *penates* functioned within the overall religious system of ancient Rome is contained in Robert Turcan, *The Gods of Ancient Rome,* esp. pp. 14–50. For a classic interpretation of the social purpose of the *lares,* see Georges Dumézil, *La Religion romaine archaïque,* esp. pp. 335–40.

I would not want to commit myself to the empirical assertion that there is no such thing as a house without windows, since no doubt someone could always come forward with an example that falsifies it; nevertheless, exceptions to that rule—if they do indeed exist—have little bearing on the meditation I am proposing here. So let me phrase my claim in these terms: a house without windows or windowlike openings is not a house as I understand it. For what it is worth, the *Encyclopaedia Brittanica* states: "Windows are a very ancient invention, probably coincident with the development of fixed and enclosed houses," citing representations of windows in ancient Egyptian and Assyrian art. (*The New Encyclopaedia Britannica*, 15th ed., s.v. "window").

In *The First House* R. D. Dripps offers an extended and very interesting meditation on the first theorist of the house, Vitruvius, whose ancient treatise *Ten Books of Architecture* describes mankind's building of houses as inextricably intertwined with his awareness of dwelling in the world, a notion Dripps sees as fundamental for revitalizing architectural philosophy. On the house as the foundational structure protecting and allowing daydreaming and thus imagination, see Gaston Bachelard, *Poetics of Space*. In *Architecture and Nihilism* Massimo Cacciari offers a compelling discussion of modernist architectural reflections on the nature and role of dwellings, and of the relation of such architectural theory to modernist literature and philosophy.

On Thoreau's treatment of dwelling and architecture, and his attempt to conceive the necessities of the latter on the basis of the demands of the former, see W. Barksdale Maynard, "Thoreau's House at Walden"; also, Elsie Leach, "Building One's Own House." For a reading of Thoreau's *Walden* project in relation to nineteenth-century paradigms of domesticity, see Cecelia Tichi, "Domesticity on Walden Pond." Regarding Thoreau's relation to and reappropriation of the classics, see the thorough discussion of Ethel Seybold in *Thoreau: The Quest and the Classics;* and Robert D. Richardson Jr. in *Henry Thoreau: A Life of the Mind*. For a comprehensive analysis and bibliography of Thoreau's sources, see Robert Sattelmeyer, *Thoreau's Reading*. On Thoreau's relation to classical genres, see Linck C. Johnson, "Revolution and Renewal." Stanley Cavell's *Senses of Walden* remains for me the most inspiring meditation on Thoreau's literary project as a whole in *Walden*, with profound insights into his use and "retrieval" of the classics as well as Judeo-Christian Scriptures. Cavell also discusses the various ghosts that Thoreau brought with him to Walden, especially those of his Puritan forebears.

In *Demons, Dreamers, and Madmen* Harry G. Frankfurt draws attention to Descartes's fire in the First Meditation, suggesting that the presence of the fire (as Descartes describes it) indicates that Descartes does not dismiss outright all sensory perception (p. 36). While this may be true, I wonder whether we must take the fire as belonging solely to the sensory, external world, or take it rather as the symbol or externalized figure (perhaps even the "objective correlative") of that intimate psychic life of the meditating mind. In that case the fire in fact creates a calorific intimacy that is at once internal and external in nature (like the house in the closure of its walls and openness of its windows). Michel Foucault offers a brief analysis of the First Meditation in *Histoire de la folie* (pp. 56–59, not included in the abridged English translation)—an analysis that drew critical attention from Jacques Derrida in his essay "Cogito and the History of Madness" (in *Writing and Difference*, pp. 31–63.) For Foucault the fire is evidence that the force of the senses' illusions "laisse toujours un résidu de vérité." Its presence adds to the meditation's entire domestic scene of bourgeois security, which not by chance (Foucault suggests) serves as the scene of a systematic doubting that in the final analysis never doubts the essential soundness (i.e., nonmadness) of the doubting mind. Derrida's response to Foucault, in which Derrida presumed to instruct his one-time teacher about the "hyperbolic" drive of philosophy itself, deserved, in my opinion, the demolition visited upon it by Foucault in an appendix to the 1972 edition of *Folie et déraison* (pp. 583–603). The appendix, entitled "Mon corps, ce papier, ce feu," was removed from subsequent editions.

On homelessness, alienation, and nihilism in *The Notebooks of Malte Laurids Brigge* see Thomas J. Harrison, *1910*, pp. 108–17 (pp. 111–12 for a discussion of the demolished wall passage in particular). See also Walter H. Sokel, "The Devolution of the Self in *The Notebooks of Malte Laurids Brigge*"; and Sokel, "The Blackening of the Breast." For an interesting and, from the perspective of this chapter, very relevant analysis of the anguish of being outside walls in Rilke's *Malte*, see Christian Doumet, "Malte devant les parois." Less directly relevant, but essential nonetheless, are the pages devoted to Rilke and anguish by Maurice Blanchot in *Faux Pas*, pp. 47–52.

For a thorough analysis of the *Duino Elegies* see Kathleen L. Komar, *Transcending Angels* (on the Ninth Elegy and the question of the earth and sayability, see pp. 155–68). In *The Space of Literature* Maurice Blanchot meditates on Rilke's notion of transmutation and metamorphosis in their relation both to death and poetry (pp. 120–60). On the relationship to death in general in the *Duino Elegies*, see Torsten Pettersson, "Internalization and Death."

For a discussion of the coffin in *Moby Dick*, see William Rosenfeld, "Uncertain Faith." On nihilism in Melville generally, see Leon F. Seltzer, *The Vision of Melville and Conrad*, pp. 35–53; and Kingsley Widmer, *The Ways of Nihilism*.

4. The Voice of Grief

Ernesto De Martino's *Morte e pianto rituale* is the most probing, insightful, documented, and rigorous psycho-anthropological account of ritualized mourning practices that I know of. Its uniqueness, in my opinion, stems from a combination of factors, beginning with the extensive fieldwork the author undertook in Lucania at a time when, and a place where, it was still possible to observe firsthand various highly formal rituals, ceremonies, and lamentation chants whose origins receded into the Euro-Mediterranean night of time, as it were, and whose basic forms had persisted relatively unchanged since antiquity. Yet De Martino was not only an ethnographer. He was also a classicist, a philologist, and a psychologist well versed in contemporary theories of trauma, panic, and psychosis. Above all he was also a philosopher who had an exceptional capacity to theorize his empirical findings on the basis of a broad, ontological conception of human being: a conception influenced in part by Heidegger's existentialism and in part by Croce's Hegelian-based psychological idealism (De Martino's work as a whole was indebted to but in no way derivative of these influences). The result of this unusual (I would say Vichian) admixture is an astonishingly original book that offers a comprehensive philosophical anthropology and/or psychology of ritualized mourning.

As far as I know, *Morte e pianto rituale* is available only in Italian. It certainly deserves to be widely translated even now, five decades after its publication. Indeed, the book only gains in importance, in my opinion, by the fact that its thesis about the depersonalizing, objectifying drive of mourning rituals adds De Martino's voice to a chorus of theorists and anthropologists (Radcliffe-Brown, Langer, Levi-Strauss, Bloch, Moore and Myerhoff, Tambiah, and many others) who in the past several decades have stressed the distancing, performative aspects of ritual and ceremony in general. Suzanne Langer, for example, remarks that, far from being a "free expression of emotions," ritual is a diligent performance—"not a sign of the emotion it conveys but a symbol of it" (*Philosophy in a New Key*, p. 123, quoted by Stanley Jeyraja Tambiah, *Culture, Thought and Social Action*, p. 133). The distinction, so pertinent to

De Martino's work, is an important one. An emotion is symbolized when its psychic content is objectified in "formalized gestures" that distance the actors from the spontaneity of the feelings they "denote" through ritualized enactment. Taking up Langer's theories in his work on the performative dimensions of ritual, Tambiah states that the distancing mechanism of ritual "separates the private emotions of the actors from their commitment to a public morality" (*Culture, Thought and Social Action*, p. 133). For De Martino mourning rituals involve precisely such a separation, in the sense that their performative protocols get the griever to recommit himself or herself to the world of the living instead of dying (inwardly) with the dead. The "separation of the private emotions" marks the first stage in the process of separation from the deceased. The formal articulation of emotion—what Langer calls the ritualistic "denotation of feeling" as opposed to its natural expression—is where grief's work of objectification, for De Martino, begins.

For an overview of theories of mourning with a comprehensive bibliography on the subject, see John S. Stephenson, *Death, Grief, and Mourning*. For a classic, comprehensive anthropological treatment of mourning rituals, see Peter Metcalf and Richard Huntington, *Celebrations of Death*. See also Jean-Pierre Mohen, *Les Rites de l'au-delà*. For a comprehensive psychological study of mourning in different cultures, see Paul C. Rosenblatt, R. Patricia Walsh, and Douglas A. Jackson, *Grief and Mourning in Cross-Cultural Perspective*. For a psychoanalytically informed discussion of the mourning process in relation to the love-object as represented in literature throughout history, see Henry Staten, *Eros in Mourning*. For an examination of the importance of mourning ritual in literature, see Susan Letzler Cole, *The Absent One*. For a feminist analysis of mourning and lamentation in Greek culture and literature, see Gail Holst-Warhaft, *Dangerous Voices*. For an interesting recent analysis of bereavement as a historically conditioned process, see Sarah Tarlow, *Bereavement and Commemoration*. For a detailed archeological study of lamentation in ancient Egypt, but with relevant associations with the lamentations discussed in this chapter, see Marcelle Werbrouck, *Les Pleureuses dans l'Egypte ancienne*. I would mention, finally, two excellent studies on the work of mourning in the poetic text: *The English Elegy* by Peter M. Sacks, and *The Poetry of Mourning* by Jahan Ramazani.

For detailed studies of Rousseau's *On the Origin of Language*, see Dominique Bourdin, *Essai sur l' "Essai sur l'origine des langues" de Jean-Jacques Rousseau;* and André Wyss, *Jean-Jacques Rousseau*. On the question of music and language in Rousseau, see John T. Scott, "The Harmony between Rousseau's Musical Theory and His Philosophy"; and Ronald P. Bermingham, "Le Cri de la nature et la nature du cri." For philosophical discussions of Rousseau's linguistic theories, see for example Jean Starobinski, "Rousseau et l'origine des langues"; and Jacques Derrida, *Of Grammatology*, esp. pp. 165 ff.

While I do not deal with Johann Gottfried Herder's theories of the gestural and cantatory origins of language explicitly in this chapter, they are nevertheless directly relevant to the discussion. For a fine comparison of Herder and Vico on this score, see Jürgen Trabant's essay, "Parlare cantando." Along similar lines, see also John Ole Askedal, "Johann Gottfried Herder's Conception of the Origin of Language"; and Charles Taylor, *Philosophical Arguments*, pp. 79–99.

For an interesting study relating Vico's theories of the origin of language to current research in glottogenetics, or scientific theories of language origin, see Marcel Danesi, *Vico, Metaphor, and the Origin of Language*. On Vico's ideas of language origin, see Rosario Salamone, *Lingua e linguaggio nella filosofia di Giambattista Vico*. See also Roberto Maria Dianotto, "Vico's Beginnings and Ends"; Frank Nuessel, "Vico's Views on Language and Linguistics"; and Annabella d'Atri, "The Theory of Interjections in Vico and Rousseau."

(I would mention here that to speak of the cantatory origins of language means perforce to speak of the origins of poetry, as Vico reminds us time and again. Both can be traced, in a purely speculative manner, to mourning rituals. For Ernesto De Martino, rhythm and repetition—whether in the swaying and rocking of the body or in the lamentation chants themselves—figure as the most important elements when it comes to objectifying and mastering the chaotic impulse at the heart of grief through ritualized performance. Both rhythm and repetition give recursive measure to gesture and voice, allowing for an iterable communal participation. Thus it would hardly be farfetched to suggest that the meters, antiphonies, and alliterations of ancient poetry are at bottom the distillation of formal elements that first arose in the threnodies of archaic grief.)

The Hegel passage about how "every animal finds a voice in its violent death" and thereby "expresses itself as a sublated self" comes from Hegel's Philosophy of Nature lectures of 1805/6, which as far as I can tell have not been translated into English yet. Special thanks to Matthew Tiews for helping me with the German original. In *Hegel's Development*, H. S. Harris paraphrases the passage as follows: "Only in its self-expressive cries does the beast come to the boundary of really theoretical awareness (or so Hegel believes)" (p. 462); and then in a footnote Harris explains: "Hegel says that the animal facing violent death 'expresses itself as a sublated *Selbst*'" (p. 462 n. 3). Harris notes (p. 292 n. 3) that there are two places in Hegel's corpus where it is the death cry that epitomizes the "demand to be recognized": the quotation referenced above, and a quotation from *System of Ethical Life*, the extended version of which reads as follows:

> An animal's voice comes from its inmost point, or from its conceptual being, but like the whole animal, it belongs to feeling. Most animals scream at the danger of death, but this is purely and simply an outlet of subjectivity, something formal, of which the supreme articulation in the song of the birds is not the product of intelligence, of a preceding transformation of nature into subjectivity. The absolute solitude in which nature dwells inwardly at the level of intelligence is missing in the animal which has not withdrawn this solitude into itself. The animal does not produce its voice out of the totality contained in this solitude; its voice is empty, formal, void of totality. But the corporeality of speech displays totality resumed into individuality, the absolute entry into the absolute [monadic] point of the individual whose ideality is inwardly dispersed into a system. (pp. 115–16)

A fascinating discussion of how the human voice prolongs in its articulate speech the voice of the dying animal, with explicit reference to Hegel, can be found in Giorgio Agamben's *Language and Death*, pp. 44–47. While Agamben makes no deliberate connection between the human voice and grief, many of the claims put forward in this chapter sympathize with the links between language and death that he establishes in his book. Other claims of mine are of course at odds with his thesis, in the way they are at odds with Hegel's. For me it is in the objectified death of the other, not in the internalized nullity of the linguistic subject, that we must first look for the ground of the conjunction between language and death.

In the extended passage from *A System of Ethical Life* quoted above, Hegel declares that the "the supreme articulation in the song of the birds is not the product of intelligence, of a preceding transformation of nature into subjectivity." Thanks in large part to the rise of evolutionary psychology, the question of the origin of language has received renewed attention in the last thirty years, much of the current research seeing birdsong as the closest animal parallel to human language in its incipient vocalizations. A small sampling of recent studies includes Michael C. Corballis, *From Hand to Mouth;* Alison Wray, ed., *The Transition to Language;* Robin Allott, *The Great Mosaic Eye;* Jean Atchison, *The Seeds of Speech;* and Derek Bickerton, *Language and Species.*

Susan Stewart's poem "O" comes from her new collection *Columbarium.* Copyright © 2003 by The University of Chicago. All rights reserved. I thank Susan Stewart and the University of Chicago Press for permission to reproduce it here.

5. *The Origin of Our Basic Words*

For the reconstructed Indo-European root of the Greek *logos* and the Latin *lex* I have relied on Calvert Watkins, *The American Heritage Dictionary of Indo-European Roots* (see the entry for *leg*-1, p. 47). For an overview of the literature on linguistic reconstruction, with a discussion of the history of the reconstruction of a putative Indo-European protolanguage, and positions taken for and against linguistic reconstruction, see Konrad Kerner, "Comments on Reconstructions in Historical Linguistics." For technical studies on the history and methodology of the reconstruction of Indo-European, see Frederick W. Schwink, *Linguistic Typology, Universality, and the Realism of Reconstruction* and the numerous perspectives collected in Edgar C. Polomé and Werner Winter, eds., *Reconstructing Languages and Cultures.*

On the connection between Ungaretti and Leopardi, see Joseph Cary's superb *Three Modern Italian Poets,* pp. 166–77 (my discussion of Ungaretti's inheritance of Leopardi and Petrarch is indebted to these pages); also, Franco Di Carlo, *Ungaretti e Leopardi.* On the temporality at work in Leopardi's poetics of the *parola,* see Margaret Brose's *Leopardi sublime,* esp. pp. 83–118.

The bibliography on Shakespeare's manipulation and reinvention of the English language is vast, much of it of interest primarily to specialists in historical linguistics. For a thorough, if somewhat technical, study of Shakespeare's linguistic environment and his contributions to it, with a comprehensive bibliography on the topic, see N. F. Blake, *A Grammar of Shakespeare's Language.* For a more accessible presentation of the same material, see his *Shakespeare's Language.* For an earlier study focusing on Shakespeare's mixing of registers and use of archaisms and neologisms, see Ifor Evans, *The Language of Shakespeare's Plays.* For an overview of different disciplinary perspectives on the question, see Vivian Salmon and Edwina Burness, eds., *A Reader in the Language of Shakespearean Drama.*

There are a great number of excellent introductions to, and more specialized studies of, Vico in English. Of the former variety, see, for example, the three vast interdisciplinary compendia of essays edited by Giorgio Tagliacozzo on various aspects of Vico's thought and influence. Peter Burke's *Vico* offers an excellent short overview of Vico's development and major aspects of his *New Science,* as does Thomas Bergin and Max Fisch's long introduction to their translation of Vico's *Autobiography* (pp. 1–107). The most probing book on Vico's career as a whole in recent years is, in my opinion, Giuseppe Mazzotta's *New Map of the World,* which at once places Vico in his historical and intellectual context and maps out his relevance to our own late-modern preoccupations with the vocation of knowledge, morality, and political theory. For another recent study of Vico's philosophy, see Gennaro Carillo's *Vico.*

On Vico and philology, see Erich Auerbach, "Vico et la philologie"; Robert A. Caponigri, "Filosofia et filologia: La 'nuova arte della critica' di Giambattista Vico"; René Wellek, "Auerbach and Vico"; and Donald R. Kelly, "Vico's Road: from Philology to Jurisprudence and Back". See also Gianfranco Cantelli, *Mente Corpo Linguaggio;* and Francesco Botturi, *Tempo Linguaggio e Azione.* For meditations on Vico and Heidegger, see Ernesto Grassi, *Vico and Humanism.* For an explication of his thought as grounded in the concept of imagination, see Luigi Pareyson, *L'estetica e I suoi problemi,* pp. 351–77; also, Donald Phillip Verene's excellent comprehensive study, *Vico's Science of Imagination;* also, Stefano Velotti, *Sapienti e bestioni* (esp. pp. 105–44), stressing how knowledge, for Vico, arises in and from ignorance by way of the imagination. For a discussion of Vico's philosophy in political context, see Antonino Pennisi, *La Linguistica dei Mercatanti.* See also the classic study of Vico and his role in intellectual history by Isaiah Berlin: *Vico and Herder;* and the equally classic study by Benedetto Croce, *La Filosofia di Giambattista Vico.*

On the "verum-factum" principle, see Rodolfo Mondolfo, *Il "Verum-Factum" Prima di Vico;* Robert C. Miner, "Verum-Factum and Practical Wisdom in the Early Writings of Giambattista Vico"; Donatella Di Cesare, "Verum, Factum, and Language"; James C. Morrison, "Vico's Principle of Verum in Factum and the Problem of Historicism"; Karl Lowith, "Verum et factum convertuntur"; and the excellent pages in L. M. Palmer's introduction to Vico's *On the Most Ancient Wisdom of the Italians,* esp. pp. 17–34. See also the following more general works on Vico with discussions of the principle: Enrico Nuzzo, *Tra ordine della storia e storicità;* Robert C. Miner, *Vico;* Richard Manson, *The Theory of Knowledge of Giambattista Vico;* Franceso Botturi, *La Sapienza della storia;* Paolo Rossi, *The Dark Abyss of Time;* Cecilia Miller, *Giambattista Vico;* and Paolo Cristofolini, *Vico et l'histoire.* Mark Lilla, in *G. B. Vico,* presents the principle in a slightly different light by focusing on Vico's earlier thought and his political philosophy as the foundation of his philosophy of history. The latter also offers an important perspective on Vico's unorthodox and, as it were, "politically incorrect" modernity.

The most lucid and compelling analysis of Heidegger's radically desecularizing and decontextualizing obsession with a few select Greek words is found in Glenn Most's recent article "Heidegger's Greeks." I thank Glenn Most for making this article available to me in manuscript prior to publication.

For an assortment of critical perspectives on Giorgio Caproni's oeuvre, including statements by Giuseppe de Robertis, Pier Palo Pasolini, Pietro Citati, Giorgio Agamben, and others, see Caproni, *Tutte le poesie,* pp. 981–1027.

6. Choosing Your Ancestor

On the place of death in Western thought generally, from the perspective of a history of ideas, see Jacques Choron's classic *Death and Western Thought* (the pages on Heidegger [230–40] are somewhat misleading, yet compelling nonetheless). The classic comprehensive treatment of the place of death in Heidegger's thought is still James M. Demske, *Being, Man & Death.* On Heidegger's view of death and its sources in Nietzsche's thought, see Sean Ireton, "Heidegger's Ontological Analysis of Death and Its Prefiguration in Nietzsche." Heidegger's ontological analysis of death has had an enormous influence on several French philosophers. Sartre, for instance, is critical of certain aspects of that analysis in *Being and Nothingness* (esp. pp. 531–53), yet his concept of nothingness is also thoroughly indebted to it. Albert Camus takes Heidegger's ontology of death as a point of departure in *The Myth of Sisyphus;* Alexandre Kojéve (a French philosopher by association) insinuates it into almost every page of his powerful existentializing interpretation of Hegel; Maurice Blanchot adopts it wholesale in *The Space of Literature,* making of literature the space of death as such, Heideggerianly understood; and Jean-Luc Nancy extends it into a sociopolitical sphere in *The Birth to Presence,* among other works. Among Italian thinkers, Giorgio Agamben, Gianni Vattimo, Massimo Cacciari, Mario Perniola, Vincenzo Vitiello, Carlo Sini, Marco Guzzi, and many others have also reappropriated Heidegger's ontology of death, as have many twentieth-century Italian poets, including Eugenio Montale, Andrea Zanzotto, Mario Luzzi, Giorgio Caproni, Nanni Cagnone, Fabrizio Falconi, and others.

On the topic of Heidegger and repetition, the most illuminating commentaries known to me are those of Thomas Sheehan, especially "Choosing One's Fate," which offers an in-depth explication-commentary on section 74 of *Being and Time;* see also Sheehan, "Heidegger's New Aspect" and "On the Way to *Ereignis.*" See also Charles Spinosa, "Derrida and Heidegger"; and E. M. Henning, "Destruction and Repetition." For a complex study on Heidegger, sketching out the consequences of his thinking on repetition and on responsibility, see David Wood, *Thinking after Heidegger.* For a broader meditation on our late- or postmodern relation to the historical past, as well as the various modes by which we in fact disinherit the past in the guise of revering it as "heritage," see Jeremy Tambling, *Becoming Posthumous.*

For an overview of the importance of the corpse through the ages and a taxonomy of the many rituals and responses it has elicited, see Christine Quigley, *The Corpse.*

In his 1915 essay "Thoughts for the Times on War and Death," Freud writes (as if in deliberate response to Heidegger's subsequent claims in *Being and Time*) the following: "It is indeed impossible to imagine our own death; and whenever we attempt to do so we can perceive that we are in fact still present as spectators. Hence the psycho-analytic school could venture on the assertion that at bottom no one believes in his own death, or, to put the same thing in another way, that in the unconscious every one of us is convinced of his own immortality" (p. 289). Carl Jung either inherited this same conviction from Freud or (as he claimed) arrived at it independently through his own clinical experience. In his 1934 essay "The Soul and Death," Jung writes: "In my rather long psychological experience I have observed a great many people whose unconscious psychic activity I was able to follow into the immediate presence of death. . . . On the whole, I was astonished to see how little ado the unconscious psyche makes of death. It would seem as though death were something relatively unimportant, or perhaps our psyche does not bother about what happens to the individual" (p. 411). Despite his sustained criticism of psychoanalysis, Sartre seems to have taken to heart Freud's remarks about the self's lack of any innate sense of its own death. In *Being and Nothingness* he writes (again, against Heidegger): "Thus death is in no way an ontological structure of my being, at least not in so far as my being is *for itself;* it is the Other who is mortal in his being. There is no place for death in being-for-itself; it can neither wait for death nor realize it nor project itself toward it; death is in no way a foundation of the finitude of the for-itself" (pp. 546–47). For a detailed discussion of Freud's views on death, see William Kerrigan, "Death and Anxiety."

For a book-length study on the underworld in epic poetry, see Ronald R. MacDonald, *The Burial-Places of Memory,* esp. pp. 17–56 on Virgil. On the underworld in Virgil as a commentary on the nature of Rome and Roman politics, see D. C. Feeney, "History and Revelation in Vergil's Underworld." Regarding the connections I seek to establish between the underworld, the anachronic matrix of the institutional order, and what Heidegger calls *das Nichte,* I would draw attention to Richard Polt's essay, "The Question of the Nothing," in which he traces the evolution of Heidegger's concept of the Nothing and argues that, for the later Heidegger, "the happening of

Be-ing brings with it the happening of Nothing, the tracing of a fragile frontier beyond which things can belong no more to the realm of the accessible and acceptable." It is that other realm, or what Polt calls "the shadows and enigmas of the frontier" (p. 82), that interests me here.

For a treatment of Heidegger's concept of the call of conscience and its relevance to his views on rhetoric, see Michael J. Hyde, "The Call of Conscience." Also, Karen S. Feldman's doctoral dissertation, "On Rhetoric, Performativity and the Example of Conscience in Hobbes, Leibniz, Hegel and Heidegger."

On Rimbaud's *Season in Hell* as a farewell to literature, see Maurice Blanchot, "Rimbaud et l'oeuvre final"; and Alain Coelho, *Arthur Rimbaud fin de la littérature*. Steve Murphy argues for a continuity between *Illuminations* and *Une saison en enfer* in "Une saison en enfer et les 'derniers vers' de Rimbaud" For a classic study on Rimbaud and particularly the relationship between the *Illuminations* and *Une saison en enfer*, with interesting reflections on the phenomenon of "depth" in the latter (in contrast with the former), see Jean-Pierre Richard, *Poésie et profondeur*, esp. pp. 189–250.

For a classic discussion of Baudelaire's literary affiliation with Poe, see editor W. T. Bandy's introduction to Baudelaire's *Edgar Allan Poe*, pp. xi–xlvi. For a theoretical argument on the reasons for Baudelaire's affinity with Poe, see Jonathan Culler, "Baudelaire and Poe." For a treatment of the question of Poe's effect on Baudelaire's poetic compositions, see Yves Bonnefoy, "La Septième Face du bruit."

7. Hic Non Est

For an excellent comprehensive study that puts Saint Perpetua in her social and historical context and offers a condensed account of the underground spread of Christian faith throughout the Roman Empire during the first and second centuries AD, see Joyce Salisbury's *Perpetua's Passion* (on the Dinocrates dream, see pp. 104–6). For a brilliant, more literary analysis of Perpetua's dream, see Peter Dronke's *Women Writers of the Middle Ages*, pp. 11–13.

Plinio Prioreschi offers a succinct and learned account of the changes that Christianity brought about in Western conceptions of death and the afterlife in *A History of Human Responses to Death*, esp. pp. 141–54. Prioreschi's encyclopedic compendium has been a useful reference for me throughout this book.

The secondary literature on Jesus' empty tomb and Resurrection is enormous and, for a nonspecialist, exceedingly daunting. The book I have benefited from the most, and with whose thesis I am most sympathetic, is Thomas Sheehan's *First Coming*. Among other things, Sheehan reminds us of the following: "Popular devotion and bad theology notwithstanding, Christians do not believe in the resurrection of Jesus *because* of the empty tomb. No matter how vigorously the church may proclaim the Easter stories found in the Gospels, she does not believe in what those stories say. She believes, rather, in what those stories *mean*. Saint Thomas Aquinas is clear on this point: The object of faith is not the words of a text but the divine reality they point to" (p. 163). It is to this reminder that I appeal when I declare: "Whether the historical Jesus was ever laid in a tomb or not is of little concern here. It is the *meaning* of the Easter story as it comes to us through the Gospels, and mediated through our own interpretation, that is of primary interest." I also share Sheehan's claim that the meaning of Easter lies in the breaking into history of the present-future of the kingdom—an event that I understand as inextricably linked to Catholicism's resacralization of the earth and its "dead matter."

Reginald Fuller recounts the development of the Resurrection stories in *The For-*

mation of the Resurrection Narratives. For an account of the Resurrection that emphasizes the events surrounding the empty tomb, see Willi Marxsen's foundational study *The Resurrection of Jesus of Nazareth;* also, Peter Walker, *The Weekend That Changed the World.* For a speculative meditation on the phenomenon of the empty tomb and the reactions of its discoverers, see Georges Haldas, *Mémoire et résurrection.* For an impressive synthesis of ancient epistemology and postmodern theology in a reading of the meanings of the empty tomb and the Resurrection, see Marianne Sawicki, *Seeing the Lord.* For a collection of essays situating the resurrection in its cultural and theological historical context, see Odette Mainville and Daniel Marguerat, eds., *Résurrection.* For a philosophical, deconstructive analysis of the empty tomb, see Gérard Bucher, *L'imagination de l'origine,* pp. 159–67, where he writes: "Mais le tombeau vide tient lieu surtout de *trace* de l'Absent. Comme pure 're-marque' de la disparition du Crucifié, il est *l'equivalent* de la lettre ou du text évangélique tout entier" (p. 164).

None of the sources I have consulted regarding the Pauline definition of faith as "the substance of things hoped for and the evidence of things unseen" make any explicit connection to the empty tomb, and perhaps for good reason: Paul seems to have known nothing about an empty tomb. Nevertheless, given that the Gospel stories were redacted in the wake of Paul's preaching, the connection is not simply arbitrary. For a classic discussion of the Pauline notion of faith in its sociotheological context, see William Henry Paine Hatch, *The Pauline Idea of Faith in Its Relation to Jewish and Hellenistic Religion.* For a detailed analysis of the role of faith in Pauline thought, see Mark A. Seifrid, *Justification by Faith.* For a semiotic analysis of Paul's writings on faith, see John D. Moores, *Wrestling with Rationality in Paul.*

For an overview of the history of the foundation of the Christian church, see Henry Chadwick, *The Early Church.* For a more detailed and comprehensive study, see Philip Esler, ed., *The Early Christian World.*

For the standard critical treatment of "Marius the Epicurean," see editor Michael Levey's introduction to *Marius the Epicurean* by Walter Pater, pp. 7–26. For a treatment of *Marius* in relation to other historical narratives set in early Christian times, see Curtis Dahl, "Pater's *Marius* and Historical Novels in Early Christian Times." For a study of the theological dimensions of Pater's text, see Martha Vogeler, "The Religious Meanings of *Marius the Epicurean.*" For a more detailed textual analysis, see Edmund Chandler, *Pater on Style,* pp. 24–78.

Chadwick recounts in succinct fashion the development of the Christian sacraments in *The Early Church* (pp. 258–72), as do Jules Lebreton and Jacques Zeiller in *The History of the Primitive Church* (pp. 335–45). See also Robert Kress, *The Church.*

On the role of the catacombs in the early Roman church, see Jérôme Carcopino, *De Pythagore aux Apôtres,* esp. pp. 225–332; Leonard Victor Rutgers, *Subterranean Rome;* and Charles Maitland's old but still inspiring *Church in the Catacombs.*

My discussion of the role and place of relics in the history of the Catholic Church is based principally on the historical and theological data provided by F. Chiovaro, ed., in the *New Catholic Encyclopedia* (s.v. "relics"). See also James Bentley, *Restless Bones.* For a more detailed treatise on the changing status of relics in church history, see Nicole Herrmann-Mascard, *Les Reliques des saints.*

The remark about Marcus Aurelius being "one of the best men who ever lived," from Joseph Brodsky's "Homage to Marcus Aurelius" in *On Grief and Reason,* deserves to be quoted in context. Speaking to Marcus, Brodsky writes:

Wasn't it your extraordinary appetite for the infinite that drove you to the most minute self-scrutiny, since you considered yourself a fragment, no mat-

ter how tiny, of the Whole of the Universe—and the Universe, you maintained, changes constantly. . . . The eventual dance of particles [that comes
with death], you held, should have no bearing on the animated body, not to
mention on its reason. You were an island, Caesar, or at least your ethics
were, an island in the primordial and—pardon the expression—postmordial
ocean of free atoms. And your statue [in Rome's Campidoglio] just marks the
place on the map of the species' history where this island once stood: unin-
habited, before submerging. The waves of doctrine and of creed—of the
Stoic doctrine and the Christian creed—have closed over your head, claiming
you as their own Atlantis. The truth, though, is that you never were either's.
You were just one of the best men that ever lived, and you were obsessed with
your duty because you were obsessed with virtue." (pp. 290–91)

On Roman blood sport and the culture of death, see Paul Plass, *The Game of Death
in Ancient Rome;* Thomas Wiedemann, *Emperors and Gladiators;* Alison Futrell, *Blood in
the Arena;* and Keith Hopkins, *Death and Renewal.*

8. The Names of the Dead

An earlier version of this chapter appeared as "The Names of the Dead" in *Critical Inquiry* 24 (autumn 1997): 176–90. Copyright © 1997 by The University of Chicago.
All rights reserved. Many thanks to the university for permission to reprint it.

For a discussion of Ungaretti's poetic response to his experiences in World War I,
see Desmond O'Connor, "The Poetry of a Patriot." For a comparison of his war poetry
with other World War I poetry, see Walter Musolino, "Physics and Metaphysics." For a
biographical perspective, see Walter Mauro, *Vita di Giuseppe Ungaretti,* pp. 37–50.

The literature on genre is vast. For a concise but comprehensive discussion of
genres and genre theory which isolates essential features distinguishing epic from
lyric (including the personal versus collective dynamic that is of interest to me here
above all), see Gérard Genette and Tzvetan Todorov, eds., *Théorie des genres.* For a rea-
soned study tracing the continuity of genres from Aristotle's initial distinction between the lyric, the epic, and the dramatic, through the innumerable subsequent
theories of genre, see Dominique Combe, *Les Genres littéraires.* In my book *The Body of
Beatrice* I theorize further the lyric and epic "alternatives" in the context of Dante's
shift from his early lyric production to the epic magnitudes of the *Divine Comedy* (see
pp. 129–43, 159–70).

For an intensive analysis of the deeper theological meaning of the title of Dante's
poem, see Giorgio Agamben, "Comedìa"; also, Robert P. Harrison, "Dante and
Modernity."

For a comprehensive bibliography of critical readings of the snow imagery in
Joyce's story "The Dead," see Daniel R. Schwarz, "A Critical History of 'The Dead,'"
in *James Joyce: The Dead,* ed. Daniel R. Schwarz, esp. pp. 80–81. In the same volume
see John Paul Riquelme's deconstructionist reading of the snow imagery in his con-
tribution, "For Whom the Snow Taps." See also the other essays collected in that volume for a variety of theoretical perspectives on Joyce's story. For a study tracing the
source of Joyce's snow imagery to the work of George Moore, see Adam Parkes,
"Moore, Snow, and the Dead." For a Barthesian reading of the end of the story, see
Gerald Doherty, "Shades of Difference." Vincent Pecora discusses the story and its
imagery from the point of view of the waning modernist self in its social context in
Self & Form in Modern Narrative, pp. 214–59.

The literary history of the image I trace in this chapter has, in addition to the declensions analyzed here, an important Miltonian version as well. Speaking of the fallen angels, Milton employs the simile in *Paradise Lost* (1.299–313):

> Nathless he so endur'd, till on the Beach
> Of that inflamed Sea, he stood and call'd
> His Legions, Angel Forms, who lay in trans't
> Thick as Autumnal Leaves that strow the Brooks
> In *Vallombrosa*, where th' *Etrurian* shades
> High overarch't imbow'r; or scatter'd sedge
> Afloat, when with fierce Winds *Orion* arm'd
> Hath vex'd the Red-Sea Coast, whose waves o'erthrew
> *Busiris* and his *Memphian* Chivalry,
> While with perfidious hatred they pursu'd
> The Sojourners of *Goshen*, who beheld
> From the safe shore their floating Carcasses
> And broken Chariot Wheels; so thick bestrown
> Abject and lost lay these, covering the Flood,
> Under amazement of their hideous change.

The most comprehensive study of the trajectory of this simile throughout epic literature is Sergio Baldi, "Folte come le foglie (e lo scudo di Satana)". For a detailed study of the simile in Milton with a comprehensive bibliography of its provenance and of the secondary sources treating it, see Neil Harris, "The Vallombrosa Simile and the Image of the Poet in *Paradise Lost*," esp. p. 72 n. 3. C. M. Bowra traces the simile through Homer, Bacchylides, Virgil, Dante, Tasso, Marlowe, and Milton in *From Virgil to Milton*, pp. 240–41. For a brief discussion of this simile as a formal device in Homer, Virgil, and Milton, see James P. Holoka, "Thick as Autumnal Leaves."

The idea of a monument that would feature the names of all the men and women who never made it back from Vietnam we owe not to Maya Ying Lin, the wall's designer, but to Jan Scruggs, who founded the Vietnam Veterans Memorial Fund in 1979. Every design submitted to the nationwide contest had to meet this condition of a complete listing of the names of the dead and missing. For Lin's own assessment of her project, see Maya Lin, Andrew Barshay, Stephen Greenblatt, and others, *Grounds for Remembering*, esp. p. 13; and Maya Lin, *Boundaries*. For a comprehensive discussion of the memorial, see Jan Scruggs and Joel Swerdlow, *To Heal a Nation*. For an inspired meditation on names, memorials, and the dead, with reference to the Vietnam Veterans Memorial, see Peter. S. Hawkings, "Naming Names." In a forthcoming essay that looks at the "performative" power of the Vietnam Veterans Memorial, Karen Feldman makes creative connections between the wall and Heidegger's concept of repetition. Feldman:

> But insofar as it is a work, the memorial is in any case not a final statement, a last word; it is not a tomb where the dead are finally and for all time laid to rest. It is rather a repository of potential readings, returns and repetitions. There is indeed something quite right in Jan Scruggs' association of the memorial with a boomerang. With regard to the purpose of the memorial and of memorials *per se,* namely as commemorating loss and trauma, in part a memorial works precisely in reevoking the event of loss again and again. The memorial does and should in some regard function precisely as a boomerang. Traumas and losses are like boomerangs—one cannot throw them away, rather the attempts to get rid of them effect their very return.

Feldman's essay, "The Shape of Mourning," is forthcoming in the journal *Word & Image*. I thank her for permission to quote from it here.
For criticisms of the memorial see Tom Carhart, "Insulting Vietnam Vets" (Carhart famously called the wall a "black gash of shame"). See also Paul Gapp, "Clouds of Doubt Engulf Viet Nam War Memorial"; and Kristin Ann Hass, *Carried to the Wall*, p. 16.

9. The Afterlife of the Image

In addition to the relevant bibliography about the corpse cited in the notes to chapter 6 (i.e., Christine Quigley's excellent study *The Corpse* [on body disposal see pp. 78–104]), see Mike Parker Pearson, *The Archeology of Death and Burial*, pp. 45–71. Pearson also discusses some of the political and legal issues surrounding the right of ownership to the corpse in his chapter "The Politics of the Dead" (pp. 171–92). For a historical look at issues of body disposal, see the essays collected in Peter C. Jupp and Glennys Howarth, eds., *The Changing Face of Death*. For a reading of funerary ritual as a symbolic means of disposing of the dead, see Jean-Thierry Maertens, *Le Jeu du mort*. On the widespread, presumably nondiffusionary phenomenon of the so-called double burial in both primitive and modern cultures, see Robert Hertz's foundational study, *Sociologie religeuse et folklore*. See also Philippe Aries' invaluable magnus opus, *L'homme devant la mort* (in English *The Hour of Our Death*), which offers an encyclopedic history-anthropology of changing Western attitudes toward death from the medieval period to our own times. For a more whimsical, or what he calls "lively," account of various cultural forms of dealing with the dead, see Nigel Barley, *Grave Matters*.
The incident of the Greek generals who were tried and hung in Athens after their naval victory is told by Xenophon in *Hellenica*, 1.7. Fustel de Coulanges discusses the incident in *La cité antique*, pp. 11–12.
The undead have had their most illustrious career in the cinema, as many studies of horror films attest. Among these see Gregory A. Waller, *The Living and the Undead;* also, Cynthia A. Freeland, *The Naked and the Undead*. For anthropological studies of the undead in various cultures, see for example Wade Davis, *Passage of Darkness;* Yves Saint-Gérard, *Le Phénomène zombi;* and Luise White, *Speaking with Vampires*.
There are at least two issues at stake in the absence of the corpse which should be distinguished, albeit I sometimes treat them under the same rubric. On the one hand there is an absent body in the certainty of death, as for example with Priam after the slaying of Hector, or the widows of the Whaleman's Chapel in *Moby Dick*, and so forth. On the other, there is uncertainty about the person's fate and/or uncertainty about the *location* of the person's remains. The one certainty that the loved ones of the victims of the September 11 tragedy have is that of location, which in its own relative way has a certain power of consolation. On the importance for survivors of the location of the corpse and the accomplishment of funerary rites, see Louis-Vincent Thomas, *Rites de mort*. For a critical application of the notion of "disappearance" to the current state of nonacceptance of death, see Patrick Baudry, *La Place des morts*, esp. pp. 81–122. Much of my discussion of the *desaparecidos* in Argentina is indebted to Zoë Crossland's article "Buried Lives." I am grateful to Ewa Domanska for bringing it to my attention. For more about *desaparecidos* of Latin America, see Marjorie Agosin, ed., *Surviving beyond Fear*.
Regarding the claim that the underlying "matter" of *The Iliad* could be seen as the warriors' dread of remaining unburied, see Jasper Griffin's excellent discussion in *Homer on Life and Death and Life* (pp. 112–20). See also James Redfield, *Nature and*

Culture in the Iliad. Redfield points out that the poem never actually represents the scene of dead bodies being consumed by dogs or birds, as if the abomination of it were too great for Homer's audiences. Nevertheless, the specter of such a fate figures as the ultimate taunt, threat, or calamity in *The Iliad.* Polydamas, for instance, warns his fellow Trojans that if they do not return to the city for the night "there will be many Trojans the vultures / and dogs will feed on" (18.270–71). Urging his men to battle, Agamemnon declares that, for the slackers, "no longer / will there be any means to escape the dogs and the vultures" (2.392–93). Hector taunts Ajax: "you will glut the dogs and birds of the Trojans / with fat and flesh" (13.831–32). And Achilles to Hector before killing him: "on you the dogs and vultures / shall feed and foully rip you; [but] the Achaians will bury Patroklos" (22.335–36). For a full catalogue of the motif in *The Iliad* see Griffin, pp. 116–17.

For a speculative essay on the relation between the image and death in the context of mass media and representations of the Holocaust, see Jay Cantor, "Death and the Image." On the use of photography from its earliest days to memorialize the newly dead and preserve their image for posterity, see Audrey Linkman, *The Victorians,* pp. 119–23. Consider in this regard the remarks of William Lake Price in his *Manual of Photographic Manipulation* (1858): "Posterity by the agency of photography will view the faithful image of our times: the future student, in turning the pages of history, may at the same time look at the very skin, into the very eyes, of those, long since mouldered to dust, whose lives and deeds he traces in the text" (cited in Peter Hamilton and Roger Hargreaves, *The Beautiful and the Damned,* p. 51. See also pp. 43–56 for a discussion of initial responses to the photographic medium in terms of capturing images for the future). On postmortem memorializing photography in nineteenth-century America, see Karen Sánchez-Eppler, "Then When We Clutch Hardest."

For Homer's Greeks the shadow images of the dead were not only *like* dream images, they were ontologically continuous with them. As Erwin Rohde declares in his foundational study *Psyche,* the Greeks saw dream images as "veritable realities and not empty fancies," especially when it came to epiphanies of the dead in sleep. These oneiric visitations were taken as proof of the dead's continued existence beyond the grave: "Since this shape can show itself to a dreamer, it must of necessity exist; consequently it survives death, though, indeed, only as a breath-like image" (p. 7). Understood in these terms, we could say that Hades figures as a realm of dreams, and Odysseus as a lucid dreamer.

One of the best-known and compelling interpretations of Orpheus's turn to look back at Eurydice—an interpretation with which my own is, to a certain extent, in sympathy—is Maurice Blanchot's in *The Gaze of Orpheus,* esp. pp. 99–104. For a speculative overview of the importance of the Orpheus myth in Western culture, with a discussion of various treatments of his descent into the underworld and his fatal glance at Euridyce, see Joan M. Erikson, *Legacies,* pp. 77–118, esp. pp. 83–89. For a book-length analysis of the use of the Orpheus myth in modernist literature, see Walter A. Strauss, *Descent and Return.* For an explanation of the Orphic tragedy in the context of ancient theogony, see Simonne Jacquemard and Jacques Brosse, *Orphée ou l'initiation mystique,* esp. pp. 37–43. For a philological discussion of the sources of the Orpheus myth and their consequences for its understanding, see W. K. C. Guthrie, *Orpheus and Greek Religion,* esp. pp. 25–68.

Regarding the invention of voice-recording technologies, Edison, in an 1878 article in the *North American Review,* envisioned ten possible uses for his phonograph. One of them was to record "the last words of dying persons" (quoted by Friedrich A.

Kittler, *Gramophone, Film, Typewriter*, p. 12). Kittler himself remarks: "In 1902 in the first German monograph on *Care and Usage of Modern Speaking Machines*, Alfred Parzer-Muehlbacher promises that gramophones . . . will be able to build 'archives and collections' for all possible 'memories.'" He goes on to quote Parzer-Muehlbacher: "'Cherished loved ones, dear friends, and famous individuals who have long since passed away will years later talk to us again with the same vividness and warmth; the wax cylinders transport us back in time to the happy days of youth— we hear the speech of those who lived countless years before us, whom we never knew, and whose names were only handed down by history'" (p. 55). For a detailed discussion of the gramophone as a medium and its impact on modernity, see pp. 1–114.

Paul de Man has dealt with the figure of prosopopeia extensively, although from a different perspective than the one I adopt in this chapter. See his essays, "Anthropomorphism and Trope in the Lyric" and "Lyrical Voice in Contemporary Theory." See also Michel Riffaterre's response to de Man in his essay "Prosopopeia." Barbara Johnson speaks insightfully about the trope in "Apostrophe, Animation, and Abortion."

J. J. Wilhelm reviews Ezra Pound's war years and the dawning of his political awareness in *Ezra Pound in London and Paris (1908–1925)*, pp. 167–221. In *Ezra Pound and Italian Fascism* Tim Redman discusses Pound's gradual shift from aloofness to social engagement because of the horrors of the war, which Redman sees as the roots of the economic theories that dominate Pound's social commentary in the '30s and '40s. (pp. 25–50). Daniel Tiffany's thought-provoking book *Radio Corpse Imagism and the Cryptaesthetic of Ezra Pound* is especially relevant in this context, for it is concerned primarily with the influence of the corpse on Pound's writings, the birth of imagism in the negativity of death, and the importance of the disembodied voice of radio for Pound's aesthetic—all elements of the prosopopeia that dominated Pound's career as a whole.

Regarding Christ's death, one might say that it is at the moment of his perishing on the cross that he entrusts his death (and with it the meaning of his life) to the world. The Synoptic Gospels emphasize the perishing aspect of Christ's demise, to be sure, describing the moment as an expiration (in Mark and Luke, *exepneusen*, "he expired"; in Matthew, *apheken to pneuma*, "he let go of his breath"). By contrast, the Gospel of John describes the moment as a transmission or handing over: *paredoken to pneuma*, "he handed over his spirit" (from *paradidoni*, "to hand over"). The Vulgate (unlike most English translations) is careful to preserve the communicative, entrusting action contained in the Greek original: *tradidit spiritum*. Whether or not with this phrase John alludes to the communication of the Holy Spirit promised by Jesus to his disciples after his glorification, one could say that, in the final analysis, to be mortal means to hand over the spirit of our death to one another constantly.

WORKS CITED

Agamben, Giorgio. "Comedìa: La svolta comica di Dante e la concezione di colpa." *Paragone* 346 (December 1978): 1–19.

———. *Language and Death.* Translated by Karen E. Pinkus. Minneapolis: Minneapolis University Press, 1991.

Agosin, Marjorie, ed. *Surviving beyond Fear: Women, Children and Human Rights in Latin America.* Freedonia, N.Y.: White Pine Press, 1993.

Albritton, Claude C. Jr. *The Abyss of Time: Changing Conceptions of the Earth's Antiquity after the Sixteenth Century.* San Francisco: Freeman, Cooper & Company, 1980.

Alexander, Michael, trans. *The Earliest English Poems.* Harmondsworth: Penguin Books, 1966. 3d ed. revised, London: Penguin Books, 1991.

Allen, Jerry. *The Sea Years of Joseph Conrad.* New York: Doubleday, 1965.

Allott, Robin. *The Great Mosaic Eye: Language and Evolution.* Sussex: The Book Guild Ltd., 2001.

Amanat, Abbas, and Magnus T. Bernhardsson, eds. *Imagining the End: Visions of Apocalypse from the Ancient Middle East to Modern America.* London: I. B. Tauris, 2002.

Ammons, A. R. *Sumerian Vistas.* New York: Norton, 1987.

Aries, Philippe. *L'homme devant la mort.* 2 vols. Paris: Seuil, 1977. Published in English under the title *The Hour of Our Death,* translated by Helen Weaver (New York: Knopf, 1980).

Arnault, Antoine-Vincent. *Anthologie de la poesie française. VIII siècle, IX siècle, XX siècle,* textes choisis, présentés et annotés par Martine Bercot, Michel Collot, et Catriona Seth. Paris: Gallimard Editions de la Pléiade, 2000.

Askedal, John Ole. "Johann Gottfried Herder's Conception of the Origin of Language." In *Semiotics around the World: Synthesis in Diversity: Proceedings of the Fifth Congress of the International Association for Semiotic Studies, Berkeley, 1994,* edited by Irmengard Rauch and Gerald F. Carr, pp. 183–86. Berlin: Mouton de Gruyter, 1997.

Atchison, Jean. *The Seeds of Speech: Language Origin and Evolution.* Cambridge: Cambridge University Press, 1996.

Auerbach, Erich. "Farinata and Cavlacante." In *Mimesis: The Representation of Reality in Western Literature,* translated by William R. Trask, pp. 174–202. Princeton, N.J.: Princeton University Press, 1953.

———. "Vico et la philologie." Translated by Robert Kahn. *Poésie* 86 (1998): 83–94.

Augustine. *Confessions.* Translated by Rex Warner. New York: Mentor, 1963.

———. *The City of God.* Translated by Henry Bettenson. London: Penguin Books, 1972.

Bachelard, Gaston. *Poetics of Space.* Translated by Maria Joles. Boston: Beacon Press, 1969.

Baldi, Sergio. "Folte come le foglie (e lo scudo di Satana)." In *Critical Dimensions,* ed. Mario Curreli and Alberto Martino, pp. 221–40. Cuneo: SASTE, 1978.

Barley, Nigel. *Grave Matters: A Lively History of Death around the World.* New York: Henry Holt & Co. Inc., 1995.

Batchelor, John. *The Life of Joseph Conrad: A Critical Biography.* Oxford: Blackwell, 1994.

Baudelaire, Charles. *Baudelaire: Oeuvres complètes.* Paris: Seuil, 1968.

———. *Edgar Allan Poe: Sa vie et ses ouvrages.* Edited by W. T. Bandy. Toronto: University of Toronto Press, 1973.

Baudry, Patrick. *La Place des morts. Enjeux et rites.* Paris: Armand Colin, 1999.

Bentley, James. *Restless Bones: The Story of Relics.* London: Constable, 1985.

Berlin, Isaiah. *Vico and Herder: Two Studies in the History of Ideas.* London: Hogarth Press, 1976.

Bermingham, Ronald P. "Le Cri de la nature et la nature du cri: Etude d'une rupture épistemologique." In *Etudes sur les Discours de Rousseau/Studies on Rousseau's Discourses,* edited by Jean Terrasse, pp. 179–92. Ottawa: North American Association for the Study of Jean-Jacques Rousseau, 1988.

Bickerton, Derek. *Language and Species.* Chicago: University of Chicago Press, 1990.

Blake, N. F. *Shakespeare's Language: An Introduction.* New York: St. Martin's Press, 1983.

———. *A Grammar of Shakespeare's Language.* Basingstoke, Hampshire: Palgrave, 2002.

Blanchot, Maurice. "Rimbaud et l'oeuvre final." *La Nouvelle Revue française* 104 (August 1, 1961): 293–303.

———. *The Gaze of Orpheus.* Translated by Lydia Davis. Barrytown, N.Y.: Station Hill Press, 1981.

———. *The Space of Literature.* Translated by Ann Smock. Lincoln: University of Nebraska Press, 1982.

———. *Faux Pas.* Translated by Charlotte Mandell. Stanford, Calif.: Stanford University Press, 2001.

Bonnefoy, Yves. "La Septième Face du bruit." *Europe: Revue littéraire mensuelle* 70, no. 760–61 (August-September 1992): 5–19.

Botturi, Francesco. *La Sapienza della storia. Giambattista Vico e la filosofia pratica.* Milan: Vita e pensiero, 1991.

———. *Tempo Linguaggio e Azione: Le strutture vichiane della "storia ideale eterna."* Naples: Alfredo Guida Editore, 1996.

Bourdin, Dominique. *Essai sur l' "Essai sur l'origine des langues" de Jean-Jacques Rousseau. Pour une étude pragmatique du texte.* Geneva: Editions Slatkine, 1994.

Bowra, C. M. *From Virgil to Milton.* London: Macmillan & Co Ltd., 1963.

Brodsky, Joseph. *Less than One.* New York: Farrar & Strauss, 1986.

———. *On Grief and Reason.* New York: Farrar & Strauss, 1995.

Brose, Margaret. *Leopardi sublime.* Translated by Elisabetta Bertoli. Bologna: Re Enzo, 1998.

Bucher, Gérard. *L'imagination de l'origine.* Paris: L'Harmattan, 2000.

Burchfield, Joe D. *Lord Kelvin and the Age of the Earth.* New York: Science History Publications, 1975.

Burke, Peter. *Vico.* Oxford: Oxford University Press, 1985.

Burkert, Walter. *Greek Religion.* Translated by John Raffan. Cambridge, Mass.: Harvard University Press, 1988.

Cacciari, Massimo. *Architecture and Nihilism: On the Philosophy of Modern Architecture.* Translated by Stephen Sartarelli. New Haven, Conn.: Yale University Press, 1993.

Cantelli, Gianfranco. *Mente Corpo Linguaggio: Saggio sull'interpretazione vichiana del mito.* Florence: Sansoni Editore, 1987.

Cantor, Jay. "Death and the Image." In *Beyond Document: Essays on Nonfiction Film,* edited by Charles Warren, pp. 23–49. Hanover, N.H.: Wesleyan University Press, 1996.

Caponigri, Robert A. "Filosofia et filologia: La 'nuova arte della critica' di Giambattista Vico." Translated by M. P. Fimiani. *Bollettino del centro di Studi Vichiani* 12–13 (1982–83): 29–61.

Caproni, Giorgio. *Tutte le poesie.* Milan: Garzanti, 1999.

Carcopino, Jérôme. *De Pythagore aux Apôtres: Etudes sur la conversion du monde romain.* Paris: Flammarion, 1968.

Carhart, Tom. "Insulting Vietnam Vets." *New York Times,* 24 October 1981, sec. 1.

Carillo, Gennaro. *Vico: Origine e genealogia dell'ordine.* Naples: Editoriale Scientifica, 2000.

Cary, Joseph. *Three Modern Italian Poets.* Chicago: University of Chicago Press, 1969.

Casey, Edward S. *The Fate of Place: A Philosophical History.* Berkeley and Los Angeles: University of California Press, 1997.

Cavell, Stanley. *The Senses of Walden: An Exploration of Thoreau's Masterpiece.* New York: Viking, 1972.

Chadwick, Henry. *The Early Church.* Pelican History of the Church, part 1. Grand Rapids, Mich.: Wm. B. Eerdmans Publishing Company by arrangement with Penguin Books Limited, 1967.

Chandler, Edmund. *Pater on Style: An Examination of the Essay on "Style" and the Textual History of "Marius the Epicurean."* Copenhagen: Rosenkilde and Bagger, 1958.

Chantraine, Pierre. *Dictionnaire étymologique de la langue grecque.* Paris: Editions Klincksieck, 1984.

Chiovaro, F. "Relics." In *New Catholic Encyclopedia,* vol. 12. New York: McGraw-Hill Book Company, 1967.

Choron, Jacques. *Death and Western Thought.* New York: Collier Books, 1973.

Coelho, Alain. *Arthur Rimbaud fin de la littérature: Lecture d'Une saison en enfer.* Paris: Joseph K., 1995.

Cole, Susan Letzler. *The Absent One: Mourning Ritual, Tragedy, and the Performance of Ambivalence.* University Park: Pennsylvania State University Press, 1985.

Coleridge, Samuel Taylor. *The Statesman's Manual.* In *Lay Sermons,* edited by R. J. White. Vol. 6 of *The Collected Works of Samuel Coleridge,* edited by Kathleen Coburn and Bart Winder. Princeton, N.J.: Princeton University Press, 1972.

Combe, Dominique. *Les Genres littéraires.* Paris: Hachette, 1992.

Connolly, Thomas E. *Swinburne's Theory of Poetry.* Albany: SUNY Press, 1964.

Corballis, Michael C. *From Hand to Mouth: The Origins of Language.* Princeton, N.J.: Princeton University Press, 2002.

Costello, Bonnie. *Marianne Moore: Imaginary Possessions.* Cambridge, Mass.: Harvard University Press, 1981.

Cousineau, Robert Henri. *Humanism and Ethics: An Introduction to Heidegger's "Letter on Humanism."* Louvain: Editions Nauwelaerts, 1972.

Cristofolini, Paolo. *Vico et l'histoire.* Paris: Presses Universitaires de France, 1995.

Croce, Benedetto. *Frammenti d'etica.* Bari: Gius. Laterza & Figli, 1922.

———. *La Filosofia di Giambattista Vico.* Edited by Felicita Andisio. Naples: Bibliopolis, 1997.

Crossland, Zoë. "Buried Lives: Forensic Archaeology and the Disappeared in Argentina." *Archaeological Dialogues* 7, no. 2 (2000): 146–59.

Culler, Jonathan. "Baudelaire and Poe." *Zeitschrift für französische Sprache und Literatur* 100 (1990): 61–73.

Dahl, Curtis. "Pater's *Marius* and Historical Novels in Early Christian Times." *Nineteenth-Century Fiction* 28 (1973): 1–24.

Danesi, Marcel. *Vico, Metaphor, and the Origin of Language.* Bloomington: Indiana University Press, 1993.

Dante Alighieri. *Inferno.* Translated by Allen Mandelbaum. New York: Bantam Books, 1980.

———. *Purgatory.* Translated by Allen Mandelbaum. New York: Bantam Books, 1980.

D'Atri, Annabella. "The Theory of Interjections in Vico and Rousseau." Translated by Christine Dodd. In *Historical Roots of Linguistic Theories,* ed. Lia Formigari and Daniele Gambarara, pp. 115–27. Amsterdam: Benjamins, 1995.

Davis, Wade. *Passage of Darkness: The Ethnobiology of the Haitian Zombie.* Chapel Hill: University of North Carolina Press, 1988.

De Martino, Ernesto. *Morte e pianto rituale: Dal lamento funebre antico al pianto di Maria.* Turin: Bollati Boringhieri, 1975. Reprint, Turin: Bollati Boringhieri, 2000.

Demske, James M. *Being, Man & Death: A Key to Heidegger.* Lexington: University Press of Kentucky, 1970.

Derrida, Jacques. *Writing and Difference.* Translated by Alan Bass. Chicago: University of Chicago Press, 1978.

———. "Speech and Writing according to Hegel." Translated by Alfonso Lingis. In *G. W. F. Hegel: Critical Assessments,* vol. 2, edited by Robert Stern. London: Routledge, 1993.

———. *Of Grammatology.* Corrected edition. Baltimore: Johns Hopkins University Press, 1997.

Dianotto, Roberto Maria. "Vico's Beginnings and Ends: Variations on the Theme of the Origin of Language." *Annali d'Italianistica* 18 (2000): 13–28.

Di Carlo, Franco. *Ungaretti e Leopardi.* Rome: Bulzoni, 1979.

Di Cesare, Donatella. "Verum, Factum, and Language." *New Vico Studies* 13 (1995): 1–13.

Doherty, Gerald. "Shades of Difference: Tropic Transformations in James Joyce's 'The Dead.'" *Style* 23, no. 2 (summer 1989): 225–37.

Doumet, Christian. "Malte devant les parois." In *Rainer Maria Rilke et "Les Cahiers de Malte Laurids Brigge": Ecriture romanesque et modernité,* edited by Christian Klein, pp. 71–82. Paris: Armand Colin/Masson, 1996.

Dripps, R. D. *The First House: Myth, Paradigm, and the Task of Architecture.* Cambridge: MIT Press, 1997.

Dronke, Peter, ed. *Women Writers of the Middle Ages.* Cambridge: Cambridge University Press, 1984.

Dufresne, Todd. *Tales from the Freudian Crypt: The Death Drive in Text and Context.* Stanford, Calif.: Stanford University Press, 2000.

Dumézil, Georges. *La Religion romaine archaïque.* Paris: Payot, 1966.

Edmunds, Lowell. *Theatrical Space and Historical Place in Sophocles's "Oedipus at Colonus."* Lanham, Md.: Rowman & Littlefield Publishers, Inc., 1996.

Emerson, Ralph Waldo. *Essays: Second Series.* Vol. 3 of *The Complete Works of Ralph Waldo Emerson,* edited by Edward Waldo Emerson. Boston: Houghton Mifflin, 1903.

Engle, Bernard F. *Marianne Moore.* New York: Twayne Publishers, Inc., 1964.

Erikson, Joan M. *Legacies. Prometheus, Orpheus, Socrates.* New York: W. W. Norton & Company, 1993.

Euripides. *Andromache.* Translated by Susan Stewart and Wesley D. Smith. Oxford: Oxford University Press, 2001.

Esler, Philip F., ed. *The Early Christian World.* 2 vols. London: Routledge, 2000.

Evans, Ifor. *The Language of Shakespeare's Plays.* London: Methuen & Co. Ltd., 1952.

Feeney, D. C. "History and Revelation in Vergil's Underworld." In *Why Vergil? A Collection of Interpretations,* edited by Stephanie Quinn, pp. 108–22. Wauconda, Ill.: Bolchazy-Carducci Publishers, Inc., 2000.

Feldman, Karen S. "On Rhetoric, Performativity and the Example of Conscience in Hobbes, Leibniz, Hegel and Heidegger." Ph.D. diss., DePaul University, 1999.

———. "The Shape of Mourning: Reading, Aesthetic Cognition, and The Vietnam Veterans Memorial." *Word & Image,* forthcoming.

Feuerbach, Ludwig. *The Essence of Christianity.* Translated by George Eliot. New York: Harper & Row, 1957.

Foscolo, Ugo. *Opere.* Edited by Mario Puppo. Milan: Mursia & C., 1966.

———. *On Sepulchres: An Ode to Ippolito Pindemonte.* Translated by Thomas G. Bergin. Bethany, Conn.: The Bethany Press, 1971.

Foster, Hal. *The Anti-Aesthetic: Essays on Postmodern Culture.* New York: New Press, 1998.

Foucault, Michel. *Histoire de la folie à l'âge classique.* Paris: Gallimard, 1972.

Frampton, Kenneth. "Toward a Critical Regionalism: Six Points for an Architecture of Resistance." In *The Anti-Aesthetic: Essays on Postmodern Culture,* edited by Hal Foster, pp. 16–30. Port Townsend, Wash.: Bay Press, 1983.

Frankfurt, Harry G. *Demons, Dreamers, and Madmen: The Defense of Reason in Descartes's "Meditations."* Indianapolis: The Bobbs-Merrill Company, Inc., 1970.

Freeland, Cynthia A. *The Naked and the Undead: Evil and the Appeal of Horror.* Boulder, Colo.: Westview Press, 2000.

Freud, Sigmund. *Civilization and Its Discontents.* New York: W. W. Norton & Co., 1961.

———. *Beyond the Pleasure Principle.* New York: W. W. Norton & Co., 1961.

———. "Thoughts for the Times on War and Death." In *The Standard Edition of the Complete Psychological Works of Sigmund Freud,* translated and edited by James Strachey in collaboration with Anna Freud, assisted by Alix Strachey and Alan Tyson, 14:273–302. London: The Hogarth Press and the Institute of Psycho-Analysis, 1957. Originally published under the title "Zeitgemaesses ueber Krieg und Tod," *Imago* 4, no. 1 (1915): 1–21.

Fuller, Reginald. *The Formation of the Resurrection Narratives.* New York: Macmillan-Collier, 1971.

Fustel de Coulanges, Numa Denis. *La cité antique* [1864]. Preface by François Hartog. Paris: Flammarion, 1984. Published in English under the title *The Ancient City* (Baltimore: Johns Hopkins University Press, 1980).

Futrell, Alison. *Blood in the Arena: The Spectacle of Roman Power.* Austin: University of Texas Press, 1997.

Gamberini, Spartaco. *Analisi dei "Sepolcri" foscoliani.* Messina: G. D'Anna, 1982.

Gapp, Paul. "Clouds of Doubt Engulf Viet Nam War Memorial." *Chicago Tribune,* June 28, 1981, sec. 6.

Genette, Gérard, and Tzvetan Todorov, eds. *Théorie des genres.* Paris: Editions du Seuil, 1986.

Gould, Stephen Jay. *Time's Arrow, Time's Cycle: Myth and Metaphor in the Discovery of Geological Time.* Cambridge, Mass.: Harvard University Press, 1987.

Grassi, Ernesto. *Vico and Humanism: Essays on Vico, Heidegger, and Rhetoric.* New York: Peter Lang, 1990.

Grene, David. "Introduction: The 'Theban Plays of Sophocles.'" In *Sophocles I/Three Tragedies,* edited by David Grene and Richmond Lattimore. Chicago: University of Chicago Press, 1954.

———. *Aeschylus II.* Edited by David Grene and Richmond Lattimore. 2d ed. Chicago: Chicago University Press, 1991.

Griffin, Jasper. *Homer on Life and Death.* Oxford: Clarendon, 1980.

Grubb, Nancy. *Revelations: Art of the Apocalypse.* New York: Abbeville Press, 1997.

Guthrie, W. K. C. *Orpheus and Greek Religion: A Study of the Orphic Movement.* New York: Norton. 1967.

Hadas, Pamela White. *Marianne Moore: Poet of Affection.* Syracuse, N.Y.: Syracuse University Press, 1977.

Haldas, Georges. *Mémoire et résurrection: chronique extravagant.* [Lausanne]: L'Age de l'Homme, 1991.

Hamilton, Peter, and Roger Hargreaves. *The Beautiful and the Damned: The Creation of Identity in Nineteenth Century Photography.* Aldershot: Lund Humphries in association with The National Portrait Gallery, London, 2001.

Harries, Karsten. *The Ethical Function of Architecture.* Cambridge, Mass.: MIT Press, 1998.

Harris, H. S. *Hegel's Development: Night Thoughts (Jena 1801–1806).* Oxford: Clarendon Press, 1983.

Harris, Neil. "The Vallombrosa Simile and the Image of the Poet in *Paradise Lost.*" In *Milton in Italy: Contexts, Images, Contradictions,* pp. 71–94. Binghamton, N.Y.: Medieval & Renaissance Texts & Studies, 1991.

Harrison, Robert P. "Dante and Modernity." *MLN* 102, no. 5 (December 1982): 1043–61.

———. *The Body of Beatrice.* Baltimore: Johns Hopkins University Press, 1988.

———. *Forests: The Shadow of Civilization.* Chicago: University of Chicago Press, 1992.

———. "Tombstones." In *Complexities of Motion: New Essays on A. R. Ammons's Long Poems,* edited by Steven P. Schneider. Madison, Wisc.: Associated University Presses, 1999.

Harrison, Thomas J. *1910: The Emancipation of Dissonance.* Berkeley and Los Angeles: University of California Press, 1996.

Hass, Kristin Ann. *Carried to the Wall: American Memory and the Vietnam Veterans Memorial.* Berkeley and Los Angeles: University of California Press, 1998.

Hatch, William Henry Paine. *The Pauline Idea of Faith in Its Relation to Jewish and Hellenistic Religion.* Cambridge, Mass.: Harvard University Press, 1917.

Hawkings, Peter S. "Naming Names: The Art of Memory and the NAMES Project AIDS Quilt." *Critical Inquiry* 19 (summer 1993): 752–79.

Hegel, G. W. F. ———. *Gesammelte Werke.* Edited by Rolf-Peter Horstmann and Johann Heinrich Trede. Hamburg: Felix Meiner Verlag, 1976.

———. *System of Ethical Life (1802/3) and First Philosophy of Spirit (Part III of the System of Speculative Philosophy).* Edited and translated by H. S. Harris and T. M. Knox. Albany: SUNY Press, 1979.

Heidegger, Martin. ———. *Being and Time.* Translated by John Macquarrie and Edward Robinson. New York: Harper & Row, 1962.

———. *Poetry, Language and Thought.* New York: Harper & Row, 1971.

———. "Art and Space." *Man and World* 6 (1973): 3–8.

———. *Early Greek Thinking.* New York: Harper & Row, 1975.

———. *Basic Writings.* Edited by David Krell. New York: Harper & Row, 1977.

———. *Nietzsche,* vol. 1. New York: Harper and Row, 1979.

Henning, E. M. "Destruction and Repetition: Heidegger's Philosophy of History." *Journal of European Studies* 12, no. 4 (December 1982): 260–82.

Herrmann-Mascard, Nicole. *Les Reliques des saints: Formation coutumière d'un droit.* Paris: Editions Klincksieck, 1975.

Hertz, Robert. *Sociologie religeuse et folklore.* Paris: PUF, 1928.

Hölderlin, Friedrich. "Vorrede" to the "Vorletzte Fassung" of *Hyperion.* In *Sämtliche Werke,* edited by Friedrich Beissner ("Stuttgarter Ausgabe"), 3:235. Stuttgart: W. Kohlhammer Verlag, 1957.

Holoka, James P. "Thick as Autumnal Leaves: The Structure and Generic Potentials of an Epic Simile." *Milton Quarterly* 10, no. 3 (October 1976): 78–83.

Holst-Warhaft, Gail. *Dangerous Voices: Women's Laments and Greek Literature.* London: Routledge, 1992.

Homer. *The Iliad.* Translated by Richard Lattimore. Chicago: University of Chicago Press, 1951.

———. *The Odyssey.* Translated by Richard Lattimore. New York: Harper Perennial, 1965.

Hopkins, Gerard Manley. *The Poems of G. M. Hopkins.* London: Oxford University Press, 1967.

Hopkins, Keith. *Death and Renewal.* Sociological Studies in Roman History, vol. 2. Cambridge: Cambridge University Press, 1983.

Hyde, Michael J. "The Call of Conscience: Heidegger and the Question of Rhetoric." *Philosophy and Rhetoric* 27, no. 4 (1994): 374–96.

Ireton, Sean. "Heidegger's Ontological Analysis of Death and Its Prefiguration in Nietzsche." *Nietzsche Studien: Internationales Jahrbuch für die Nietzsche-Forschung* 26 (1997): 405–20.

Jacquemard, Simonne, and Jacques Brosse. *Orphée ou l'initiation mystique.* Paris: Bayard Editions, 1998.

Johnson, Barbara. "Apostrophe, Animation, and Abortion." *Diacritics* 16 (spring 1986): 29–39.

Johnson, Linck C. "Revolution and Renewal: The Genres of *Walden.*" In *Critical Essays on Henry David Thoreau's Walden,* edited by Joel Meyerson, pp. 215–34. Boston: G. K. Hall & Co., 1988.

Joyce, James. *Dubliners.* London: Penguin Books, 1967.

Joyner, Michael A. "Of Time and the Garden: Swinburne's 'A Forsaken Garden.'" *Victorian Poetry* 35, no. 1 (spring 1997): 99–105.

Jung, C. G. "The Soul and Death." In *Collected Works*, translated by R. F. C. Hull, 8:410–11. 2d ed. Princeton, N.J.: Princeton University Press, 1969.

Jupp, Peter C., and Glennys Howarth, eds. *The Changing Face of Death: Historical Accounts of Death and Disposal.* New York: St. Martin's Press, Inc., 1997.

Kant, Immanuel. *Critique of Pure Reason.* Translated by Werner S. Pluhar. Indianapolis: Hackett, 1996.

Kay, Shirley. *The Bedouin.* New York: Crane, Russak & Company Inc., 1978.

Kelly, Donald R. "Vico's Road: from Philology to Jurisprudence and Back." In *Giambattista Vico's Science of Humanity*, edited by Giorgio Tagliacozzo, pp. 15–29. Baltimore: Johns Hopkins University Press, 1976.

Kerner, Konrad. "Comments on Reconstructions in Historical Linguistics." In *The New Sound of Indo-European: Essays in Phonological Reconstruction*, edited by Theo Vennemann, pp. 1–13. Berlin: Mouton de Gruyter, 1989.

Kerrigan, William. "Death and Anxiety: The Coherence of Late Freud." *Raritan* 16, no. 3 (winter 1997): 64–80.

Kittler, Friedrich A. *Gramophone, Film, Typewriter.* Translated by Geoffrey Winthrop-Young and Michael Wutz. Stanford, Calif.: Stanford University Press, 1999.

Kockelmans, Joseph J., ed. *On Heidegger and Language.* Evanston, Ill.: Northwestern University Press, 1972.

Kojéve, Alexandre. *Introduction to the Reading of Hegel.* Translated by James H. Nichols Jr. Ithaca, N.Y.: Cornell University Press, 1969.

Kolb, David. *Postmodern Sophistications: Philosophy, Architecture and Tradition.* Chicago: University of Chicago Press, 1990.

Komar, Kathleen L. *Transcending Angels: Rainer Maria Rilke's Duino Elegies.* Lincoln: University of Nebraska Press, 1987.

Kress, Robert. *The Church: Communion, Sacrament, Communication.* New York: Paulist Press, 1985.

Lacan, Jacques. *The Four Fundamental Concepts of Psychoanalysis.* Translatede by Alan Sheridan. New York: Norton, 1977.

———. *The Ethics of Psychoanalysis.* Translated by Dennis Porter. New York: Norton, 1992.

Lahr, Oonagh. "Greek Sources of 'Writ in Water.'" In *Keats-Shelley Journal* 21–22 (1972–73): 17–18.

Langer, Suzanne. *Philosophy in a New Key.* New York: New American Library. 1951. Reprint, Cambridge, Mass.: Harvard University Press, 1963. Quoted by Stanley Jeyraja Tambiah, *Culture, Thought and Social Action* (Cambridge, Mass.: Harvard University Press, 1985), p. 133.

Leach, Elsie. "Building One's Own House: *Walden* and *Absalom, Absalom.*" *San Jose Studies* 17, no. 2 (spring 1991): 62–83.

Lebreton, Jules, and Zeiller, Jacques. *The History of the Primitive Church.* Translated by Ernest C. Messenger. 2 vols. New York: Macmillan, 1949.

Leibniz, G. W. *New Essays concerning Human Understanding* (bk. 2, chap. 27, par. 3). Translated by Alfred Gideon Langley. Chicago: The Open Court Publishing House, 1916. [Translation modified.]

Leopardi, Giacomo. *Zibaldone: A Selection.* Translated by Martha King and Daniela Bini. New York: Peter Lang, 1992.

Lilla, Mark. *G. B. Vico: The Making of an Anti-Modern.* Cambridge, Mass.: Harvard University Press, 1993.

Lin, Maya. *Boundaries.* New York: Simon and Schuster, 2000.

Lin, Maya, Andrew Barshay, Stephen Greenblatt, and others. *Grounds for Remembering: Monuments, Memorials, Texts.* Berkeley, Calif.: Doreen B. Townsend Center for the Humanities.

Linkman, Audrey. *The Victorians: Photographic Portraits.* London and New York: Tauris Park Books, 1993.

Loos, Adolf. "Architektur" (1910). Cited in Ludwig Münz and Gustave Künstler, *Adolf Loos: Pioneer of Modern Architecture,* translated by Harold Meek, p. 192. New York: Praeger, 1966.

Lowith, Karl. "Verum et factum convertuntur: Le premesse teologiche del principio di Vico et le loro consequenze secolari." In *Omaggio a Vico,* edited by A. Corsano, Paolo Rossi, A. M. Jacobelli Isoldi, and F. Tessitore, pp. 75–112. Naples: Romano, 1968.

MacDonald, Ronald R. *The Burial-Places of Memory: Epic Underworlds in Vergil, Dante, and Milton.* Amherst: University of Massachusetts Press, 1987.

Macri, Oreste. *Semantica e metrica dei Sepolcri del Foscolo: Con uno studio sull'endecasillabo.* Roma: Bulzoni, 1978.

Maertens, Jean-Thierry, with Marguerite Debilde. *Le Jeu du mort: Essai d'anthropologie des inscriptions du cadavre.* Paris: Aubier Montaigne, 1979.

Magrelli, Valerio. *The Contagion of Matter.* Translated by Anthony Molino. New York: Holmes & Meier Publishers, 2000.

———. "Il ventunesimo compleano." *Trame di letteratura comparata,* 2 (I semestre 2001): 121–28.

Mainville, Odette, and Daniel Marguerat, eds. *Résurrection. L'après-mort dans le monde ancien et le Nouveau Testament.* Montréal: Médiaspaul, 2001.

Maitland, Charles. *The Church in the Catacombs: A Description of the Primitive Church of Rome, Illustrated by Its Sepulchral Remains.* London: Longman, Brown, Green, and Longmans, 1847.

Man, Paul de. "Anthropomorphism and Trope in the Lyric,." In *The Rhetoric of Romanticism,* pp. 239–62. New York: Columbia University Press, 1984, pp. 239–62.

———. "Lyrical Voice in Contemporary Theory." In *Lyric Poetry: Beyond New Criticism,* edited by Chaviva Hosek and Patricia Parker, pp. 55–72. Ithaca, N.Y.: Cornell University Press, 1985, pp. 55–72.

Mansbach, Abraham. *Beyond Subjectivism: Heidegger on Language and the Human Being.* Westport, Conn.: Greenwood Press, 2002.

Manson, Richard. *The Theory of Knowledge of Giambattista Vico.* [Hamden, Conn.]: Archon Books, 1969.

Marxsen, Willi. *The Resurrection of Jesus of Nazareth.* Translated by Margaret Kohl. Philadelphia: Fortress, 1970.

Mauro, Walter. *Vita di Giuseppe Ungaretti.* Milan: Camunia, 1990.

Maynard, W. Barksdale. "Thoreau's House at Walden." *Art Bulletin* 81, no. 2 (June 1999): 303–25.

Mazzotta, Giuseppe. *The New Map of the World: The Poetic Philosophy of Giambattista Vico.* Princeton, N.J.: Princeton University Press, 1999.

McNeill, William, ed. *Pathmarks.* Cambridge: Cambridge University Press, 1998.

Melville, Herman. *Moby Dick.* New York: The Modern Library, 1992.

Metcalf, Peter, and Richard Huntington. *Celebrations of Death: The Anthropology of Mortuary Ritual.* 2d ed. Cambridge: Cambridge University Press, 1991.

Miller, Cecilia. *Giambattista Vico: Imagination and Historical Knowledge.* New York: St. Martin's Press, 1993.

Mills, Sophie. *Theseus, Tragedy and the Athenian Empire.* Oxford: Clarendon Press, 1997.

Milton, John. *Complete Poems and Major Prose.* Edited by Merritt Y. Hughes. Indianapolis: The Bobbs-Merrill Company, Inc., 1957.

Miner, Robert C. "Verum-Factum and Practical Wisdom in the Early Writings of Giambattista Vico." *Journal of the History of Ideas* 59, no. 1 (January 1998): 53–73.

——. *Vico: Genealogist of Modernity.* Notre Dame, Ind.: University of Notre Dame Press, 2002.

Mitchell, W. J. T. "Holy Landscape: Israel, Palestine and the American Wilderness." *Critical Inquiry* 26, no. 2 (winter 2000): 193–223. Reprinted in *Landscape and Power,* edited by W. J. T. Mitchell, 2d ed. (Chicago: University of Chicago Press, 2002).

Mohen, Jean-Pierre. *Les Rites de l'au-delà.* Paris: Editions Odile Jacob, 1995.

Mondolfo, Rodolfo. *Il "Verum-Factum" Prima di Vico.* Naples: Guida Editori, 1969.

Moore, Marianne. *Complete Poems.* New York: Macmillan, Viking Books, 1981. Reprint, New York: Macmillan Publishing Company, Penguin Books, 1994.

Moores, John D. *Wrestling with Rationality in Paul: Romans 1–8 in a New Perspective.* Cambridge: Cambridge University Press, 1995.

Morrison, James C. "Vico's Principle of Verum in Factum and the Problem of Historicism." *Journal of the History of Ideas* 39 (1978): 579–95.

Morrison, Jim. *The American Night.* New York: Villard Books, 1990.

Most, Glenn. "Heidegger's Greeks." *Arion: A Journal of Humanities and the Classics* 10, no. 1 (spring-summer 2002): 83–98.

Mumford, Lewis. *The City in History: Its Origins, Its Transformations, and Its Prospects.* New York: Harcourt, Brace & World, Inc., 1961.

Münz, Ludwig, and Künstler, Gustave. *Adolf Loos, Pioneer of Modern Architecture.* Translated by Harold Meek. New York: Praeger, 1966.

Murphy, Steve. "Une saison en enfer et les 'derniers vers' de Rimbaud: Rupture ou continuité?" *Revue d'histoire littéraire de la France* 95, no. 6 (November–December 1995): 958–73.

Musolino, Walter. "Physics and Metaphysics: Capture and Escape. Two War Poems of Wilfred Owen and Giuseppe Ungaretti." *Forum Italicum* 30, no. 2 (fall 1996): 311–19.

Nancy, Jean-Luc. *The Birth to Presence.* Translated by Brian Holmes. Stanford, Calif.: Stanford University Pres, 1993.

Nietzsche, Friedrich. *The Gay Science.* Translated by Walter Kaufmann. New York: Random House, 1974.

Nitchie, George W. *Marianne Moore: An Introduction to the Poetry.* New York: Columbia University Press, 1969.

Nuessel, Frank. "Vico's Views on Language and Linguistics." *Romance Languages Annual* 9 (1997): 280–87.

Nuzzo, Enrico. *Tra ordine della storia e storicità: Saggi sui saperi della storia in Vico.* Rome: Edizione di storia e letteratura, 2001.

O'Connor, Desmond. "The Poetry of a Patriot: Ungaretti and the First World War."

AUMLA: Journal of the Australasian Universities Language and Literature Association 56 (November 1981): 201–18.

O'Neill, Tom. *Of Virgin Muses and of Love: A Study of Foscolo's "Dei Sepolcri."* Dublin: Foundation for Italian Studies, University College Dublin/Irish Academic Press, 1981.

Paparelli, Gioacchino. *Ugo Foscolo: I sepolcri; lezioni di letteratura italiana raccolte da Carlo Chirico.* Pompei: Tip I.P.S.I., 1966.

Pareyson, Luigi. *L'estetica e I suoi problemi.* Milan: Marzortai, 1961.

Parkes, Adam. "Moore, Snow, and the Dead." *English Literature in Transition (1880–1920)* 42, no. 3 (1999): 265–82.

Pater, Walter. *Marius the Epicurean.* Edited with introduction and notes by Michael Levey. Harmondsworth, England: Penguin Books Ltd., 1985.

Pearson, Mike Parker. *The Archeology of Death and Burial.* College Station: Texas A&M University Press, 1999.

Pecora, Vincent. *Self & Form in Modern Narrative.* Baltimore: Johns Hopkins University Press, 1989.

Pennisi, Antonino. *La Linguistica dei Mercatanti: Filosofia linguistica e filosofia civile da Vico a Cuoco.* Naples: Guide editori, 1987.

Pettersson, Torsten. "Internalization and Death: A Reinterpretation of Rilke's *Duineser Elegien.*" *Modern Language Review* 91, no. 3 (July 1999): 731–43.

Pirandello, Luigi. *Novelle per un anno.* Milan: Mondadori, 1956.

Plass, Paul. *The Game of Death in Ancient Rome: Arena Sport and Political Suicide.* Madison: University of Wisconsin Press, 1995.

Plato. *Complete Works.* Edited by John M. Cooper. Indianapolis: Hackett Publishing Company, 1997.

Pöggler, Otto. "Heidegger's Topology of Being." In *On Heidegger and Language,* edited by Joseph J. Kockelmans, pp. 107–46. Evanston, Ill.: Northwestern University Press, 1972.

Poissonier, Dominique. *La Pulsion de mort de Freud à Lacan.* Ramonville Saint-Agne: Editions Erès, Collection "Point Hors Ligne," 1998.

Polomé, Edgar C., and Werner Winter, eds. *Reconstructing Languages and Cultures.* Berlin: Mouton de Gruyter, 1992.

Polt, Richard. "The Question of the Nothing." In *A Companion Guide to Heidegger's "Introduction to Metaphysics,"* edited by Richard Polt and Gregory Fried. New Haven, Conn.: Yale University Press, 2001.

Pound, Ezra. *Collected Early Poems of Ezra Pound.* New York: New Directions Books, 1976.

Powell, James Lawrence. *Mysteries of Terra Firma. The Age and Evolution of the World.* New York: The Free Press, 2001.

Prioreschi, Plinio. *A History of Human Responses to Death: Mythologies, Rituals, and Ethics.* Lewiston, Australia: The Eden Mellen Press, 1990.

Quigley, Christine. *The Corpse: A History.* Jefferson, N.C.: McFarland & Company, 1996.

Ramazani, Jahan. *The Poetry of Mourning.* Chicago: University of Chicago Press, 1994.

Ranta, Jerrald. "Marianne Moore's Sea and the Sentence." In *Essays in Literature* 15, no. 2 (fall 1998): 245–57.

Redfield, James M. *Nature and Culture in the Iliad: The Tragedy of Hector.* Expanded edition. Durham, N.C.: Duke University Press, 1994.

Redman, Tim. *Ezra Pound and Italian Fascism.* New York: Cambridge University Press, 1991.

Richard, Jean-Pierre. *Poésie et profondeur.* Paris: Editions du Seuil, 1955.

Richardson, Robert D. Jr. *Henry Thoreau: A Life of the Mind.* Berkeley and Los Angeles: University of California Press, 1986.

Riede, David G. *Swinburne: A Study of Romantic Mythmaking.* Charlottesville: University Press of Virginia, 1978.

Riffaterre, Michel. "Prosopopeia." In *Lessons of Paul de Man,* edited by Peter Brooks, Shoshana Felman, and J. Hillis Miller, pp. 107–23. Yale French Studies, no. 69. New Haven, Conn.: Yale University Press, 1986.

Rilke, Rainer Maria. *The Letters of Rainer Maria Rilke: 1910–26.* Translated by Jane Bannard Greene and M. S. Herder Norton. Vol. 2. New York: W. W. Norton, 1947.

———. *Duino Elegies.* Translated by C. F. MacIntyre. Berkeley and Los Angeles: University of California Press, 1961.

———. *The Notebooks of Malte Laurids Brigge.* Translated by M. D. Herter Norton. New York: W. W. Norton, 1949.

Rimbaud, Arthur. *A Season in Hell.* Translated by Louise Varèrse. New York: New Directions, 1961.

———. *Oeuvres complètes d'Arthur Rimbaud.* Edited by Rolland de Renéville and Jules Mouquet. Paris: Bibliothèque de la Pléiade, 1963.

Riquelme, John Paul. "For Whom the Snow Taps." in *James Joyce: The Dead,* edited by Daniel R. Schwarz, pp. 219–34. New York: St. Martin's Press, Bedford Books, 1993.

Rohde, Erwin. *Psyche: The Cult of Souls and Belief in Immortality among the Greeks.* Translated by W. B. Hills. Chicago: Ares Publishers, 1925. Reprint, Chicago: Ares Publishers, 1987.

Rollins, Hyder. *The Keats Circle; Letters and Papers 1816–1878.* Cambridge, Mass.: Harvard University Press, 1948.

Rooksby, Rikky, and Shrimpton Nicholas, eds. *The Whole Music of Passion: New Essays on Swinburne.* Hants, England: Scolar Press, 1993.

Rosenblatt, Paul C., R. Patricia Walsh, and Douglas A. Jackson. *Grief and Mourning in Cross-Cultural Perspective.* New Haven, Conn.: HRAF Press, 1976.

Rosenfeld, William. "Uncertain Faith: Queequeg's Coffin and Melville's Use of the Bible." *Texas Studies in Literature and Language: A Journal of the Humanities* 7 (1966): 317–27.

Rossi, Paolo. *The Dark Abyss of Time: The History of the Earth and the History of Nations from Hooke to Vico.* Translated by Lydia G. Cochrane. Chicago: University of Chicago Press, 1984.

Rotella, Guy. *Reading and Writing Nature: The Poetry of Robert Frost, Wallace Stevens, Marianne Moore, and Elizabeth Bishop.* Boston: Northeastern University Press, 1991.

Rousseau, Jean-Jacques. *On the Origin of Language.* Translated by John H. Moran and Alexander Gode. Chicago: University of Chicago Press, 1966.

Rutgers, Leonard Victor. *Subterranean Rome: In Search of the Roots of Christianity in the Catacombs of the Eternal City.* Leuven: Peeters; Hadleigh: BRAD, 2000.

Sacks, Peter M. *The English Elegy: Studies in the Genre from Spencer to Yeats.* Baltimore: Johns Hopkins University Press, 1985.

Saint-Gérard, Yves. *Le Phénomène zombi: La Présence en Haïti de sujets en état de non-être.* Toulouse: Erès, 1992.

Salamone, Rosario. *Lingua e linguaggio nella filosofia di Giambattista Vico.* Rome: Edizioni dell'Ateneo, 1984.

Salisbury, Joyce E. *Perpetua's Passion.* New York: Routledge, 1997.

Salmon, Vivian, and Edwina Burness, eds. *A Reader in the Language of Shakespearean Drama.* Amsterdam: John Benjamins Publishing Company, 1987.

Sánchez-Eppler, Karen. "Then When We Clutch Hardest: On the Death of a Child and the Replication of an Image." In *Sentimental Men: Masculinity and the Politics of Affect in American Culture,* edited by Mary Chapman and Glenn Hendler. Berkeley and Los Angeles: University of California Press, 1999.

Sartre, Jean-Paul. *Being and Nothingness.* Translated by Hazel E. Barnes. New York: Philosophical Library, 1956.

Sattelmeyer, Robert. *Thoreau's Reading: A Study in Intellectual History with Bibliographic Catalogue.* Princeton, N.J.: Princeton University Press, 1988.

Sawicki, Marianne. *Seeing the Lord: Resurrection and Early Christian Practices.* Minneapolis: Fortress Press, 1994.

Schwarz, Daniel R. "A Critical History of 'The Dead.'" In *James Joyce: The Dead,* edited by Daniel R. Schwarz, pp. 63–84. Boston: St. Martin's Press, Bedford Books, 1993.

Schwink, Frederick W. *Linguistic Typology, Universality, and the Realism of Reconstruction.* Washington, D.C.: Institute for the Study of Man, 1994.

Scott, John T. "The Harmony between Rousseau's Musical Theory and His Philosophy." *Journal of the History of Ideas* 59, no. 2 (April 1998): 287–308.

Scruggs, Jan, and Joel Swerdlow. *To Heal a Nation: The Vietnam Veterans Memorial.* New York: Harper & Row, 1985.

Seifrid, Mark A. *Justification by Faith: The Origin and Development of a Central Pauline Theme.* Leiden: E. J. Brill, 1992.

Seltzer, Leon F. *The Vision of Melville and Conrad: A Comparative Study.* Athens: Ohio University Press, 1970.

Serres, Michel. *Statues: Le Livre des fondations.* Paris: François Bourdin, 1987.

Seybold, Ethel. *Thoreau: The Quest and the Classics.* New Haven, Conn.: Yale University Press, 1951.

Sheehan, Thomas, ed. *Heidegger: The Man and the Thinker.* Chicago: Precedent, 1981.

———. "On the Way to *Ereignis:* Heidegger's Interpretation of *Physis.*" In *Continental Philosophy in America: Prize Essays,* edited by John Sallis, 1:131–64. Pittsburgh: Duquense University Press, 1983.

———. *The First Coming: How the Kingdom of God Became Christianity.* New York: Random House, 1986.

———. "Heidegger's New Aspect: On *In-Sein, Zeitlichkeit,* and the Genesis of *Being and Time.*" *Research in Phenomenology* 25 (November 1995): 207–25.

———. "Choosing One's Fate: A Re-reading of *Sein und Zeit,* § 74." *Research in Phenomenology* 28 (1999): 63–83.

Sokel, Walter H. "The Devolution of the Self in *The Notebooks of Malte Laurids Brigge.*" In *Rilke: The Alchemy of Alienation,* edited by Frank Baron, Ernst S. Dick, and Warren R. Maurer, pp. 171–90. Lawrence: The Regents Press of Kansas, 1986.

———. "The Blackening of the Breast: The Narrative of Existential Education and R. M. Rilke's *The Notebooks of Malte Laurids Brigge.*" In *Reflection and Action: The German Bildungsroman,* edited by James Hardin, pp. 329–61. Columbia: University of South Carolina Press, 1991.

Spinosa, Charles. "Derrida and Heidegger: Iterability and Ereignis." In *Heidegger: A Critical Reader,* edited by Hubert Dreyfus and Harrison Hall, pp. 270–97. Oxford: Blackwell, 1992.

Starobinski, Jean. "Rousseau et l'origine des langues." In *Europäische Aufklarung: Herbert Dieckmann zum 60. Geburtstag,* edited by Hugo Friedrich and Fritz Schalk, pp. 281–300. Munich: W. Fink, 1967.

Staten, Henry. *Eros in Mourning: Homer to Lacan.* Baltimore: Johns Hopkins University Press, 1995.

Stephenson, John S. *Death, Grief, and Mourning: Individual and Social Realities.* New York: The Free Press, Macmillan, 1985.

Stevens, Wallace. *The Collected Poems of Wallace Stevens.* New York: Vintage, 1983.

Stewart, Susan. *Columbarium.* Chicago: University of Chicago Press, 2003.

Stillinger, Jack, ed. *The Letters of Charles Armitrage Brown.* Cambridge, Mass.: Harvard University Press, 1966.

Strauss, Walter A. *Descent and Return: The Orphic Theme in Modern Literature.* Cambridge, Mass.: Harvard University Press, 1971.

Swinburne, Algernon Charles. *Swinburne: Selected Poetry and Prose.* Edited by John D. Rosenburg. New York: Modern Library, 1968.

Tafuri, Manfredo. *The Sphere and the Labyrinth: Avant Gardes and Architecture from Piranesi to the 1970s.* Translated by Pellegrino d'Acierno and Robert Connolly. Cambridge, Mass: Harvard University Press, 1987.

Tagliacozzo, Giorgio, ed. *Giambattista Vico's Science of Humanity.* Baltimore: Johns Hopkins University Press, 1976.

———. *Vico: Past and Present.* Atlantic Highlands, N.J.: Humanities Press, 1981.

Tagliacozzo, Giorgio, with Hayden V. White, eds. *Giambattista Vico: An International Symposium.* Baltimore: Johns Hopkins University Press, 1969.

Tambiah, Stanley Jeyraja. *Culture, Thought and Social Action: An Anthropological Perspective.* Cambridge, Mass.: Harvard University Press, 1985.

Tambling, Jeremy. *Becoming Posthumous: Life and Death in Literary and Cultural Studies.* Edinburgh: Edinburgh University Press, 2001.

Tarlow, Sarah. *Bereavement and Commemoration: An Archaeology of Mortality.* Oxford: Blackwell, 1999.

Taylor, Charles. *Philosophical Arguments.* Cambridge, Mass.: Harvard University Press, 1995.

Thomas, Louis-Vincent. *Rites de mort: Pour la paix des vivants.* Paris: Fayard, 1985.

Thoreau, Henry David. *"Walden" and "Civil Disobedience."* Edited by Owen Thomas. New York: Norton, 1966.

Tichi, Cecelia. "Domesticity on Walden Pond." In *A Historical Guide to Henry David Thoreau,* edited by William E. Cain, pp. 95–122. Oxford: Oxford University Press, 2000.

Tiffany, Daniel. *Radio Corpse Imagism and the Cryptaesthetic of Ezra Pound.* Cambridge, Mass.: Harvard University Press, 1995.

Trabant, Jürgen. "Parlare cantando: Language Singing in Vico and Herder." *New Vico Studies* 9 (1991): 1–16.

Travis, Roger. *Allegory and the Tragic Chorus in Sophocles' "Oedipus at Colonus."* Lanham, Md.: Rowman & Littlefield Publishers, Inc., 1999.

Turcan, Robert. *The Gods of Ancient Rome: Religion in Everyday Life from Archaic to Imperial Times.* Translated by Antonia Nevill. Edinburgh: Edinburgh University Press, 2000.

Ungaretti, Giuseppe. *Saggi e interventi.* Milan: Mondadori, 1974.

———. *Vita d'un uomo*. Reprint edition. Milan: Mondadori, 1988.

Velotti, Stefano. *Sapienti e bestioni: Saggio sull'ignoranza, il sapere e la poesia in Giambattista Vico*. Parma: Pratiche Editrice, 1995.

Verene, Donald Phillip. *Vico's Science of Imagination*. Ithaca, N.Y.: Cornell University Press, 1989.

Vico, Giambattista. *The New Science*. Translated by Thomas Bergin and Max Fisch. Ithaca, N.Y.: Cornell University Press, 1958.

———. *Autobiography*. Translated by Thomas Bergin and Max Fisch. Ithaca, N.Y.: Cornell University Press, 1969.

———. *On the Most Ancient Wisdom of the Italians*. Translated by L. M. Palmer. Ithaca, N.Y.: Cornell University Press, 1988.

Virgil. *The Aeneid*. Translated by Allen Mandelbaum. New York: Bantam, 1972.

Vogeler, Martha Salmon. "The Religious Meanings of *Marius the Epicurean*." *Nineteenth-Century Literature* 19 (1964): 287–99.

Walker, Peter. *The Weekend That Changed the World: The Mystery of Jerusalem's Empty Tomb*. Louisville, Ky.: Westminster John Knox Press, 2000.

Waller, Gregory A. *The Living and the Undead: From Stoker's Dracula to Romero's Dawn of the Dead*. Urbana: University of Illinois Press, 1986.

Watkins, Calvert, ed. *The American Heritage Dictionary of Indo-European Roots*. 2d ed. Boston: Houghton Mifflin Co., 2000.

Weber, Eugene. *Apocalypses: Prophecies, Cults, and Millennial Beliefs through the Ages*. Cambridge, Mass.: Harvard University Press, 1999.

Wellek, René. "Auerbach and Vico." In *Vico: Past and Present*, edited by Giorgio Tagliacozzo, 2:85–96. Atlantic Highlands, N.J.: Humanities Press, 1981.

Werbrouck, Marcelle. *Les Pleureuses dans l'Egypte ancienne*. Brussels: Editions de la fondation égyptologique Reine Elisabeth, 1938.

White, Luise. *Speaking with Vampires: Rumor and History in Colonial Africa*. Berkeley and Los Angeles: University of California Press, 2000.

Whitman, Walt. "When Lilacs Last in the Dooryard Bloom'd." In *American Poetry: The 19th Century*, 1:895–904. New York: The Library of America, 1978.

Widmer, Kingsley. *The Ways of Nihilism: A Study of Herman Melville's Short Novels*. Los Angeles: The California State Colleges, 1970.

Wiedemann, Thomas. *Emperors and Gladiators*. New York: Routledge, 1992.

Wilhelm, J. J. *Ezra Pound in London and Paris (1908–1925)*. University Park: Pennsylvania State University Press, 1990.

Wilner, Eleanor. *Reversing the Spell*. Port Townsend, Wash.: Copper Canyon Press, 1998.

Wilson, Joseph P. *The Hero and the City: An Interpretation of Sophocles' "Oedipus at Colonus."* Ann Arbor: University of Michigan Press, 1997.

Wood, David. *Thinking after Heidegger*. Cambridge: Polity, 2002.

Woodman, A. J. "Greek Sources of 'Writ in Water': A Further Note." *Keats-Shelley Journal* 24 (1975): 12–13.

Wordsworth, William. *Selected Poetry of William Wordsworth*. Edited by Mark Van Doren. New York: Random House, Modern Library, 2001.

Wray, Alison, ed. *The Transition to Language*. Oxford: Oxford University Press, 2002.

Wright, Frank Lloyd. *American Architecture*. Edited by Edgar Kaufmann. New York: Horizon Press, 1955.

Wyss, André. *Jean-Jacques Rousseau: L'Accent de l'écriture*. Neuchâtel: A la Baconnière, 1988.

Xenophon. *Hellenica*, books I–V. Translated by Carleton L. Brownson. London: William Heinemann, 1918.

Young, Julian. "What Is Dwelling? The Homelessness of Modernity and the Worlding of the World." In *Heidegger, Authenticity and Modernity: Essays in Honor of Hubert Dreyfus,* ed. Mark Wrathall and Jeff Malpas, pp. 187–204. Cambridge, Mass.: MIT Press, 2000.

Zimmerman, Michael E. *Heidegger's Confrontation with Modernity.* Bloomington: Indiana University Press, 1990.

Zucker, Paul. *Fascination of Decay.* Ridgewood, N.J.: The Gregg Press, 1968.

INDEX